MEMOIR

OF

MAJ.-GEN. GEORGE H. THOMAS.

BY

RICHARD W. JOHNSON,
BRIGADIER-GENERAL U.S.A.
(RETIRED).

PHILADELPHIA:
J. B. LIPPINCOTT & CO.
1881.

Copyright, 1881, by R. W. Johnson.

Printing Statement:

Due to the very old age and scarcity of this book, many of the pages may be hard to read due to the blurring of the original text, possible missing pages, missing text, dark backgrounds and other issues beyond our control.

Because this is such an important and rare work, we believe it is best to reproduce this book regardless of its original condition.

Thank you for your understanding.

TO MY SONS,

ALFRED B., RICHARD W., JR., AND HENRY S. JOHNSON,

THIS VOLUME

IS AFFECTIONATELY DEDICATED

BY THEIR FATHER,

THE AUTHOR.

PREFACE.

In presenting this volume to the public the writer desires to state that it is not designed as a history of the war of the rebellion. The events of that terrible period in our country's history are referred to only so far as the character and services of Major-General George H. Thomas are brought to light, and in describing battles others who took prominent parts are not mentioned, for the reason that it has been the design of the author, so far as possible, to avoid entering into the details which have hitherto been so well and so accurately portrayed by others. The subject of this volume is worthy of an abler biographer, but as ten years have elapsed since his death, and no history of him has yet appeared, I have felt myself called upon to prepare a brief sketch of his life and services. For thirteen years the writer was associated with General Thomas, and had as good opportunities of studying and understanding his character as any one not of his own family. It will be the aim to give the incidents of his life, which lie like massive facts upon the face of our national history, without embellishment, and certainly without a desire to make him prominent by dwarfing the services of those who labored side by side with him. The thrilling events of the period covered by the life of General Thomas followed each other in such rapid succession that the public could scarcely become interested in any one, or in any combination of events, before others would appear and command attention, hence but little is known of the private lives of our great military leaders. Looking back at the achievements of Thomas he is seen in his true character,—an incorruptible patriot, a brave, wise, and skilful soldier. And as years pass by and the bitter wounds engendered by the war have been healed, his honored name will be more and more venerated by the people of America, as they will see in his life those noble traits of character which distinguish him, in an eminent degree, in every period of his manhood. Let the young study his character and strive to imitate his noble example. No better model can be placed before them than that "completely rounded, skilful, judicious, modest soldier," that wise, calm, self-poised, steadfast chieftain, the hero of Chickamauga and Nashville, the able commander of the Army of the Cumberland.

CONTENTS.

CHAPTER I.

Early Life—Appointment to a Cadetship—His Graduation and Assignment to a Regiment—His Services in the Everglades of Florida—Campaigns against the Seminoles—Capture of a Large Body of Indians—Complimentary Notice by Colonel Worth   11

CHAPTER II.

From the Everglades to New Orleans—Baltimore—Recruiting Service—Ordered to join General Taylor at Corpus Christi—Defence of Fort Brown—Battle of Monterey—Services with Bragg's Battery—At Mouth of Rio Grande—Again in Florida, and thence to West Point—Popularity with Cadets—Marriage—Service in California—Fort Yuma—Major Second Cavalry—Indian Campaigns in Texas—Opinion of General Patterson 22

CHAPTER III.

Commands a Brigade under General Patterson—Promoted—City Troop—Falling Waters—Capture of Martinsburgh—Movement on Bunker Hill and Winchester—Appointed Brigadier-General —Assigned to Duty in Kentucky—Camp Dick Robinson—Scarcity of Arms—States' Rights and Peace Men—Suggests Campaign to Knoxville—Despatches from General Sherman—Commands

First Division—How composed—At Crab Orchard—Defeat of the Rebel Forces under General G. B. Crittenden—Battle of Mill Spring, and Report of same 40

CHAPTER IV.

In Camp at Somerset, Kentucky—Movement to Bowling Green—To Nashville—Bitterness of Feeling in Nashville—Movement to the Relief of General Grant at Pittsburg Landing—Battle of Shiloh—Siege of Corinth—March to Huntsville—Pursues Bragg to Kentucky—Thomas's Unselfishness 64

CHAPTER V.

Thomas offered Buell's Command—Declined—Battle of Perryville—Rosecrans succeeds Buell—March to Nashville—Battle of Stone River—Capture of Murfreesboro'—Colonel Buckner's Seventy-ninth Illinois Volunteers—Capture of Tullahoma—Chickamauga Campaign—Rosecrans relieved by Thomas—Short Rations—Driving Enemy from the River—Grant at Chattanooga—Thomas's Plans Approved—Opinion of W. F. G. Shanks, Esq. 71

CHAPTER VI.

Appearance of Chattanooga—Thomas's Staff—General W. D. Whipple, Chief—Who planned Battle of Mission Ridge—Thomas's Report—Mr. Shanks again—Pursuit of Enemy to Ringgold—Demonstration against Rocky Face and Buzzard's Roost—March to Atlanta—Battles—Captain Wells, A.A.G.—General Palmer's Coolness and Gallantry 115

CHAPTER VII.

Closing in around Atlanta—Hood offers Battle on 20th, 22d, and 28th Days of July—Defeated on each Occasion—McPherson killed—Howard succeeds him—Atlanta captured—Thomas's Report of Operations preceding and during the Battle, etc. 154

CHAPTER VIII.

Sherman goes to the Sea—Other Important Battles to be fought by Thomas in Tennessee—Concentrates his Forces at Nashville—Importuned to attack Enemy before Arrangements were completed—Despatches from General Grant, etc.—Final Contest and Great Victory—President Lincoln congratulates Thomas and his Army—Pursuit of Hood—Consequences had Thomas been defeated—Wilson's Cavalry—Thomas's Report of the Battle of Nashville . 173

CHAPTER IX.

Thomas careful of those under him—Never sacrificed them uselessly—Vote of Thanks of Congress and Legislature of the State of Tennessee—Medal presented by Latter—Promoted Major-General U.S.A.—Building up Waste Places—Reconstruction—Civil Duties—On Leave of Absence—Headquarters removed to Louisville—Declines a Present from Admirers in Ohio—The Presidency—Brevet Rank declined—Brevets conferred without much Reference to Service—Dyer Court of Inquiry—Transferred to California—Inspects his Command—Visits his Old Post—Fort Yuma—Thomas as a Public Speaker 228

CHAPTER X.

Thomas's Loyalty—Pen-Portrait by William Swinton . . . 244

CHAPTER XI.

Nature and Character of Last Illness—Death—General Sherman's Order announcing Death—Received by the Country with Universal Sadness—Remains taken to Troy, N. Y., for Interment—Funeral Services—Pall-Bearers—Comments of the *Albany Evening Journal*, furnished by Mr. George C. Bishop—Action of the Society of the Army of the Cumberland—Equestrian Statue decided

10   CONTENTS.

PAGE

upon—Unveiling of the same—Letters of Distinguished Gentlemen regretting their Inability to be present—High Opinions held by them of Deceased—Speeches of General Sherman and Others . 254

CONCLUSION 292

APPENDIX.

Address by Colonel Stanley Matthews on the Occasion of the Unveiling of the Statue 293

LIST OF ENGRAVINGS.

MAJOR-GENERAL GEORGE H. THOMAS . . .	*Frontispiece*
GENERAL U. S. GRANT	Facing page 24
GENERAL W. T. SHERMAN	" 46
LIEUTENANT-GENERAL P. H. SHERIDAN . . .	" 76
MAJOR-GENERAL W. S. ROSECRANS	" 104
MAJOR-GENERAL A. McD. McCOOK	" 140
MAJOR-GENERAL L. H. ROUSSEAU	" 176
MAJOR-GENERAL W. D. WHIPPLE	" 206
MAJOR-GENERAL D. S. STANLEY	" 246
MAJOR-GENERAL W. B. HAZEN	" 280

MEMOIR

OF

MAJ.-GEN. GEORGE H. THOMAS.

CHAPTER I.

Early Life—Appointment to a Cadetship—His Graduation and Assignment to a Regiment—His Services in the Everglades of Florida—Campaigns against the Seminoles—Capture of a Large Body of Indians—Complimentary Notice by Colonel Worth.

SINCE the close of the Rebellion many of the prominent men of that eventful period have passed away, and their histories can now be written unbiassed by partiality or prejudice which would have influenced, to a greater or less extent, the biographer at an earlier period and during the lifetime of his subject.

The name of George H. Thomas has been written upon the highest pinnacle of Fame's proud temple, and the pages of American history have been made to glow with the record of his brilliant achievements. It is but just that his life, character, and services should be embodied in one volume, so that a knowledge of his many noble qualities of head and heart may be convenient of access to the rising generation, in order that they may venerate the hero who by his courage, his ability, and his devotion to duty did so much in the great struggle to suppress the Rebellion, and whose deeds of valor have exalted and illustrated the annals of war.

George Henry Thomas was born in Southampton County, Virginia, on the 31st day of July, 1816. His father was of Welsh and his mother of French-Huguenot descent. They were persons of education and refinement, and, having amassed a comfortable fortune, lived in luxury and ease; yet their sons were taught to believe that it would be necessary for them to rely wholly upon themselves, and from early age they gave evidence of future usefulness. George was born at the close of the war of 1812–15, and when he arrived at that age when children are so deeply interested in the stories told them by their loving parents, he was told of the dangers, trials, and hardships through which our brave soldiers passed in that unequal contest.

It is not strange that he early decided upon the life of a soldier, which he seems to have done at an early age, and set his face in the direction of West Point. These stories taught him lessons of patriotism, which grew with his growth and strengthened with his strength, and produced such rich fruit in his after-years. Born in a slave State, where the plantations were large, there were not enough white children convenient to any given point for school purposes, and hence schools were scarce and of a low order, yet he had all the educational advantages afforded by the country.

From childhood he evinced a positive character, an individuality which adhered to him throughout his eventful life.

He seems to have passed from childhood to manhood without passing through the intermediate grade of boyhood. Steady, thoughtful, studious, he was conscientious in the discharge of every duty, however disagreeable and unpleasant it may have been. His early teachers spoke of him as an apt scholar, one of unusual sprightliness and ability, and predicted for him a distinguished career. Truthfulness and unswerving integrity were early instilled in him by his parents, and these he never forgot, but always practised them in every walk of life and under all circumstances. Not one of his many acquaintances in the army or in civil life can truthfully say that he ever wronged them by word or deed. The beauty of his character was, in a great measure, due to his parents, who laid its foundation upon the broad and enduring basis of truth and honor; but he showed himself to be a master builder by erecting thereon a symmetrical and graceful superstructure.

With such parents, and with such training, is it surprising that the boy should develop into the man distinguished alike for his patriotism, integrity, and high sense of honor? So even was his disposition, so amiable yet so firm, so positive in his convictions, so manly, and so dignified, that he was known among his youthful associates by the name of George Washington.

In the year 1836 he received an appointment as cadet at the United States Military Academy, whither he repaired in the month of June and reported to the superintendent. During his *plebe* year he was subjected to the same trying ordeals through which all of his predecessors had passed, but he endured them all without murmur or complaint. At the close of the first year, when he was advanced to the grade and dignity of a third classman, his time arrived to haze the *plebes*, but this he never did. Well did he remember the insults and outrages which had been heaped upon him, and his innate sense of justice enabled him to see the wrong that he had been compelled to endure, and he gave the poor homesick *plebes* the benefit of his counsel and advice. In this way he gained their confidence, and he was regarded as a friend and benefactor, and the attachments thus formed bound many friends to him in life, and at his death they ceased not to claim proud friendship with his hallowed mould.

Thomas graduated twelfth in a class of forty-two members, and among his classmates were Generals W. T. Sherman, Stewart Van Vliet, G. W. Getty, Colonel Pinckney Lugenbeel, and many others distinguished in the late war on the Union side, while B. R. Johnson and R. H. Ewell of his class united their fortunes with the Confederacy. The class of 1840 was one of unusual ability, and the fact that Thomas graduated twelfth shows him to have been not only a good student, but one of no ordinary capacity.

The Military Academy turns out every year a number of graduates, all of whom are proficient in the arts and sciences taught in that institution. To master the numerous subjects in the short space of time allotted to each requires not only close application, but a quick and active mind to comprehend, and when once understood to retain. Thomas was a close student, probably not as quick as some, but he continued to apply himself until he had fairly mastered any of the difficult subjects in the higher branches; then he would store them away in the recesses of his great brain, there to remain until he was ready to apply them. The writer remembers with what ease and certainty he could solve difficult problems in mathematics long years after he left the Academy, showing as much familiarity with the principles involved as if they had just been investigated. Thomas never forgot anything, and his mind was a storehouse filled with useful and valuable information on all subjects which have engaged the thoughts of men of letters and of science.

In the month of June, 1840, Thomas received his diploma, and with it the usual leave of absence to enable him to visit his home and await his assignment to a regiment. On the 1st day of July following he was assigned to the Third Regiment of Artillery as second lieutenant, and ordered to report to the commanding officer at Fort Columbus, New York Harbor, on the expiration of his leave of absence. Fort Columbus, then as now, was a rendezvous for recruits, and the young graduates were sent there to drill and prepare them for the active duty of the field, and when a certain proficiency was attained they were assigned to regiments and sent to the frontier, the young officers taking charge of those attached to their respective regiments.

Thomas remained at Fort Columbus only a few months, when he was sent to Florida with a detachment of recruits for his regiment. The Indian war was then in progress, and active duty was required of him in the Everglades of Florida.

That war was unnecessarily prolonged, because the government officers failed to comprehend its magnitude. Defeat and massacre followed each other in rapid succession, and yet the government did not seem to realize the extent of the opposition of the Seminole chiefs and their copper-colored followers. The cost of that war was immense compared with the insignificant number of the hostiles, but in their native wilds they could secrete themselves when a large force was in their immediate vicinity, to come forth from their hiding-places when a small detachment appeared, and by force of numbers overpower and massacre the last one of the party. In this kind of warfare the nation lost many valuable officers and men without inflicting any very serious damage to the Indians, and this waste of life and treasure was continued for years, whereas had a large force been placed in the field a sharp and decisive campaign would have resulted in the subjection of the Indians at a very small outlay compared with the enormous expenditures of the government in carrying out the wretched plan adopted. To some extent this same policy seems to prevail to-day. Our army is entirely too small to successfully contend with the savage foe of the frontier. The massacre of the gallant Custer with his three hundred brave followers of that magnificent regiment, the Seventh Cavalry, the killing of that fine soldier Lieutenant-Colonel W. H. Lewis, and the sad affair wherein the brave Thornburgh lost his life, all, all show that our military force is too weak to protect the extended frontier, and massacres and defeats may be looked for until Congress is aroused to the fact that the fighting force of the country should be augmented. This cannot be long delayed. General Sherman is of the opinion that the army should be much larger than it is; yet he has, in deference to the views of Congress, reluctantly consented to fixing it at about twenty-five thousand men. For some years Congress has been discussing the propriety of a very great reduction, but the members are not agreed among themselves as to the best plan. Some have favored the reduction to a skeleton and the starving of the skeleton, while others have favored abolishing it altogether. These are, however, ultra views, and will in process of time yield to a more conservative policy towards the army. After the next apportionment the great West will control the legislation of the country, and Western men, who know the wants of their constituents, will regulate the size of the army to the necessity of our extended frontier. The blood of our murdered soldiers and frontier settlers, the little mounds that mark the last resting-places of gallant men and murdered women and children to be found upon every hill-top and in every valley, from the Red River of the North to the Rio Grande on the south, the terrible carnage of the brave Custer with its hallowed sadness, speak most earnestly in favor of an increase of the army. The effective strength should be great enough so that when detachments are ordered out they can be made sufficiently strong to overcome all Indian opposition, and in case of conflict deal such heavy blows that the savages will not care to encounter them. When the Indians are made to understand that detachments sent out will be able to whip them on every field and under all circumstances, troubles on the frontier will cease, and the bold settlers who have pushed out beyond the general line of civilization will not be kept in constant dread of savage outbreaks. The writer would be false to his deep and honest convictions if he failed to place himself on record as in favor of transferring the Indian from the Interior to the War Department. The Indian problem is not a civil but a military question, and military men who have been on duty on the frontier for years, and who are familiar with the Indian character, are the ones to treat with them. A short time since, in conversation with an intelligent Indian from one of the reservations, he remarked that he wished the care of his people was in the hands of the War Department; for, said he, "the officers know what we want and will treat us honestly, but, alas! we have an agent who came to us recently, and when he arrived at our camp he did not know an Indian from a buffalo calf."

When Thomas arrived in Florida he reported for duty to Captain R. D. A. Wade, Third Artillery, and served with his company in all of its marches during that eventful campaign, and participated in the capture of a number of the savage foe. The facts in this case are so minutely set forth in the report of Captain Wade—a copy of which has been kindly furnished by Adjutant-General Townsend—that it is given in full :

"FORT LAUDERDALE, E. F., November 13, 1841.

"SIR,—In pursuance to the instructions contained in your communication of the 24th September, I set out on the morning of the 5th inst., accompanied by Lieutenant Thomas, Third Artillery, Assistant Surgeon Emerson, and sixty non-commissioned officers and privates, embarked in twelve canoes

CAPTURE OF A LARGE BODY OF INDIANS. 19

and provisioned for fifteen days. We proceeded by the inland passage to the northward, coming out in the bay at the Hillsborough Inlet, and in such manner that our canoes were concealed from the view of an Indian whom I there discovered fishing on the northern point of the inlet. I made the requisite dispositions immediately to land, and succeeded in surprising him. By operating on his hopes and fears, I induced him to lead us to his Indian village, fifteen miles distant in a westerly direction. This we reached on the morning of the 6th; surprised and captured twenty Indians, men, women, and children; took six rifles, destroyed fourteen canoes and much provisions of the usual variety. Of those who attempted to escape eight were killed by our troops. We returned to our boats the same forenoon with our prisoners, and proceeded up a small stream towards the Orange Grove haul-over, where we encamped for the night. On the morning of the 7th, after proceeding three miles farther north, the stream became too shallow for canoe navigation, and we made here a camp, leaving the prisoners, the boats, and a sufficient guard in charge of Dr. Emerson. Under the guidance of an old Indian found among our prisoners, who is called Chia-chee, I took up the line of march through nearly a mile of deep bog and saw-grass, then through the pine barren and some hummocks to a cypress swamp a distance of some thirty miles northward. Here (on the 8th inst.) we were conducted to another village, which we also surrounded, and surprised and captured twenty-seven Indians, took six rifles and one shot-gun, and destroyed a large quantity of provisions and four canoes. The next morning (November 9) we set out on our return to the boats, on a more easterly route than the former, which led us to the shores of Lake Worth, where we found and destroyed a canoe, a field of pumpkins, and an old hut. In the afternoon of this day one man came in and surrendered himself, thus making the whole number of our Indian prisoners forty-nine. At 11 A.M. of the 10th we arrived at our boats and proceeded to the little Hillsborough bar by evening, and in the afternoon of the next day (November 11) we returned to Fort Lauderdale without any loss on our part, after an absence of six days. Having seen much in the old man Chia-chee to inspire my confidence in his integrity, I permitted him to go out from our camp (on the 10th November) to bring in other Indians, which he promised to do in three or four days. This promise he subsequently redeemed, having on the 14th inst. brought in six (four men and two boys) at Fort Lauderdale.

"My warmest thanks are due to Dr. Emerson and Lieutenant Thomas for their valuable and efficient aid in carrying out my orders; and of the conduct of the troops likewise, without any exception, I can speak only in terms of the highest praise.

"I have the honor to be, very respectfully,
"Your obedient servant,
[Signed] "R. D. A. WADE,
"Captain Third Artillery,
"Commanding Expedition."

Colonel W. J. Worth, then commanding the army in Florida, in forwarding Captain Wade's report to the adjutant-general of the army endorsed thereon:

"I have the satisfaction to forward the accompanying report of the successful operations of Captain Wade, Third Artillery, acting under the orders of his immediate commander, Major Childs. This very creditable affair will operate the most favorable influence upon the closing scenes of this protracted contest, and I but do equal justice to the distinguished

COMPLIMENTARY NOTICE BY GENERAL WORTH.

merit and conduct of Captain Wade, and the expectations of the service, in respectfully asking that the special notice of the Department of War may be extended to him and his gallant assistant, Second Lieutenant G. H. Thomas, of the same regiment.

* * * * * *

"Respectfully, etc.,
[Signed] "W. J. WORTH,
"Colonel Commanding."

The War Department, acting on the recommendation of Colonel Worth, recognized the valuable services of Thomas in this expedition, and conferred upon him the brevet rank of first lieutenant, to date from November 6, 1841, "for gallantry and good conduct in the war against the Florida Indians."

The service above referred to may seem small and, in fact, insignificant when compared with the heavy battles of more recent dates, but it should be remembered that the country traversed was almost a bottomless bog, through which the command struggled with the greatest difficulty. Thomas, unaccustomed to such service, was not heard to complain of its hardships, but like a true soldier led the way and called upon his men to follow. This was the bursting of the germ,—the very beginning of a career which was destined to render his name immortal and place him in the front rank with the great military leaders of the nineteenth century.

CHAPTER II.

From Everglades to New Orleans—Baltimore—Recruiting Service—Ordered to join General Taylor at Corpus Christi—Defence of Fort Brown—Distinguished for Coolness and Courage—Battle of Monterey—With Bragg's Famous Battery—At Mouth of Rio Grande—Again in the Swamps of Florida—Thence to West Point—Popularity with Cadets—Married—Ordered to California—Fort Yuma—Major Second Cavalry—At Jefferson Barracks—Court-Martial Duty—Ordered to Utah — Order Countermanded — Indian Campaigns in Texas — Wounded—Opinion of General Patterson.

THE services required of an officer of the army are so multifarious that one can hardly expect to remain at a given station any great length of time. This constant moving around breaks the monotony and renders army life endurable. If one has a disagreeable station, he consoles himself with the thought that he will not remain there long; and although he may go to a still less desirable post, yet it is attended with change of associations and surroundings, and adds a little more spice to a life made up pretty much of allspice.

Following Thomas's career, it is seen that he was not an exception,—that an easy, quiet life was not in store for him: From the Everglades of Florida, in 1841, to New Orleans Barracks, in 1842, thence to Fort Moultrie, South Carolina, where he remained for a few months only, for at the close of the year we find him stationed at Fort McHenry, near Baltimore. Service at stations near New Orleans and Baltimore was quite agreeable to him, then a gay, dashing young officer of artillery, who had just "won his spurs" by gallant and meritorious services in the field. Being a man of fine address, and handsome withal, with a mind well stored by miscellaneous reading, polite and agreeable, he was not only a valuable acquisition, but very justly a great favorite in society circles.

He had scarcely become settled at Fort McHenry when an order was received at the post requiring the colonel commanding the Third Artillery to detail a subaltern for the general recruiting service. Thomas's exemplary conduct and soldierly bearing secured the detail for him, and he was accordingly designated and ordered to report in person to superintendent of the recruiting service in New York City. Although this frustrated his plans for the future, yet with the true instincts of a good soldier he obeyed without a murmur.

The war with Mexico appeared imminent, and Thomas was relieved from duty on the recruiting service and ordered to report to his company preparatory to embarking for Texas to join the Army of Occupation under General Taylor. This order was obeyed with alacrity, for active service in preference to a life of gayety in a city was more in accordance with his wishes.

In the defence of Fort Brown, Texas, from May 3 to May 9, 1846, Thomas was distinguished for his coolness and bravery, showing himself worthy of the commission of a general officer, but in those days it was thought unsafe and unwise to trust young men with large commands. Only officers who had grown gray in the service were considered reliable commanders. In the great Rebellion it did not take any great length of time to learn that in the reeling shock of conflict, and the seething, surging struggle of battle, fiery, dauntless commanders, whose hearts spoke in their blades, and whose voices rang through their actual victories, were the men whose services the country required. Like flaming meteors, Grant, Sherman, Sheridan, Thomas, Hancock, Schofield, Terry, and a host of others appeared in response to the nation's call or the nation's need. George H. Thomas was particularly conspicuous in this grand meteoric display.

At the battle of Monterey, September 21–23, 1846, his skill and daring brought him prominently to the notice of his commander, and again he received evidence of a nation's gratitude by the bestowal of brevet rank, that of captain, for "gallant conduct in the several conflicts at Monterey, Mexico." As a lieutenant in Bragg's famous battery, it was Thomas who let loose the dogs of war which belched forth from their brazen throats iron, shot, and shell in obedience to the order of "Old Rough and Ready,"—"a little more grape, Captain Bragg." The admirable manner in which he managed his section of the battery once more secured the favorable notice of General Taylor, upon whose recommendation he was brevetted major " for gallant and meritorious conduct in the battle of Buena Vista, Mexico."

Hostilities having ceased, the company to which Thomas

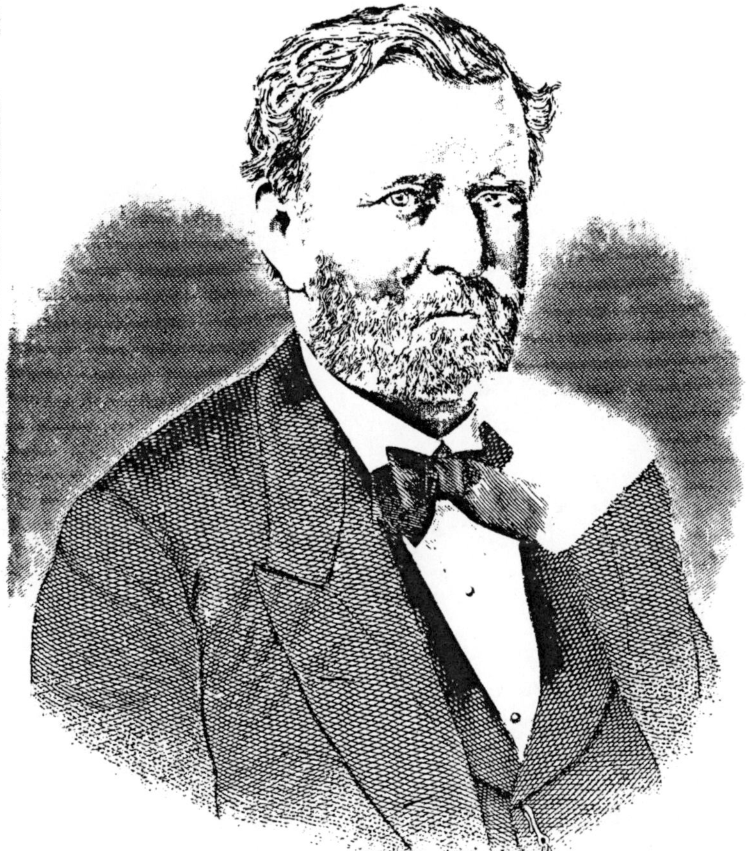

was attached was ordered into camp at the mouth of the Rio Grande, Texas.

Routine duty in camp or garrison was distasteful to him at all times, but especially so after passing through the excitement incident to active operations in an enemy's country and in front of an opposing army, but he was soon removed from that camp and transferred to the swamps of Florida to engage once more in the Seminole troubles, which still remained unsettled. Here he remained for a year; at the expiration of that time he was ordered to Fort Independence, in Boston Harbor.

Thomas had now been in service for ten years, had passed through two wars, but was still a subaltern. A man whose skill and courage eminently fitted him for the highest command was retained as a lieutenant for the reason that the government had not yet learned that young men of dash were better fitted for active service than those who had grown old in the service, and whose efficiency was necessarily impaired by bodily infirmities incident to age and long exposure in the line of duty. Thomas had faith that his time would come, some day, and he patiently waited for it.

It must be evident to any one having any knowledge of the heads of the various staff departments as they existed thirty years ago that they had become too old to expand so as to meet the wants of a large army. It was necessary to displace them and appoint young and active men to fill their places, and this infusion of new and young blood became a necessity not only in the staff, but the line of the army. In the year 1851 the subject of this volume was ordered to West Point to assume the duties of instructor in artillery and cavalry, and there he remained until the year 1854. He was very popular with the cadets,—not because he was lax in discipline, for he was quite the reverse, but for the reason that he was eminently just. It gave him great pain to be compelled to punish a cadet, and he never did so unless duty imperatively demanded it. Cadets sometimes imagine that the officers of the Academy often report them on suspicion and for trifling offences, thus giving them demerit marks, which indirectly lower their standing in scholarship and subject them to unnecessary punishment. Thomas's keen sense of justice prevented him from taking an undue advantage of any one. General M. R. Morgan, now a distinguished officer of the army, was, at the time Thomas was stationed at the Academy, a cadet, and so fond of fun and frolic that he often neglected some of his studies, and Thomas reported him for such neglect on one occasion. Morgan knew that the report was just and proper, suffered the penalty, and forgot the circumstance. Not so Thomas. Years afterwards they met, and Thomas, thinking that Morgan still treasured it against him, spoke of it, and expressed deep sorrow at being compelled to take notice of such neglect and hoped that he would forgive and forget it.

This little circumstance, trifling, it may be, illustrates the character of the man. If he ever did an act of injustice to any one, it arose from an error of the head and not of the heart. A man of such clear ideas and with the principles of justice so thoroughly inwrought into his very nature is not likely to treat those under or associated with him unjustly or ungentlemanly. Thomas's intercourse with all men was characterized by the greatest dignity, and when one came into his presence he felt the influence of his high character, of his spotless purity, and was irresistibly drawn to him by invisible cords of love and genuine affection. This was the secret of his great popularity. It was this that made his soldiers love him, that made them willing to follow wherever he led the way. He was not demonstrative in his attachments to men, but a more kind and affectionate heart never pulsated in man than the one that throbbed in his manly bosom. While on duty at West Point he met Miss Frances L. Kellogg, to whom he was married, Nov. 17, 1852.

Miss Kellogg was a lady of rare accomplishments. Her mind was well filled with all that is taught in the best schools, to which she had added a fund of information drawn from travels and the study of the best authors. As she was pleasing in her manner, handsome in her appearance, with a fluency in conversation rarely equalled, it was not strange that they should be mutually fascinated with each other. As he was the noblest type of manhood, so she was the purest and best type of womanhood. As his wife she made his home the earthly paradise he had sought, and her noble, generous hospitality rendered it a pleasant place for all who enjoyed her acquaintance. After his death she returned to her former home, in Troy, New York, where she now resides, and the nation mourns with her the loss she sustained in the death of her gallant husband while yet in the prime of his life.

On the 24th day of December, 1853, Thomas was promoted to the full rank of captain in his regiment, and in 1854 was placed in command of a battalion of the Third Artillery and ordered to march therewith to Benicia, California. On his arrival in that department he was assigned to the command of Fort Yuma, where he remained until the spring of 1855. As a company commander he had no superior. He had one of the best-disciplined companies in the service. His men seemed to model themselves after their soldierly captain, and it is said that no company in the army had fewer trials by courts-martial.

Fort Yuma was one of the most disagreeable posts garrisoned by the army,—disagreeable from various causes, but more particularly on account of the excessive heat of summer. The hills around the garrison seemed to concentrate the rays of the sun upon the parade-ground, and it was not an unusual circumstance to have the thermometer indicate one hundred and sixteen degrees in the shade. The nights were so hot and oppressive that sleep was quite out of the question until after midnight, and then only on the housetops. Thomas often referred to his service at that post, and illustrated the extreme temperature of the place by the relation of a story the old soldiers were in the habit of telling to the recruits. A notoriously bad man belonging to the command died and was buried. His character and habits had been such as to leave but little doubt in the minds of those who believed in a future state of rewards and punishments as to his final destination. One night, shortly after his funeral, he was seen to enter the squad-room, looking as he did in life. His general appearance was such that every one who saw the apparition recognized it at once, and his old "bunkie" called out to him, "I say, Bill, what do you want?" In answer to this he replied, "Boys, I have been to h——l and came near freezing to death, so I just asked the 'boss' for a pass for an hour to enable me to come here for my blankets. Boys, hell is only about a half-mile from Fort Yuma." Several of his old chums gave him their wrappings, and Bill departed never to return again.

Thomas could enjoy a good story and laugh as heartily as any one, yet he rarely ever attempted to repeat the witty sayings of others. When not engaged in the weighty affairs of official business he would sit for hours with those with whom he was familiar and listen to their stories, and enjoy them as keenly as any one, provided they were of such a character that they might be told in a company of ladies, not otherwise.

On the 12th day of May, 1855, Thomas was appointed major of the Second Regiment of Cavalry, a new regiment organized under the act of Congress approved March 3 of that year. As soon as he received his commission he left Fort Yuma for the States without any delay whatever. The field-officers of the regiment were: Colonel, Albert Sydney Johnston; Lieutenant-Colonel, Robert E. Lee; Majors, William J. Hardee, GEORGE H. THOMAS.

Louisville, Kentucky, was designated as the headquarters of the regiment, and the colonel took his station at that point with his regimental staff. The other field-officers were ordered to Jefferson Barracks, near St. Louis, Missouri. As rapidly as the companies were recruited they were forwarded to that point and subjected to drills, while the officers had not only to drill, but to be drilled and to recite lessons in the school of the trooper, mounted and dismounted. These duties followed each other in such rapid succession that about all the time was taken up by them. Half of the company officers were from civil life, and all had to undergo, like the recruits, the "setting up" process. This in part was entrusted to Thomas, and the subsequent soldierly record of the young officers of this regiment demonstrated very clearly how thoroughly he performed his duty. This regiment gave to the Federal cause Generals Thomas, Oakes, Palmer, Stoneman, Colonels Brackett, Royall, and others, and to the Confederate army Generals A. S. Johnston, R. E. Lee, Hardee, Van Dorn, E. K. Smith, Fitz-Hugh Lee, Hood, Cosby, and others. It is thus seen that the Second Cavalry supplied to both sides in the struggle some of the ablest and best officers in either army. In the latter part of October, 1855, the regiment, having been filled up to the maximum and mounted on the best horses ever purchased for the cavalry service, was ordered to Texas, and within ten days after the receipt of the order the command moved out on its long and tedious journey. The writer desires to be indulged here in a slight divergence from the main subject in order to remark upon the manner of mounting the cavalry arm of service. The usual rule is to fix a limit to the price to be paid for horses, and beyond this the purchasing officer cannot go. The result of this is to secure for the use of the army an inferior lot of horses, which rarely ever survive the campaigns of a single year. Authority was granted the colonel of the Second Cavalry to send a board of officers selected by him to Kentucky and elsewhere to buy the best horses they could get, without regard to price. These horses were carefully examined and inferior ones rejected. The regiment was mounted on splendid animals, and the result proved that the best horses, after all, are the cheapest. The writer knows of one company (F) in the Second which, after the rough, hard service of six years, had forty-four of its original " mount." If the regiment had been furnished with cheap horses, half of them would have fallen by the wayside on the march to Texas. Cheap horses are not the best for cavalry; they cannot endure the hard marches which they are often called on to undergo.

One would naturally suppose when all the field-officers of a regiment are present with it that the position of second major is somewhat of a sinecure, but the second major in this case was not willing to occupy a position devoid of duty and responsibility. He proved himself to be a very efficient assistant to the colonel, and relieved him of many of the vexatious details which usually devolve upon a regimental commander. When about twenty days out from Jefferson Barracks he was ordered back on court-martial duty, and did not join the regiment again until after its arrival in Texas.

The business of the court having been completed, Thomas was placed temporarily on the recruiting service with a view to the enlistment of musicians for his regiment. This duty having been performed, he joined the regiment at Fort Mason, Texas, where he remained until the spring of 1857, when he was detailed as a member of a general court-martial for the trial of Major Giles Porter. Porter, who was well informed in regard to the technicalities and intricacies of the law, kept the court in session for a period of six months. On the final adjournment of that military tribunal he returned to his station at Fort Mason, where he was permitted to remain until the spring of 1858. Trouble with the Mormons in Utah having assumed an alarming aspect, Colonel A. S. Johnston was relieved from duty in Texas, and ordered to assume command of all the troops then in motion in the direction of Salt Lake.

After Johnston arrived at Fort Bridger, he became aware of the magnitude of the contemplated resistance on the part of Brigham Young and his followers, and, seeing the necessity of a larger cavalry force, applied to the War Department for an entire regiment. His application was approved, and General D. E. Twiggs, commanding the Department of Texas, was instructed to cause the concentration of the Second Cavalry at Fort Belknap, Texas, preparatory to an overland march to that remote region, then much more remote than now, for at that time there were no railroads in that portion of the country. The regiment assembled, and every preparation was made. The ladies and children were sent off hurriedly, baggage reduced to the lowest limit, and the command placed on a war-footing and ready for active field-service; but to the disgust of Thomas, and, in fact, of every officer and soldier in the command, the order was countermanded, and the regiment was doomed to further service in Texas.

During the Mexican war Thomas incurred the displeasure of General Twiggs because he refused to give up a fine mule-team, which he had with his battery, to be used by Twiggs at his headquarters. After much discussion and the use of quantities of red tape, Thomas thwarted Twiggs's plans and retained possession of his team. It greatly incensed Twiggs to think that he should be defeated by a lieutenant, and he swore that he would yet get even with the impudent subaltern who dared to oppose him.

Trifling as this offence was, Twiggs never forgot it, and he never allowed to pass unimproved an opportunity to heap an indignity upon or do an underhanded injustice to Thomas.

After the order was countermanded by which the regiment was to be sent to Utah, an opportunity was given Twiggs to revenge himself in part. The entire regiment was at Fort Belknap, and he made the following disposition of the companies: Two were sent to Camp Cooper, on the Clear Fork of the Brazos; eight companies were sent on an expedition to the Wichita Mountains, under command of Captain and Brevet-Major Earl Van Dorn; while Thomas was left at Fort Belknap with the non-commissioned staff, band, and the sick of the regiment. He protested against such flagrant outrage to his rights as commander of the regiment, and in course of time the general-in-chief considered the subject, deciding in favor of Thomas, and directing Twiggs to order him to join and assume command of the eight companies in the field. To avoid doing this he recalled the expedition and distributed the companies to the different posts in the department. Thomas was assigned to the command of Camp Cooper, one of the least desirable posts within the limits of Texas, and he at once organized an expedition to the Red River country, about the close of the year 1859, which remained out until the spring of 1860. Soon after his return he started on what he called the Kiowa expedition, and on the 26th day of August, 1860, near the head of the Clear Fork of the Brazos, he encountered a party of Indians, with which he had a sharp conflict, being himself wounded in the face by an arrow. This fight was a running one, and when it became evident that the entire party of Indians would be killed or captured, one old Indian, himself badly wounded, made a stand, resolved to sell his life as dearly as possible, delaying Thomas's command, and thus enabling his comrades, women, and children to make good their escape. This brave old savage was wounded about twenty times before he was finally dispatched, and managed to kill and wound quite a number of the soldiers. While this target-practice was in progress, Thomas directed the guide to say to the Indian in his own language that if he would surrender his life should be spared. His reply was, "Surrender? Never! no, never! Come on, Long-knives!" Such courage, such a spirit of self-sacrifice, deserved a better fate.

There seems to be a great difference between a wounded white man and a wounded Indian. A severe wound inflicted upon the person of the former unnerves him,—his thoughts are of death and the future state whose mysterious realms lie through and beyond the portals of the grave,—while the latter, under precisely the same circumstances, seems to be nerved for extraordinary effort. The Indian believes that his happiness in the world to come will be great or small in proportion to the number of his enemies he succeeds in killing. This belief urges him to deeds of desperation, and makes him unmindful of danger and a foe of no mean proportions.

One badly-wounded Indian is more dangerous than four not wounded, while one badly-wounded white man is not only worthless for fighting, but requires the services of four able-bodied men to carry him to the rear, where his wounds can be cared for, thus reducing the fighting force by five men, while on the other hand the effective strength of the Indians is increased by the equivalent of four men for every severely-wounded one. Every officer with experience in Indian fighting will substantiate the foregoing statement.

While the regiment was at Fort Belknap, Major Thomas directed the captains of each company to detail a man with some knowledge of music; if they could not play on an instrument, but could whistle a tune, such a one would be eligible. These men were to be placed under instruction for service in the regimental band. In obedience to this order one of the captains sent to regimental headquarters a soldier by the name of Hannah, who had no knowledge of music whatever, and it was said of him that he could not distinguish "Hail, Columbia!" from "taps" on the drum. After a thorough trial the band-master reported to Major Thomas that Hannah could not be taught so as to make him of any service as a musician, whereupon he remarked, "Well, I will order him back to his company. Poor fellow! he was mistaken: possibly he had a sister by that name who could play on some instrument."

After the return of the Kiowa expedition, Thomas obtained a leave of absence and left the State of Texas, Lieutenant-Colonel R. E. Lee having returned from leave and assumed the command of the regiment.

In February, 1861, General Scott ordered Lee to Washington for consultation. General A. S. Johnston was in command of the Department of California, and Major Hardee was on leave of absence. Thus the regiment was without a field-officer. Secession, having its origin in South Carolina, spread like wild-fire over the Southern States. One by one passed the ordinance of secession, and when once passed the Southern people appeared to believe that the way was clear to establish the Confederacy without a contest. They were foolish enough to believe, or to pretend to believe, that the Federal government would permit its dismemberment without an attempt to prevent it.

Texas, bound to the Federal government by the right of purchase, admitted into the Union on terms of equality with the other States, and permitted to retain absolute control over her public lands, should have been the last State in the Union to attempt to sever her connection, but when the treasonable tempest swept over the South, Texas was involved, and she drifted from her moorings into the deep sea of revolution and rebellion against the government. Sam Houston, then governor, did all in his power to restrain the people, but they rushed madly onward, passed the ordinance of secession, and called upon him to take the oath of allegiance to the Southern Confederacy. This he declined to do, and he was deposed. A committee of safety was appointed to receive the surrender of the United States troops, provided General D. E. Twiggs would consent to a peaceable abandonment of the government stores, arms, and ammunition. It transpired that he was anxious to comply with the demand of the committee, and at a time when most of the senior officers were away he surrendered the troops and basely deserted the flag of his country. The writer was stationed at Fort Mason, Texas, when Colonel Lee received the order to report to General Scott, and on the day he left the post, in reply to the question, "Will you remain North or go South?" he replied, "I shall never take up arms against the general government, but I shall hold myself in readiness to shoulder a musket in defence of my native State" (Virginia). General Scott was very fond of Lee and had a high estimate of his skill and ability, and to him the most important position would have been given had he chosen to remain loyal to the Union cause.

Soon after Lee left the regiment the garrison at Fort Mason was ordered to Indianola, Texas, to embark on board of transports which were in waiting to take the regiment North. Where we were to go, or what was to become of us, no one knew. Once on board, the vessel steamed out of Matagorda Bay, and after a pleasant voyage reached the harbor of New York on the 13th day of April, 1861, and at once proceeded to Carlisle Barracks; and on the 14th of April all that was left of this once splendid regiment reported to Major Thomas, who had given up his leave of absence and reported at that point to await the arrival of the command. The regimental organization had been almost broken up by the resignation of those officers who felt it to be their duty to cast their lots with the States that had given them birth. These vacancies had to be filled as rapidly as possible. Thomas was promoted lieutenant-colonel April 25 and colonel May 3. The War Department was not satisfied in regard to the loyalty of the old officers of the army, inasmuch as many had proven false to their trusts, and an order was issued that all should take the oath of allegiance to the government of the United States, notwithstanding they might have done so previously. The writer thought this action singular, to say the least of it, and spoke to Thomas in regard to it. His reply was: "I do not care; I would just as soon take the oath before each meal during my life if the department saw proper to order it."

There was much to be done to place the regiment in a condition to take the field. Horses and equipments had to be purchased, recruits disciplined, and the old soldiers to be clothed. The duties were sufficient to break down any ordinary man, but Thomas gave them his individual attention both day and night. Six of the companies were forwarded to Washington as soon as they were remounted, and on May 27 he reported the remaining four companies ready for service. These, with Thomas in command, were ordered to report to General Robert Patterson at Chambersburg, Pennsylvania, which was accomplished on the 1st day of June, 1861.

The veteran General Patterson served with great distinction as a captain in the war of 1812 and as a major-general in the war with Mexico. When Fort Sumter was fired upon and the tocsin of war was again sounded, he felt that the trumpet called the old war-worn veterans to duty again. Accordingly, he was among the very first to offer his services to President Lincoln. The writer has received the following letter from the gallant old soldier, which shows his high appreciation of Thomas:

"1300 Locust Street, Philadelphia, 26th Dec., 1879.

"My dear General,—I learn with pleasure that you are engaged in writing a history of our friend General George H. Thomas, and I am quite sure that with you it must be a labor of love. No more pleasant theme, no more worthy subject, could you select, for he was certainly a thoroughbred soldier and genial gentleman. As you well know, most men in the army have two reputations,—one which exists among their brother-officers, the other that by which they are known to the public at large; the one earned by deeds done, the other by words written or spoken; the former always correct, the latter very often not so. In General Thomas the two coincide. I think that of him it can be truthfully said, 'He was without fear and without reproach.'

"Sincerely your friend,
"R. Patterson."

Such a compliment from such a distinguished source speaks volumes in Thomas's praise, and yet General Patterson only gives voice to the general sentiment of all who knew Thomas personally and officially. No man ever lived who stood higher in the affections of the American people. While recognized as a great military leader, his purity of character, his high sense of honor and deeds of noble daring, have erected for him a monument more enduring than brass or marble,—a monument that will stand and grow more beautiful as the ages pass, unless loyalty, truth, and honor cease to leaven and sanctify the minds of the American people.

CHAPTER III.

Commands a Brigade under General Patterson—Promotion—City Troop—Battle of Falling Waters—Capture of Martinsburgh—Movement on Bunker Hill and Winchester—Appointed Brigadier-General of Volunteers—Assigned to Duty in Kentucky—Camp Dick Robinson—Scarcity of Arms—States' Rights and Peace Men—Suggests Campaign to Knoxville—Despatches from General Sherman—Commands First Division—How Made up—At Crab Orchard—Defeat of the Rebel General Crittenden—Battle of Mill Spring.

THE wildest excitement prevailed throughout the country at the time General Patterson formed his camp at Chambersburg. The bombardment of Fort Sumter, the firing upon the volunteers in the streets of Baltimore, the menace of the nation's capital by a large armed force, all combined, served to fire the Northern heart and to unite all opposing factions. It was evident that the Union could not be preserved without a long and bloody war, and after a careful estimate of the cost it was resolved that an army of seventy-five thousand volunteers should be called out. Congress was not in session, but the President assumed the responsibility and issued his proclamation. In reply to it patriotic men from city and from hamlet, from the marts of traffic and the fields of toil, from the busy haunts of the East and the almost untrodden confines of the mighty West, from river and lake and prairie and glen, from every avocation and every department of business, rallied for the defence of the Union. This material was soon organized into companies, regiments, brigades, and divisions. Thomas was assigned to the command of a brigade, of which the four companies of his regiment constituted a part. The cavalry was well mounted and well drilled; the others had to be drilled and instructed in the ordinary duties of the soldier in camp, on guard, and on the march. Men just from the walks of civil life and furnished with arms, for the first few weeks are as formidable to friends as to the enemy. It was not an unusual occurrence while in camp at Chambersburg to hear, during the still, quiet hours of night, the gentle click of the trigger,—to hear the sound of the deadly musket, followed by the challenge, "Who comes there?" Instead of challenging and following that by firing, these new men, desirous of being vigilant, reversed the order, and the result was that many of our own men were compelled to bite the dust in the camp of their friends. It did not take long, however, to instruct these men. The officers were intelligent and willing to be taught, and more than anxious to prepare their commands for the fearful struggle through which it was evident they would have to pass. To accomplish all this required an immense amount of labor on the part of Thomas, but with the cheerful co-operation of the officers he soon had these raw recruits converted into good soldiers, whose brilliant exploits subsequently commanded the admiration of the loyal people of America.

There was a body of men attached to Thomas's brigade which deserves special mention,—the "Philadelphia City Troop." This organization had been maintained for many years, having a twofold object in view,—social intercourse and military instruction. No one was admitted to its ranks except by a unanimous vote, and in this way the high character of its membership was preserved. The Troop offered its services for three months, was accepted, and assigned a place in Thomas's brigade with the regular cavalry. The members of this company endured the hardships incident to active service without murmur or complaint, always ready to brave every danger and endure every trial like true soldiers and gentlemen. Captain James subsequently became a field-officer in one of the splendid regiments of Pennsylvania cavalry, while the first sergeant is now the Hon. Samuel J. Randall, Speaker of the United States House of Representatives. Nearly all the members of the Troop, after the three months' service, became officers of volunteer regiments furnished by their State, and in every case proved themselves to be brave and competent commanders.

While at Chambersburg, General Patterson urged upon the general-in-chief (Scott) to allow him to cross the Potomac and enter Virginia at or near Leesburg for reasons hereafter given, and Colonel Thomas was warmly in favor of Patterson's plan of campaign; but General Scott, for some reason probably known by him only, overruled Patterson and ordered him to cross at Williamsport. By this movement McDowell's and Patterson's armies were placed on exterior, while Beauregard and Johnston occupied interior, lines, and were thus enabled to form a junction with each other, attack and defeat McDowell, and with equal ease they might have turned against Patterson and driven him from the Shenandoah Valley, thus defeating every organized force and leaving Washington a matter of easy capture. The crossing of Patterson at either place would have threatened Johnston's communications, and his evacuation of Harper's Ferry and occupation of Winchester would have surely followed in either event. Had Patterson, however, been at Leesburg, he would have been in supporting distance of McDowell, and could have joined him sooner than Johnston could have effected a junction with Beauregard. Had Patterson and Thomas been listened to and their plan carried out, the terrible defeat of Bull Run would not have occurred. The troops in that battle were well handled, and they fought well. The result was due to yielding to the public clamor, "On to Richmond," before the necessary arrangements were perfected. The Federal army, greatly outnumbered, had to fight on the enemy's chosen ground, and any one at all versed in military matters could have foretold the final termination of such an ill-advised movement. The Federal army was overpowered and driven back to the fortifications around Washington. It was necessary that a victim should be sacrificed, and McDowell was selected and held responsible for the disaster which had fallen upon our army. Public opinion condemned him very unjustly, for he did all that could have been done under the circumstances. Defeat was organized by the disposition of Patterson's army.

On the 2d day of July the advance, under the command of Colonel J. J. Abercrombie, U.S.A., crossed the Potomac at four o'clock A.M., followed by Thomas's brigade. The line of march was along the old Martinsburgh road, excepting Negley's brigade, which was thrown out to the right to meet the enemy should he attempt to turn the flank of the main column by a movement from Hedgeville. After a march of about five miles the advance encountered the enemy's pickets, under the command of Colonel T. J. Jackson, who was subsequently distinguished and known as Stonewall Jackson, in contradistinction to some other Jackson known as Mudwall Jackson.

Abercrombie deployed his command at once. Thomas advanced rapidly, forming on Abercrombie's right, threatening the enemy's left and rear. When the necessary dispositions were made, the line moved forward; the enemy fell back, hotly contesting the ground, but the deadly fire from our line soon created a confusion which finally resulted in a panic. The pursuit was continued for some miles, when darkness ended the contest. This affair occurred near Falling Waters, and was one of the first conflicts of the war. It seemed at that time to be a sanguinary affair, but in the grand battles fought subsequently it was forgotten by all save those who participated therein. General Patterson, in his official report of this engagement, said, "I present the reports of Colonels Abercrombie and Thomas, and take much pleasure in bearing testimony as an eye-witness to the admirable manner in which their commands were handled and their commendations earned."

On the following morning the command moved forward with Thomas in advance, who drove all opposing forces before him. About noon Martinsburgh was entered, and the army pitched its tents in and around that old country village. Here the command remained until about the 15th, when a forward movement to Bunker Hill was made. In reaching that point several skirmishes with the enemy took place, in all of which Thomas participated. He remained under the command of General Patterson, taking a prominent part in all of the movements of his army, terminating with the occupation of Charlestown and Harper's Ferry. At the expiration of ninety days Patterson's term of service expired, and he was mustered out. General N. P. Banks was designated as his successor.

The following beautiful tribute to the faithful services of General Patterson by one of the greatest military men of the age is found in a letter recently published:

"HEADQUARTERS OF THE ARMY OF THE U. S.,
"WASHINGTON, D. C., Dec. 24, 1879.

"GEN. W. S. HANCOCK, U.S.A., Governor's Island:

"MY DEAR GENERAL,—I beg to acknowledge the compliment of an invitation to unite with the Aztec Club in doing honor to the venerable Major-General Robert Patterson, at a dinner to be given at Delmonico's, at 7 P.M. on January 6.

"It will be physically impossible for me to come on that day. I regret it extremely, for there is no man in America for whom I entertain more respect and affection than for General Patterson. His whole life—now measured by eighty-eight years—has not only been noble and patriotic in an eminent degree, but it has been a type of honorable industry and of the practice of the finest social qualities.

"He is in history a strong link between the men who built up this government and those who saved it in the cruel civil war. In every epoch of this century we find his name associated with the bravest and best in peace and in war, ready at all times with his pen, his purse, and his sword to sustain the right. He does possess and enjoy at this moment more of the respect and affection of his comrades and fellow-countrymen than any living man; and I pray that his life may be spared to the last minute allotted to man on earth. When you meet him at Delmonico's please explain to him why I am not there, as well as the love and affection I bear him as a gentleman, as a citizen, and as the oldest representative of our honorable profession in all America.

"Truly your friend,
"W. T. SHERMAN."

On the 3d day of August all of the mounted regiments in the regular army were consolidated into a single organization and designated cavalry. The First and Second Dragoons and Mounted Riflemen became First, Second, and Third Cavalry, and the First and Second Cavalry became the Fourth and Fifth, in the consolidation. Thomas was then known as colonel of the Fifth Cavalry. This consolidation was not favored by a large majority of the officers, for each of the regiments had legends of its own, of which the officers were justly proud, and they desired to retain the designation under which their respective histories had been made. Aside from this, the consolidation prejudiced the rank of many of the captains in the original cavalry regiments. Thomas did all in his power to prevent the union, which he saw would work injuriously to the officers of his own regiment. On August 17, Thomas was appointed brigadier-general of volunteers and ordered to report to General Anderson, in Louisville, Kentucky. He arrived in that city and complied with his orders on September 6, 1861.

When General Anderson was sent to Kentucky, Mr. Lincoln told him that he should have any officers he might designate;

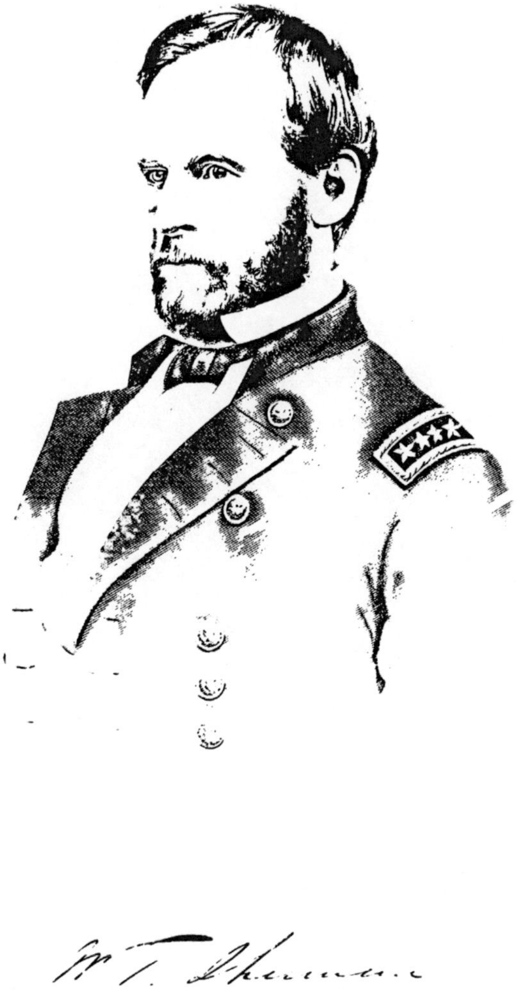

but in order that the people of that State might see that no attempt was to be made to deprive them of their negroes, he recommended that he make his selections from those of the South who were loyal. Accordingly, the following Kentuckians were made brigadiers, and ordered to report for duty,—viz., Thomas J. Wood, L. H. Rousseau, J. T. Ward, R. W. Johnson, J. T. Boyle, Wm. Nelson, and others. The arrival of such men to carry on the war convinced the people of that State that the only object the President had in view was the restoration of the Union. The freedom of the slaves became a necessity afterwards under the war-making power, and by proclamation they were declared to be free.

General Anderson had long known Thomas, and on his arrival gave him the most important position in his department,—the command of Camp Dick Robinson. This camp had been established some time previously by Lieutenant Wm. Nelson, of the U. S. Navy, a native of Kentucky, who happened to be on a visit to his old home at the beginning of our national troubles.

The difficulty in procuring arms and other supplies had very greatly retarded his progress. When it was known that Thomas was to supersede him, the secessionists made arrangements for his capture while *en route,* but from some cause unknown their plans failed, and he arrived safely at the theatre of his future operations. On his arrival he found neither quartermaster nor commissary supplies, and a very limited amount of ammunition and small-arms.

The people generally were opposed to the Federal government, although there were many loyal men ready if necessary to seal their devotion to the old government with their blood. These men flocked to Thomas's camp, and were enlisted and armed. The command to which Thomas was assigned was not organized, but he had to create it from the discordant elements around him. He relieved Nelson, and at once entered upon the great work before him. The whole State was in a feverish condition of excitement. The State government, which was loyal, did not feel secure; the loyal people were in constant dread that their lives might be taken at any moment by the roving bands of guerillas and freebooters; the secessionists were outspoken and defiant; and, added to all these, was an organized and disciplined enemy in his front, whose movements had to be watched with the greatest vigilance.

Thomas had no one upon whom he could rely for assistance, not even an experienced staff-officer, and was, therefore, compelled to give his attention to the most minute details.

He was not long in raising six regiments,—four Kentucky and two Tennessee,—and these were mustered into the service of the United States and became the nucleus around which the proud Army of the Cumberland, which was destined to perform such a prominent part in the great war, assembled and solemnly promised to bear true allegiance to the United States of America, and to defend the same against all enemies or opposers.

About this time a call was issued through the newspapers of the State to all State rights and peace men to assemble at Lexington on September 20 for the purpose of having a camp-drill, to continue for several days. These drills were

STATE RIGHTS AND PEACE MEN DISPERSED. 49

to be under the supervision of Breckenridge, Humphrey Marshall, and other men of known Southern sympathies. Thomas saw through the flimsy gauze the real object of this extraordinary gathering. He believed that it was a scheme to seize upon the arms and ammunition in Lexington, then to march to Frankfort and take violent possession of the State government, send reinforcements to Zollicoffer, and thus force the evacuation of that part of the State. To meet this measure he sent a regiment under Colonel Bramlette to camp at Lexington in the fair-grounds, with instructions to watch the assemblage closely, and if any overt act of treason was committed to arrest the leaders at once. Bramlette's approach was communicated to these misguided men and they dispersed in the wildest confusion, thus demonstrating very clearly that Thomas had correctly interpreted the character and object of the assemblage. The invasion of Kentucky by the Confederate army had the effect of stimulating enlistments and the formation of regiments in Ohio, Indiana, and Illinois, and, in fact, throughout all of the West, and troops began to pour into the State from all quarters.

These troops were undisciplined, but were better than none. They soon learned their duties, and in an incredibly short length of time became veterans. Several additional regiments were forwarded to Thomas, and he began to feel not only strong enough to hold his own, but to assume offensive operations.

The first movement that he designed to make was on Cumberland Ford. The large force under Zollicoffer increasing every day, the unprotected loyal men on the southeast border of Kentucky, who were exposed to all sorts of indignity on account of their political views, rendered a forward movement necessary so soon as it could be done with reasonable safety. But the movement of troops from Virginia to the borders of Kentucky, and the disloyal sentiments of the people generally, rendered a movement forward somewhat uncertain as to final results. The unfortunate battle of Bull Run was not to be repeated in Kentucky. Thomas, always cautious, decided to await the arrival of additional reinforcements before attempting a movement which, if unsuccessful, would prove most disastrous not only to his own command, but to that of General Sherman, operating along the line of the Louisville and Nashville Railroad.

Soon after the beginning of the war Mr. Lincoln remarked to the writer that military necessity demanded the construction of a railroad from Louisville to Knoxville, passing through Cumberland Gap; that if Knoxville could be taken it would break the backbone of the Rebellion. Looking back to that eventful period, it is easily seen that the President embraced then what it took years to demonstrate,—that Knoxville and not Richmond was the key to the Confederacy. It was not long after Knoxville was captured that it became evident that the Confederate army could not be fed without using the line of road passing through Knoxville and thence to Richmond. Thomas also saw this, and suggested to General Anderson a campaign to Knoxville for the purpose of destroying the East Tennessee and Virginia Railroad, then turning upon Zollicoffer while in the mountain-passes and capturing or dispersing his command. To accomplish this would have necessitated the concentration of nearly all the troops in the State, and General Anderson thought that such a movement might be attended by injurious results elsewhere greater than the advantage gained by the capture of Knoxville and the destruction of the East Tennessee railway system. The movement of General Zollicoffer to Loudon was one calculated to place Thomas on the defensive. He pushed forward all of the Ohio volunteers and the Third Kentucky Infantry, and ordered the obstruction of the Richmond road on the north side of Rock Castle Hills from the river to Big Hill, and the one connecting the Richmond and Mount Vernon roads, and urged General O. M. Mitchell, in command at Cincinnati, Ohio, to send reinforcements and artillery with all possible despatch. The enemy did not attempt the passage of Rock Castle Hills, but soon fell back to Cumberland Ford. The undecided course pursued by the enemy made Thomas extremely anxious to move forward to occupy his attention and prevent him from maturing his plans, and again he asked that additional troops be sent him, so that he would be in a condition to assume the offensive with a reasonable prospect of success. In furtherance of his plan he desired to send a brigade up the Big Sandy in co-operation with his movement by the way of Barbourville to East Tennessee.

After a while reinforcements arrived, but without the necessary munitions of war to render them efficient. In the early part of the war governors of States imagined that men made armies without reference to their equipments. In fact, some regiments were hastened to the front with few or no arms in the early operations in Kentucky. Crippled as Thomas was, nothing could be done except to await the enemy's movement and be prepared to meet him at whatever point he saw proper to strike. The following despatch from General W. T. Sherman, who had relieved General Anderson from the command of the department, will show that the trouble did not have its origin at his headquarters:

"LOUISVILLE, KENTUCKY, October 25, 1861.
"GENERAL GEORGE H. THOMAS, Camp Dick Robinson:

"SIR,—Don't push too far. Your line is already long and weak. I cannot now reinforce you. An interruption of the railroads by an incursion from Prestonburgh would cut you off from that source of supply. Call to your assistance the regiment from train. The State Board is impressed with the necessity of energy in the organization of volunteers, but we are still embarrassed for want of clothing and arms. Promises are a poor substitute for them, but are all we have. I will again urge on the department the pressing necessity of more good officers and large reinforcements of men."

On the 5th day of November he again telegraphed to Thomas,—

"I have done all in my power to provide men and material adequate to the importance of the crisis; but all things come disjointed,—regiments without overcoats or wagons or horses, or those essentials to movement. I can hardly sleep to think what would be your fate in case the Kentucky River bridge should be destroyed or the railroad to your rear. I have again and again demanded a force adequate to all these vicissitudes."

* * * * * *

On the 15th day of November, 1861, the designation of

the Army of the Cumberland was changed to that of the Army of the Ohio, and General D. C. Buell was assigned to the command. He at once organized the troops in the department into brigades and divisions. Thomas, being the senior brigadier-general, was assigned to the command of the First Division, which, when fully organized, was made up as follows:

FIRST BRIGADE.

Brigadier-General Albin Schoepf, Commanding.
Thirty-third Indiana Volunteers, Colonel John Coburn.
Seventeenth Ohio Volunteers, Colonel J. M. Connell.
Twelfth Kentucky Volunteers, Colonel W. A. Hoskins.
Thirty-eighth Ohio Volunteers, Colonel E. D. Bradley.

SECOND BRIGADE.

Colonel M. D. Manson, Commanding.
Fourth Kentucky Volunteers, Colonel S. S. Fry.
Fourteenth Ohio Volunteers, Colonel J. B. Steadman.
Tenth Indiana Volunteers, Colonel M. D. Manson.
Tenth Kentucky Volunteers, Colonel J. M. Harlan.

THIRD BRIGADE.

Colonel R. L. McCook, Commanding.
Eighteenth United States Infantry, Colonel H. B. Carrington.
Second Minnesota Volunteers, Colonel H. P. Van Cleve.
Thirty-fifth Ohio Volunteers, Colonel F. Vandeveer.
Ninth Ohio Volunteers, Colonel R. L. McCook.

TWELFTH BRIGADE.

Brigadier-General S. P. Carter, Commanding.
First East Tennessee Volunteers, Colonel R. R. Byrd.
Second East Tennessee Volunteers, Colonel J. P. S. Carter.
Seventh Kentucky Volunteers, Colonel T. T. Gaward.
Thirty-first Ohio Volunteers, Colonel M. B. Walker.

TROOPS NOT ASSIGNED TO BRIGADES.

First Kentucky Cavalry, Colonel F. Woolford.
Squadron Indiana Cavalry, Captain Graham.
Battery B, First Kentucky Artillery, Captain J. M. Hewitt.
Battery B, First Ohio Artillery, Captain W. B. Standart.
Battery C, First Ohio Artillery, Captain D. Kinney.
Major W. E. Lawrence, Chief of Artillery.

At the time this organization was completed the troops were raw and undisciplined, and hardly prepared to move against an enemy. To bring them up to reasonable efficiency required much labor and time. One can scarcely imagine the cares and troubles which beset Thomas. He had to watch an enterprising enemy, to provide provisions, clothes, and arms for the command, and to superintend the drills and see that every officer and soldier did his duty. The cares which devolved upon him at this critical period were numerous enough to occupy the time and attention of three or four experienced officers, and he would have failed had he been a paltry counterfeit, a human nonentity, a mere drone in this great world-hive of ours. But he was a man of iron mould and dauntless purpose,—a man who did not shrivel in the first heats of disappointment, a man whose spirits rose as obstacles thickened, acquired fresh courage with each additional responsibility, confronted new perils and difficulties, new foes and trials, with unquailing front, and gathered to his heart more of the light and essence of heaven as the world glowered and gloomed around him. Those were bleak, dark days,—not only for Thomas, but for every loyal man in the country.

It was not long before he converted this raw material into disciplined soldiers, and among his commanders were found some of the distinguished men of the war, while all the regiments under him served with great distinction throughout the contest, reflecting credit not alone upon their own organization, but upon the States which sent them forth. The veterans of the First Division are proud of their record, and very justly, while their first commander fills a dear place in their hearts. The mention of his name recalls pleasant memories of their early experience on the tented field.

On the 21st day of October, 1861, Thomas sent forward Schoepf with a part of his brigade, which met a considerable body of the enemy under General Zollicoffer, and repulsed it with slight loss on either side. On the 28th, Thomas established his headquarters at Crab Orchard, but soon after, in compliance with orders of General Buell, withdrew to Danville, and thence to Lebanon, from which latter point he moved *via* Columbia to attack the enemy, under General Crittenden, at Beech Grove. Owing to heavy rains, and consequently bad roads, he did not succeed in reaching Logan's Cross-Roads until the 17th day of November. At that point he delayed until the rear of his column came up, and endeavored to open communication with General Schoepf. The year was drawing to a close, and, with the exception of the disastrous affair at Bull Run, no engagement of any magnitude had taken place. The authorities in Washington were becoming quite anxious that some decisive blow should be delivered,—a blow with an iron hand, which would be felt from the circumference to the centre of the Confederacy and contribute in some degree to the restoration of peace. The eyes of the nation were upon Thomas and his devoted army.

On the night of January 18, 1862, the enemy, under General George B. Crittenden, moved out of his camp at Beech Grove, and on the following morning attacked Thomas's advance at Logan's Cross-Roads. A sharp engagement ensued, resulting in the defeat of the enemy, who fell back in great confusion to his intrenched camp at Beech Grove. Thomas followed up his antagonist, and at 5 o'clock P.M. formed his line in front of the enemy's works, opening a heavy artillery fire. The curtain of darkness fell, and closed the operations for the day. On the following morning it was ascertained that Crittenden had fallen back in great confusion, abandoning his artillery, wagons, munitions, and stores. Pursuit was continued as far as Monticello. In this encounter Thomas lost, in killed and wounded, two hundred and forty-six men, while the enemy's loss was three hundred and forty-nine. Only a small portion of Thomas's command was engaged, but the coolness and gallantry displayed by officers and men were highly commended by their commander. After this

BATTLE OF MILL SPRINGS. 57

engagement, small as it was, the loyal people felt encouraged, as it was the first victory of the year, and the name of Thomas was on the tongue of every loyal man in the country. The following is his modest report of this engagement:

"HEADQUARTERS FIRST DIVISION, DEPARTMENT OF THE OHIO,
"SOMERSET, KY., January 31, 1862.

"CAPTAIN,—I have the honor to report that, in carrying out the instructions of the general commanding the department, contained in his communication of the 29th December, I reached Logan's Cross-Roads, about ten miles north of the intrenched camp of the enemy on the Cumberland River, on the 17th instant, with a portion of the Second and Third Brigades, Kenney's battery of artillery, and a battalion of Woolford's cavalry. The Fourth and Tenth Kentucky, Fourteenth Ohio, and Eighteenth United States Infantry being still in rear, detained by the almost impassable condition of the roads, I determined to halt at this point, await their arrival, and to communicate with General Schoepf.

"The Tenth Indiana, Woolford's cavalry, and Kenney's battery took position on the main road leading to the enemy's camp. The Ninth Ohio and Tenth Minnesota (part of Colonel McCook's brigade) encamped three-fourths of a mile to the right of the Robertsport road. Strong pickets were thrown out in the direction of the enemy beyond where the Somerset and Mill Springs road comes into the main road from my camp to Mill Springs, and a picket of cavalry some distance in advance of the infantry. General Schoepf visited me on the day of my arrival, and after consultation I directed him to send to my camp Standart's battery, the Twelfth Kentucky, and the First and Second Tennessee Regiments, to remain until the arrival of the regiments in the rear.

"Having received information on the evening of the 17th

that a large train of wagons with its escort was encamped on the Robertsport and Danville road, about six miles from Colonel Steedman's camp, I sent an order to him to send his wagons forward under a strong guard, and to march with his regiment (the Fourteenth Ohio) and the Tenth Kentucky, Colonel Harlan, with one day's rations in their haversacks, to the point where the enemy were said to be encamped and either capture or disperse them.

"Nothing of importance occurred from the time of our arrival until the morning of the 19th, except a picket skirmish on the night of the 17th. The Fourth Kentucky, the battalion Michigan Engineers, and Wetmore's battery joined on the 18th. About half-past six o'clock on the morning of the 19th the pickets from Woolford's cavalry encountered the enemy advancing on our camp, retired slowly, and reported their advance to Colonel M. D. Manson, commanding the Second Brigade. He immediately formed his regiment (the Tenth Indiana) and took a position on the road to await the attack, ordering the Fourth Kentucky, Colonel S. S. Fry, to support him, and then informed me in person that the enemy were advancing in force and what disposition he had made to resist them. I directed him to join his brigade immediately and hold the enemy in check until I could order up the other troops, which were ordered to form immediately, and were marching to the field in ten minutes afterwards. The battalion of Michigan Engineers, and Company A, Thirty-eighth Ohio, were ordered to remain as guard to the camp. Upon my arrival on the field soon afterwards, I found the Tenth Indiana formed in front of their encampment, apparently awaiting orders, and ordered them forward to the support of the Fourth Kentucky, which was the only entire regiment then engaged. I then rode forward myself to see the enemy's position, so that I could determine what disposition to make of my troops as they arrived. On reaching the position held by the Fourth Kentucky, Tenth Indiana, and Woolford's cavalry, at a point where the roads fork to go to Somerset, I found the enemy advancing through a cornfield, and evidently endeavoring to gain the left of the Fourth Kentucky Regiment, which was maintaining its position in a most determined manner. I directed one of my aides to ride back and order up a section of artillery, and the Tennessee Brigade to advance on the enemy's right, and sent orders for Colonel McCook to advance with his two regiments (the Ninth Ohio and Second Minnesota) to the support of the Fourth Kentucky and Eighteenth Indiana.

"A section of Captain Kinney's battery took a position on the edge of the field, to the left of the Fourth Kentucky, and opened an effective fire on a regiment of Alabamians which were advancing on the Fourth Kentucky. Soon afterwards the Second Minnesota, Colonel H. P. Van Cleve, arrived, reporting to me for instructions. I directed him to take the position of the Fourth Kentucky and Tenth Indiana, which regiments were nearly out of ammunition. The Ninth Ohio, under the immediate command of Major Kaimmerling, came into position on the right of the road at the same time. Immediately after these regiments had gained their positions the enemy opened a most determined and galling fire, which was returned by our troops in the same spirit, and for nearly half an hour the contest was maintained on both sides in the most obstinate manner.

"At this time the Twelfth Kentucky, Colonel W. A. Hoskins, and the Tennessee Brigade reached the field on the left of the Minnesota regiment, and opened fire on the right flank of the enemy, who then began to fall back.

"The Second Minnesota kept up a most galling fire in front, and the Ninth Ohio charged the enemy on the left with bayonets fixed, turned their flank, and drove them from the field, the whole line giving way and retreating in the utmost disorder and confusion.

"As soon as the regiments could be formed and refill their cartridge-boxes, I ordered the whole force to advance. A few miles in rear of the battle-field a small force of cavalry was drawn up near the road, but a few shots from our artillery —a section of Standart's battery—dispersed it, and none of the enemy were seen again until we arrived in front of their intrenchments.

"As we approached their intrenchments the division was deployed in line of battle, and steadily advanced along the summit of the hill at Moulden's. From this point I directed their intrenchments to be cannonaded, which was done until dark, by Standart and Wetmore's batteries. Kinney's battery was placed in position on the extreme left of Russell's house, from which point he was directed to fire on their ferry to deter them from attempting to cross.

"On the following morning Captain Wetmore's battery was ordered to Russell's house, and assisted with his Parrott guns in firing upon the ferry. Colonel Manson's brigade took position on the left, near Kinney's battery, and every preparation was made to assault their intrenchments on the following morning. The Fourteenth Ohio, Colonel Steedman, and the Tenth Kentucky, Colonel Harlan, having joined from detached service soon after the repulse of the enemy, continued with their brigade in pursuit, although they could not get up in time to join in the fight. These two regiments were placed in front, in my advance on the intrenchments the next morning, and entered first, General Schoepf having also joined me the evening of the 19th with the Seventeenth, Thirty-first, and Thirty-eighth Ohio, his entire brigade, and entered with the other troops. On reaching the intrenchments we found that the enemy had abandoned everything and retired during the night. Twelve pieces of artillery, with their caissons packed with ammunition, one battery-wagon, and two forges, a large amount of small-arms, mostly the old flint-lock muskets, and ammunition for the same, one hundred and fifty or sixty wagons, and upwards of one thousand horses and mules, a large amount of commissary stores, intrenching tools, and camp and garrison equipage, fell into our hands. A correct list of all the captured property will be forwarded as soon as it can be made up and the property secured.

"The steam- and ferry-boats having been burned by the enemy on their retreat, it was found impossible to cross the river and pursue them; besides, their command was completely demoralized, and retreated with great haste and in all directions, making their capture in any numbers quite doubtful if pursued. There is no doubt but what the moral effect produced by their complete dispersion will have a more decided effect in re-establishing Union sentiments than though they had been captured.

"It affords me much pleasure to be able to testify to the uniform steadiness and good conduct of both officers and men during the battle, and I respectfully refer to the accompanying reports of the different commanders for the names of those officers and men whose good conduct was particularly noticed by them.

"I regret to have to report that Colonel R. L. McCook, commanding the Third Brigade, and his aide-de-camp, Lieutenant A. S. Burt, Eighteenth United States Infantry, were both severely wounded in the first advance of the Ninth Ohio Regiment, but continued on duty until the return of the brigade to camp at Logan's Cross-Roads. Colonel S. S. Fry, Fourth Kentucky, was slightly wounded while his regiment was gallantly resisting the advance of the enemy, during which time Zollicoffer fell from a shot from his pistol, which no doubt contributed materially to the discomfiture of the enemy.

"Captain George E. Hunt, assistant adjutant-general, Captain Abram C. Gillem, division quartermaster, Lieutenant J. C. Breckenridge, aide-de-camp, Lieutenant S. B. Jones, acting assistant quartermaster, Mr. J. W. Scully, quartermaster's clerk, Privates Samuel Letcher, Twenty-first Regiment Kentucky Volunteers, —— Stitch, Fourth Regiment Kentucky Volunteers, rendered me valuable assistance in carrying orders and conducting the troops to their different positions.

"Captain G. S. Roper, commissary of subsistence, deserves great credit for his perseverance and energy in forwarding commissary stores for the command as far as the hill where our forces bivouac.

"In addition to the duties of guarding the camp, Lieutenant-Colonel A. K. Hunton, commanding the Michigan Engineers, and Captain Greenwood, Company A, Thirty-eighth Regiment Ohio Volunteers, with their commands, performed very efficient service in collecting and burying the dead on both sides and removing the wounded to the hospitals near the field of battle.

"A number of flags were taken on the field of battle and in the intrenchments. They will be forwarded to department headquarters as soon as collected together.

"The loss of the enemy is as follows: Brigadier-General F. K. Zollicoffer, Lieutenant Bailey Peyton, and 120 officers, non-commissioned officers, and privates killed and buried; Lieutenant-Colonel M. B. Carter, Twentieth Tennessee, Lieutenant J. W. Allen, Fifteenth Mississippi, Lieutenant Allen Morse, Sixteenth Alabama, and 5 officers of the medical staff, and 81 non-commissioned officers and privates, taken prisoners; Lieutenant J. E. Patterson, Twentieth Tennessee,

A. J. Knapp, Fifteenth Mississippi, and 66 non-commissioned officers and privates wounded: making 122 killed, 89 prisoners, not wounded and wounded,—a total of killed and wounded and prisoners 349.

"Our loss was as follows:

KILLED.

	Com'd officers.	Non-com'd officers and privates.
Ninth Ohio	..	6
Second Minnesota	..	12
Fourth Kentucky	..	8
Tenth Indiana	..	10
First Kentucky Cavalry	1	2
	1	38

WOUNDED.

Ninth Ohio	4	24
Second Minnesota	2	31
Fourth Kentucky	4	48
Tenth Indiana	3	72
First Kentucky Cavalry	..	19
	13	194

"One commissioned officer and 38 men were killed, and 14 officers, including Lieutenant Burt, Eighteenth United States Infantry, aide-de-camp, and 194 non-commissioned officers and privates, wounded.

"A complete list of the names of our killed and wounded and of the prisoners is herewith attached.

"I am, sir, very respectfully,
"Your obedient servant,
"GEORGE H. THOMAS,
"Brigadier-General U.S.V., Commanding."

CHAPTER IV.

In Camp at Somerset—Movement to Bowling Green—To Nashville—Bitterness of Feeling in Nashville—Movement to the Relief of General Grant at Pittsburg Landing—Battle of Shiloh—Siege of Corinth—March to Huntsville—Pursues Bragg to Kentucky—Thomas's Unselfishness.

AFTER the battle of Mill Springs, Thomas established his forces in camp at Somerset, where he awaited instructions from General Buell, who had already given orders to concentrate his command for a direct movement on Bowling Green, at which point a large army, under General Albert Sydney Johnston, had been posted for some time, engaged in constructing fortifications. In a short time Thomas was ordered to move his command to Lebanon. About this time Bowling Green was evacuated, the Confederate army falling back to Nashville. Thomas moved his command to Louisville, and thence by boat to Nashville, *via* the Ohio and Cumberland Rivers.

At this time General Grant had his lines well drawn around the Confederate army at Fort Donelson, on the Cumberland, and it was evident that a crisis in the history of that command must soon arise. General Pillow, who commanded the Southern troops at that point, having no taste for prison life within the walls of a "Northern bastile," turned the command over to General Floyd, and he, for a similar reason, relinquished in favor of General S. B. Buckner, who was too honorable and too much of a soldier to run away and abandon his command to its fate, but, like a true soldier, remained to share the fortunes of his men.

Pillow and Floyd escaped by boat to Nashville, where they arrived on the Sabbath day while the good people were in attendance upon divine service in the various churches. The news of their arrival spread rapidly over the city, creating great excitement. Men, women, and children rushed frantically through the streets yelling as lustily as they could, "The Yankees are coming, the Yankees are coming!" Congregations were dismissed without the usual benediction, and every one who could get out of the city left by the first opportunity. Floyd remained long enough to cut the wires of the suspension-bridge, and precipitated that grand structure in a shapeless mass to the bottom of the river. The rear of the column of fugitives was scarcely out of the city when Buell, with his magnificent army, arrived in Edgefield, opposite Nashville. Boats were procured, and the work of crossing began at once, and continued until all were over and Nashville was in the hands of the Union army. Thomas arrived soon after and took his place in the line surrounding the city.

The Federal army found the bitterest feeling prevailing against the Union and its brave defenders. The latter were characterized as Lincoln hirelings, and "likened unto the offspring and descendants of those old Norsemen who, in the long-ago of English history, had been the terror and shame of the world." The populace had been told from pulpit and press that when the Sunny South was desecrated by the foot of the "Northern vandal," barbarities and atrocities worse than those ever perpetrated in the deepest, darkest nights of English heathenism would be heaped upon them by the mercenary soldiers of Abe Lincoln. Under the mild and gentlemanly treatment of General Buell and his able assistant, General Thomas, the citizens became convinced that the Northern people were not the cruel and inhuman monsters they had been represented.

The army remained in Nashville until about the middle of March, when a courier arrived from General Grant's camp on the Tennessee River, near Pittsburg Landing, reporting the concentration of a large force in his immediate front. Buell gave orders to prepare for a rapid march. All unnecessary baggage was stored, provisions were issued, and when all preparations had been made the order was issued and the movement began. General O. M. Mitchell was to operate from Nashville against the Memphis and Charleston Railroad, while Buell, with the divisions of Thomas, Wood, Nelson, McCook, and Crittenden, moved on the direct road to Savannah, near Pittsburg Landing, where the command arrived on the morning of April 5, 1862. Long before the arrival at Savannah the distant roar of artillery was heard, telling of a fearful struggle between the contending armies. The arrival was timely, and Buell and his army won undying honors on the memorable field of Shiloh.

Thomas did not arrive in time to participate in this battle, but his name was a potent power. His skill and courage had always been conspicuous, and he was universally regarded as worthy and qualified to fill any position to which the government might assign him. General Halleck recognized this fact, and in reorganizing his command after this battle placed Thomas in command of the right wing,—a position he held until after the siege and capture of Corinth.

The advance from the Tennessee River to Corinth was one of the most difficult campaigns of the war, and one not fully understood or comprehended by those who did not participate in it. It should be remembered that owing to the heavy spring rains it was impossible to move artillery or wagons, the wheels cutting into the ground to the hubs and rendering it out of the question to move without making corduroy roads. Miles and miles of such roads had to be constructed. With the greatest difficulty the column was moved up to the vicinity of Corinth. The lines were formed, and artillery placed within range of the town, but no assault was made. Here the army remained until after General Beauregard withdrew and allowed the Federal army to enter and take possession of his filthy camp, filled with carcasses of dead animals and overhung by an atmosphere poisoned by decaying animal matter. The fruits of this campaign can be easily summed up,—a few deserters and a few Quaker guns which Beauregard had placed in position with their frowning muzzles pointed in the direction of the Federal lines.

General Thomas was placed in command of Corinth and vicinity,—a command that he exercised until June 22, when he was transferred with his old division to the Army of the Ohio. It should be remarked that when he was placed in command of the right wing he was temporarily transferred to the Army of the Tennessee.

Leaving Corinth behind him, he took charge of the troops along the Memphis and Charleston Railroad. He was soon relieved from this duty and ordered to concentrate his division at Huntsville, Alabama, where he remained only a few days, and then pushed on with his command to Decherd, sending one brigade to Pelham. Affairs at McMinnville having assumed such a phase as to require the presence of a discreet officer, Thomas was sent thither, leaving his old division for the time in charge of General Schoepf.

The extraordinary movements of the enemy convinced Thomas that an invasion of Kentucky was contemplated, and this belief was communicated to General Buell, but the latter was of the opinion that Nashville was Bragg's objective-point. Accordingly, he made such disposition of his forces as to render it impossible for the enemy to reach that point without a desperate battle. Bragg, who was an able and cautious general, did not wish to risk a general engagement, and after having demonstrated against Nashville he changed his programme by deflecting to the right, crossing the river above that city, and pushing on in the direction of Louisville. Buell, who was always on the alert, at once proceeded to checkmate his adversary. Thomas, who had been ordered to Nashville, with his own and the divisions of Mitchell, Negley, and Paine, moved out to join Buell in Kentucky. On the 20th he effected a junction with him at Prewitt's Knob, where he found him confronted by the enemy in considerable force. The heavy skirmishing seemed to indicate an intention of offering a general battle, but on the following day Bragg withdrew, and Buell pushed on with all possible speed to Louisville, where he arrived on the 25th and the rear of his column on the 29th.

Previous to the arrival of the Federal army the Southern element was in fine spirits, while the Union people were greatly depressed; but when the advance of Buell's dusty veterans entered the city, joy and gladness filled the hearts of the loyal portion of the population. The streets were filled with the loyalists, and from doors, windows, and balconies ladies and children waved handkerchiefs and tiny flags, in exultation over their happy deliverance from anxiety and fear. The army was posted around the city, and Louisville was once more a military camp.

This march of Buell's was one of the grandest strategic movements of the war, and stamped him as a soldier with no superior in the service. Students in the military art may study this campaign with profit to themselves, feeling assured at the same time that it was one of the most brilliant exploits of the war. Buell was a soldier without a superior in the army, and had he remained in the service until the close of the Rebellion would have filled one of the highest places in public esteem. He had, at all times, the cheerful co-operation of Thomas, who was regarded by Buell as one of the most accomplished officers in the grand army.

There is something in the service calculated to engender selfishness,—probably not more so than in other professions, but certainly it is found in the army, and the older the officer the clearer does this trait show itself; but with Thomas there was no indication of it. He was ever ready to "render unto Cæsar the things that were Cæsar's." If an officer under him did anything brilliant or praiseworthy, he was sure to get the credit due him, and no man was more ready to draw the curtain of oblivion over the mishaps, misfortunes, or blunders of others. He was never willing to condemn unless the proof was positive, and even then he did so reluctantly. The more his character is studied and understood, the more we love and venerate his memory. Like Washington, "he was good because he was great, and great because he was good."

CHAPTER V.

Thomas offered Buell's Command—The Offer declined—Battle of Perryville—Rosecrans succeeds Buell—March to Nashville—Battle of Stone River—Capture of Murfreesboro'—Colonel Buckner's Seventy-ninth Illinois—Capture of Tullahoma—Chickamauga Campaign—Army saved by Thomas, who succeeds Rosecrans—Short Rations—Driving Enemy from the River—Grant at Chattanooga—Thomas's Plans Approved—Opinion of W. F. G. Shanks, Esq.

ON the 29th day of September, General Thomas received an order from the general-in-chief assigning him to the command of the Army of the Ohio, relieving General Buell, he having incurred the displeasure of the War Department by allowing the rebel army to again invade Kentucky. Instead of censure he was entitled to great praise, for it was his energy and matchless skill that prevented the capture of Louisville and saved to the cause of the Union many advantages already gained by our forces in that State. Thomas saw at once the great injustice it would be to Buell as well as to himself. His acceptance would disgrace a meritorious, worthy officer, and place one in a position for immediate service who had not studied the subject sufficiently for intelligent action. Under these circumstances, Thomas telegraphed asking for a delay in carrying out the order, and its execution was suspended. On the 1st day of October the army moved out to meet Bragg, and on that red autumnal day—the 8th day of October—a fearful battle was fought at Perryville. The success was not as complete as was expected. Some censured Buell, while he cast the blame upon others. It is not our province to decide the dispute, and hence it is left for the consideration of those who are interested to settle among themselves the true cause of the partial failure in that battle. But we will say that in our humble judgment, if any errors were commited there, they were the results of honest misapprehension of facts, and were the errors of men who have proven their mettle and chivalry in the midst of conflicts as terrible as ever shook the earth or crimsoned the soil of the battle-field.

Our loss in this battle was heavy. Prominent among the killed were Generals James S. Jackson and W. R. Terrell, who fell while gallantly leading their men against the columns of the enemy. Had these two officers survived the war, their names would now stand high on the roll of the nation's great defenders.

After this battle General Buell was relieved, and General W. S. Rosecrans, whose brilliant services in Northern Mississippi had brought him prominently forward, was his successor. When the change in the commander was made, the name of the army was also changed to that of "The Army of the Cumberland," and the troops operating in the department were consolidated and designated as the Fourteenth Corps. Rosecrans subdivided the corps into three grand divisions,—the right and left wings and centre,—and these were commanded by Major-Generals A. McD. McCook, Thomas L. Crittenden, and George H. Thomas. After the battle of Perryville

Bragg withdrew from the State, and Rosecrans concentrated his forces at Nashville on November 7. The army remained here until December 26, during which time supplies were brought forward, troops drilled, and arrangements made for an advance. The main body of the enemy was at Murfreesboro', with outposts thrown forward to the right, left, and front. Thomas moved his command by the Franklin and Wilson pikes, threatening Hardee, who retreated to Murfreesboro'. Thomas then fell in by the cross-roads to Nolensville and Stewartsboro', and from thence advanced on Murfreesboro' by the way of the Wilkinson cross-roads. On the night of December 30 the entire army was concentrated in the vicinity of Murfreesboro', or rather along the line of Stone River,—McCook on the right, Crittenden on the left, and Thomas in reserve in rear of the centre.

On the morning of the 31st the battle began by an attack on the right flank of the Federal army. It should be remarked that during the night of the 30th the enemy massed his forces opposite to our right, leaving Breckenridge with a long, weak, attenuated line in front of our left and centre. When the attack was made it was with overpowering numbers, and our right was driven back in some confusion, although obstinately contesting every inch of the ground. The lines were again reformed near the Nashville pike, where the onward rush of the enemy was checked. Here it was that the Army of the Cumberland, as such, first baptized its name in blood. Who that was there during that desperate struggle will ever forget it? We were in the midst of a population more hostile and unrelenting than that which surrounded Xenophon in his famed march from the disastrous plains of Cunaxa, or the Swedish Charles when his hitherto invincible legions were shattered by the Muscovite at Pultawa. The Federal army fought a skilful and determined enemy upon the field of his own choice, and, after a series of battles unsurpassed in the whole history of warfare for their fierceness and tenacity, defeated him whilst he was yet flushed with the excitement of his supposed success, and wrenched the garlands of victory, as it appeared, from the very hands of Fate itself.

Who shall ever tell the secrets of those cedar fastnesses or unveil the slender threads upon which the fortunes of that desperate field revolved? The brave and daring Thomas was at all times at the post of danger, and all felt secure in the thought that such a man was controlling, to some extent, the operations of the day. Then there were the brave and daring McCook and the gallant Crittenden,—men of nerve and judgment,—and these three distinguished leaders commanded the grand divisions of that magnificent army. Temporary reverses might come, but in the end victory would perch upon their banners. Such was the case at Stone River, and these three honored names will ever be associated with that battle. Rosecrans, when called to this command, took hold of a body of men whose real history had already been written so bravely at Mill Springs, Shiloh, and Perryville, and whose marches and battles had veteranized and disciplined it in the best arts of war.

Bragg fell back and the Federal army took possession of Murfreesboro', where it remained for six months,—long enough to dissatisfy the authorities in Washington, who could not understand the reason of such delay. While here Rosecrans was not idle, but was actively engaged fortifying the town, and when he had completed his various forts a small force could have held the place against the Confederate armies combined. The volunteers, who had by this time become veterans, occupied themselves in various ways. It was amusing to see some of them handling the spade and pick, instruments to which many of them had been strangers all their lives, but these same men learned before the close of the war that spades were trumps in almost every deal.

The following is Thomas's report of the battle of Stone River:

"HEADQUARTERS CENTRE FOURTEENTH ARMY CORPS,
"DEPARTMENT OF THE CUMBERLAND,
"MURFREESBORO', January 15, 1863.

"MAJOR,—I have the honor to submit to the major-general commanding the Department of the Cumberland the following report of the operations of that part of my command which was engaged in the battle of Stone River, in front of Murfreesboro'. It is proper to state here that two brigades of Fry's division and Reynolds's entire division were detained near Gallatin and along the Louisville and Nashville Railroad to watch the movements of the rebel leader Morgan, who had been for a long time on the watch for an opportunity to destroy the railroad.

"Rousseau's, Negley's, and Mitchell's divisions and Walker's brigade of Fry's division were concentrated at Nashville, but, Mitchell's division being required to garrison Nashville, my only available force was Rousseau's and Negley's divisions and Walker's brigade of Fry's division,—about 13,395 effective men.

"*December* 26.—Negley's division, followed by Rousseau's

division and Walker's brigade, marched by the Franklin pike to Brentwood, at that point taking the Wilson pike. Negley and Rousseau were to have encamped for the night at Owens's Store. On reaching the latter place, Negley, hearing heavy firing in the direction of Nolansville, left his train with a guard to follow, and pushed forward with his troops to the support of Brigadier-General J. C. Davis's command, the advance division of McCook's corps, Davis having become hotly engaged with the enemy posted in Nolansville and in the pass through the hills south of that village. Rousseau encamped with his division at Owens's Store, Walker with his brigade at Brentwood. During the night a very heavy rain fell, making the cross-roads almost impassable, and it was not until the night of the 27th that Rousseau reached Nolansville with his troops and train. Negley remained at Nolansville until 10 A.M. on the 27th, when, having brought his train across from Wilson pike, he moved to the east over an exceeding rough by-road to the right of Crittenden, at Stewartsboro', on the Murfreesboro' pike. Walker, by my orders, retraced his steps from Brentwood, and crossed over to the Nolansville pike.

"*December* 28.—Negley remained in camp at Stewartsboro', bringing his train from the rear. Rousseau reached Stewartsboro' on the night of the 28th; his train arrived early next day.

"*December* 29.—Negley's division crossed Stewart's Creek two miles southwest and above the turnpike bridge, and marched in support of the head and right flank of Crittenden's corps, which moved by the Murfreesboro' pike to a point within two miles of Murfreesboro'. The enemy fell back before our advance, contesting the ground obstinately with their cavalry rear-guard. Rousseau remained in camp at Stewartsboro', detaching Starkweather's brigade with a section of artillery to the Jefferson pike, crossing Stone River, to ob-

Phil. H. Sheridan

serve the movements of the enemy in that direction. Walker reached Stewartsboro' from the Nolansville pike about dark.

"*December* 30.—A cavalry force of the enemy, something over four hundred strong, with two pieces of artillery, attacked Starkweather about 9 A.M., but were soon driven off. The enemy opened a brisk fire on Crittenden's advance, doing but little execution, however. About 7 A.M. during the morning Negley's division was obliqued to the right, and took up a position on the right of Palmer's division of Crittenden's corps, and was then advanced through a dense cedar thicket, several hundred yards in width, to the Wilkinson cross-roads, driving the enemy's skirmishers steadily and with considerable loss—our loss comparatively small. About noon Sheridan's division of McCook's corps approached by the Wilkin's cross-roads, joined Negley's right, McCook's two other divisions coming up on Sheridan's right, thus forming a continuous line, the left resting on Stone River, the right stretching in a westerly direction and resting on high wooded ground a short distance to the south of the Wilkinson cross-roads, and, as has since been ascertained, nearly parallel with the enemy's intrenchments, thrown up on the sloping land bordering the northwest bank of Stone River, Rousseau's division, with the exception of Starkweather's brigade, being ordered up on the Murfreesboro' pike in the rear of the centre. During the night of the 30th I sent orders to Walker to take up a strong position near the turnpike bridge over Stewart's Creek and defend the position against any attempts of the enemy's cavalry to destroy it. Rousseau was ordered to move by 6 A.M. on the 31st to position in rear of Negley. This position placed his division with its left on the Murfreesboro' pike and its right extending into the cedar thicket through which Negley had marched on the 30th. In front of Negley's position, bordering a large open field reaching to the Murfreesboro' pike, a heavy growth of timber extended in a southerly direction towards the river. Across the field, running in an easterly direction, the enemy had thrown up rifle-pits at intervals from the timber to the river-bank, to the east side of the turnpike. Along this line of intrenchments, on an eminence about eight hundred yards from Negley's position, and nearly in front of his left, some cannon had been placed, affording the enemy great advantage in covering an attack on our centre. However, Palmer, Negley, and Sheridan held the position their troops had so manfully won the morning of the 30th against every attempt to drive them back, and remained in line of battle during the night.

"*December* 31.—Between 6 and 7 A.M. the enemy, having massed a heavy force on McCook's right during the night of the 30th, attacked and drove it back, pushing his division in pursuit in echelon and supporting distance until he had gained sufficient ground to our rear to wheel his masses to the right and throw them upon the right flank of the centre, at the same moment attacking Negley and Palmer in front with a greatly superior force. To counteract this movement I had ordered Rousseau to place two brigades with a battery to the right and rear of Sheridan's division, facing towards the west, so as to support Sheridan should he be able to hold his ground, or to cover him should he be compelled to fall back. About eleven o'clock General Sheridan reported to me that his ammunition was entirely out, and he would be compelled to fall back to get more. As it became necessary for General Sheridan to fall back, the enemy pressed on still farther to our rear, and soon took up a position which gave them a concentrated cross-fire of musketry and cannon on Negley's and Rousseau's troops at short range. This compelled me to fall back out of the cedar woods, and take up a line along a depression in the open ground within good musket-range of the edge of the woods, whilst the artillery was retired to the high ground to the right of the turnpike. From this last position we were enabled to drive back the enemy, cover the formation of our troops, and secure the centre on the high ground. In the execution of this last movement the regular brigade, under Lieutenant-Colonel Sheperd, Eighteenth United States Infantry, came under a most murderous fire, losing 22 officers and 508 men in killed and wounded, but, with the co-operation of Scribner's and Beatty's brigades and Guenther's and Loomis's batteries, gallantly held its ground against overwhelming odds. The centre, having succeeded in driving back the enemy from its front and our artillery concentrating its fire on the cedar thicket on our right, drove him back far under cover, from which, though attempting it, he could not make any advance.

"*January* 1, 1863.—Repeated attempts were made by the enemy to advance on my position during the morning, but they were driven back before emerging from the woods. Colonel Starkweather's brigade of Rousseau's division, and Walker's brigade of Fry's division, having reinforced us during the night, took post on the right of Rousseau and left of Sheridan, and bore their share in repelling the attempts of the enemy on the morning of the 1st instant. For the details of the most valuable service rendered by these two brigades on the 30th and 31st December, 1862, and the 1st, 2d, and 3d January, 1863, I refer you to their reports. In this connection I also refer you to the report of Lieutenant-Colonel Parkhurst, commanding Ninth Michigan Infantry (on provost duty at my headquarters), for the details of most valuable service rendered by his command on the 31st of December and 1st and 2d of January. Negley's division was ordered early in the day to the support of McCook's right, and in which position it remained during the night.

"*January* 2.—About 7 A.M. the enemy opened a direct and cross fire from his batteries in our front, and from our position on the east bank of Stone River to our left and front, at the same time making a strong demonstration with infantry, resulting, however, in no serious attack. Our artillery—Loomis's, Guenther's, Stokes's, and another battery: the commander's name I cannot now recall—soon drove back their infantry. Negley was withdrawn from the extreme right and placed in reserve behind Crittenden's right. About 4 P.M. a division of Crittenden's corps, which had crossed Stone River to reconnoitre, was attacked by an overwhelming force of the enemy, and, after a gallant resistance, compelled to fall back. The movements of the enemy having been observed and reported by some of my troops in the centre, I sent orders to Negley to advance to the support of Crittenden's troops should they want help. This order was obeyed in most gallant style, and resulted in the complete annihilation of the Twenty-sixth Tennessee rebel regiment and the capture of their flags; also in the capture of a battery, which the enemy had been forced to abandon at the point of the bayonet. (See Negley's report.)

"*January* 3.—Soon after daylight the Forty-second Indiana, on picket in a clump of woods about eight hundred yards in front of our lines, was attacked by a brigade of the enemy, evidently by superior numbers, and driven in with considerable loss. Lieutenant-Colonel Shankling, commanding regiment, was surrounded and taken prisoner whilst gallantly endeavoring to draw off his men from under the fire of such superior numbers. From this woods the enemy's sharpshooters continued to fire occasionally during the day on our pickets. About 6 P.M. two regiments from Colonel John Beatty's brigade of Rousseau's division, co-operating with two regiments of Spear's brigade of Negley's division, covered by the skilful and well-directed fire of Guenther's Fifth United States Artillery and Loomis's First Michigan batteries, advanced on the woods, and drove the enemy not only from its cover, but from their intrenchments a short distance beyond. For the details of this gallant night-attack I refer you to the reports of Brigadier-General Spear, commanding Third Brigade of Negley's division, and Colonel John Beatty, commanding Second Brigade of Rousseau's division.

"The enemy having retreated during the night of the 3d, our troops were occupied during the morning of the 4th in burying the dead left on the field. In the afternoon one brigade of Negley's division was advanced to the crossing of Stone River, with a brigade of Rousseau's division in supporting distance in reserve.

"*January 5.*—My entire command, preceded by Stanley's cavalry, marched into Murfreesboro' and took up the position we now hold. The enemy's rear-guard of cavalry was overtaken on the Shelbyville and Manchester roads, about five miles from Murfreesboro', and after sharp skirmishing for two or three hours was driven from our immediate front. The conduct of my command from the time the army left Nashville to its entry into Murfreesboro' is deserving of the highest praise, both for their patient endurance of the fatigues and discomforts of a five days' battle, and for the manly spirit exhibited by them in the various phases in this memorable contest. I refer you to the detailed reports of the division and brigade commanders, forwarded herewith, for special mention of those officers and men of their commands whose conduct they thought worthy of particular notice.

"All the members of my staff—Major G. E. Flynt, acting adjutant-general; Lieutenant-Colonel A. Von Schrader, Seventy-fourth Ohio, acting inspector-general; Captain O. A. Mack, Thirteenth United States Infantry, acting chief commissary, and Captain A. J. Mackay, chief quartermaster, were actively employed in carrying my orders to various parts of my command and in the execution of the appropriate duties of their offices. Captain O. A. Mack was dangerously wounded in the right hip and abdomen while carrying orders from me to Major-General Rosecrans. The officers of the signal corps attached to my headquarters did excellent service in their appropriate sphere when possible, and as aides-de-camp carrying orders. My escort, composed of a select detail from the First Ohio Cavalry, commanded by First Lieutenant J. D. Barker, of the same regiment, have been on duty with me for nearly a year, and deserve commendation for the faithful performance of their appropriate duties. Private Guitean was killed by a cannon-shot on the morning of January 2.

"Surgeon G. D. Beebe, medical director, deserves special mention for his efficient arrangements for moving the wounded from the field and giving them immediate attention.

"Annexed hereto is a consolidated return of the casualties of my command. The details will be seen in the accompanying reports of division and brigade commanders.

Commands.	Commissioned.	Enlisted Men.	Horses.	Guns, Artillery.	Killed. Commiss'd.	Killed. Enlisted.	Wounded. Commiss'd.	Wounded. Enlisted.	Missing. Commiss'd.	Missing. Enlisted.	Horses. Killed.	Horses. Wounded.	Horses. Missing.	Horses. Lost.	Guns. Disabled.
1st division, Maj.-Gen. Rousseau.	303	5,483	.....	18	8	171	43	903	1	324	8	5	...	...	....
2d division, Brig.-Gen Negley...	237	4,632	257	13	11	167	44	704	3	308	62	24	9	6	1
1st brigade, 3d division, Colonel M. B. Walker	97	2,243	.....	6	...	.....	4	19	.....	1	...	...	...	...	...
Total	637	12,358	257	37	19	338	94	1626	4	633	70	29	9	6	1

"Very respectfully your obedient servant,
"GEORGE H. THOMAS,
"Major-General U. S. Vols., Commanding."

The Seventy-ninth Illinois Volunteers was commanded by Colonel Buckner, a Methodist preacher, and it was said that his regiment was to a great extent composed of clergymen of that denomination. His regiment would work all day, and at night religious services of some kind were held in their camp. It is a matter well known that these Christian soldiers were among the very best in the army. Buckner was a brave soldier, and at all times ready for any service, however hazardous, and his "preacher-boys" were always anxious to be in the forefront of the battle, or to engage in any duty however difficult or dangerous. General Thomas was much attached to this regiment, was fond of hearing the songs of praise that went up from their camp every evening, which, he said, carried him back to his boyhood and called to his memory the good Christian people that surrounded him when a boy. He was not a member of the Church himself, but a firm believer in the Christian religion, and lived the life of one. His pure life, upright deportment, and general character were such as to make him a model that many professing Christians might well afford to imitate. He practised in his daily life and conversation nearly all of the Christian graces, and to all appearances was a believer in Jesus.

On June 23, 1863, the necessary orders for an advance movement were given by General Rosecrans, and these orders were hailed with delight by the troops, who had become weary of camp life and were anxious to move south and meet the defiant enemy, who boldly pressed himself against the Federal picket-line. Thomas moved out on the

Manchester pike, demonstrating towards Fairfield, arriving at the town of Manchester on the 27th. Here he detached Wilder's brigade to operate on the enemy's communications in the vicinity of Decherd. The general character of the country was such that a small force could delay the advance of the Federal line by the resolute defence of certain gaps through which the different commands had to pass. There were three of these passes or gaps,—Liberty, Hoover's, and Guy's. McCook's command, led by Johnson's division, had to pass through Liberty Gap, which was carried by Willich's and Carlin's brigades. This movement was unexpected, and the rebel troops were taken somewhat by surprise, but, after a stubborn resistance, were driven back with heavy loss and in great confusion. Thomas took Hoover's Gap, and then the lines were made to converge on Tullahoma, of which the Federal army took possession. This campaign secured Middle Tennessee, as Bragg fell back to Chattanooga, where he intrenched himself and made his arrangements to stay. Rosecrans planned his campaign well, and it was faithfully carried out, establishing for him a brilliant reputation for masterly skill and ability. Had this been the last campaign of the war none would have stood higher in the estimation of the people than he who planned it with such consummate ability. But his great success thus far seemed to have given him additional confidence in his own army and to have lessened his opinion of his adversary. Gradually he began to regard Bragg as a man of little enterprise, and finally projected a campaign into Georgia without any reference to him and the troops he commanded. Here General Rosecrans made a fearful mistake, as Bragg was a man of no mean ability and had enterprise equal to the emergency, and, aside from this, he was ably assisted by such generals as Polk, Longstreet, Hood, E. K. Smith, W. J. Hardee, P. R. Cleburn, and others, whose skill, courage, and resolute determination made them the peers of any officers of corresponding rank in the Federal army.

Thomas had served in Bragg's battery, and with E. K. Smith and W. J. Hardee, and knew them well, and did not underestimate them. When he moved against their lines or columns he did so with great caution, and it is a well-known fact that "he never made a mistake or lost a battle."

After the withdrawal of the Confederate army from Middle Tennessee, the next campaign for the Army of the Cumberland was against Chattanooga, which became its objective point.

Chattanooga was a position of great natural strength which Bragg had fortified, and within its frowning walls he felt secure against any force that could be hurled against it. Surrounded by high mountains, easily fortified, with a deep stream winding around one side, resolute and determined men could have held it against ten times their number.

The work of repairing the railroad was pushed forward with great vigor, and on the 25th day of July, 1863, a through-train from Nashville arrived at Bridgeport. Sheridan's division took possession of Stevenson and Bridgeport, and supplies were accumulated at those points as rapidly as the limited railroad facilities would permit. When it is remembered that the Federal army was wholly dependent upon one long line of railroad, passing through an enemy's country where the people were hostile, and that only certain important points could be guarded, it seems strange that trains could be passed over the road fast enough to supply an army of such magnitude. Subordinate officers know very little of the cares and responsibilities of him who has to plan campaigns to the front and preserve an unbroken line to the rear, upon which to receive supplies of food, clothing, ammunition, and the necessary materials of war. An army that is poorly fed and poorly clothed will not prove very efficient on the march or in battle, and hence supplies become a very important factor in all army movements. The general who neglects them will surely come to grief, sooner or later.

On August 16 the march over the mountains began. Crittenden's corps moved in three columns: Wood's division, from Hillsboro' *via* Pelham to Thurman, in the Sequatchie Valley; Palmer's, from Manchester *via* Hickory to Dunlap; Van Cleve's, from McMinnville to Pikeville, at the head of the Sequatchie Valley. General Thomas's corps moved in two columns: Reynolds's and Brannan's divisions *via* University and Battle Creek, and Negley's and Baird's divisions *via* Tantalon and Crow Creek. General McCook's corps moved in two columns: R. W. Johnson's division *via* Salem to Bellefonte, and J. C. Davis's division *via* Mound Top to Stevenson. General D. S. Stanley, with most of the cavalry, moved *via* Fayetteville and Athens, covering the line of the Tennessee River above Whitesburgh. Colonel Minty's cavalry moved from McMinnville to Pikeville. Colonel Wilder's brigade moved to Dunlap.

Before attempting the passage of the river the brigades of Hazen, Minty, Wagner, and Wilder were sent to demonstrate against Chattanooga from the north side of the Tennessee, guarding the line of the river from Washington down to Chattanooga.

The army commenced crossing the Tennessee River on the 29th of August, and on the 4th of September the entire command of General Rosecrans was on the south side. Thomas's corps crossed as follows: Brannan and Reynolds at the mouth of Battle Creek, Baird at Bridgeport, and Negley at Caperton's Ferry. Crittenden moved down the Sequatchie Valley and crossed at Shell Mound and at the mouth of Battle Creek. The divisions of Johnson and Davis, of McCook's corps, crossed at Caperton's Ferry, while Sheridan, of the same corps, crossed at Bridgeport. Stanley, with his cavalry, crossed partly at Caperton's Ferry and the remainder at a ford near Island Creek. Everything being in readiness the movement over the mountains began at once. Thomas moved over Sand Mountain and descended into Lookout Valley, at Trenton; thence to the summit of Lookout Mountain, at Johnson's Crook; thence, passing through Stevens's and Frick's Gaps, he descended into Chattanooga Valley. McCook moved with his corps across Sand Mountain to Valley Head, where he ascended Lookout Mountain. Crittenden with his corps moved *via* Wauhatchie and crossed over the nose of Lookout Mountain. Simultaneously with these dispositions Bragg evacuated his strong position at Chattanooga and fell back to Lafayette. McCook's corps descended Lookout Mountain and moved to Alpine. Considering the position of the enemy and the difficulty in getting the artillery and transportation down the southern slope of the mountain, and the utter impossibility of retreating if attacked by an outnumbering foe, this was one of the most hazardous undertakings of the war. From Alpine Colonel Harrison, with his splendid regiment of Indiana cavalry, was ordered to march to Lafayette and ascertain the strength of the enemy at that point. He was not long in learning that Polk's corps, and possibly other Confederate corps, were there in force. About the time Harrison made his report, instructions were received from Rosecrans directing McCook to reascend the mountain and close to the left on Thomas with all possible despatch. An entire day was consumed in getting the transportation up the mountain, but, when that was accomplished, McCook and his officers felt thankful that Bragg had not moved against the corps while at Alpine, for had he done so it would have been impossible to have saved the artillery and baggage-train.

Rosecrans, through his perfect system of secret service, learning that heavy reinforcements had been received from Virginia, and that it was Bragg's intention not to abandon Northern Georgia without a struggle, saw the immediate necessity of concentrating his widely-dispersed army, to accomplish which he issued orders to the various commanders to close in on Crawfish Spring. Thomas crossed the upper end of Mission Ridge and moved down the Chickamauga Valley to the appointed place. Crittenden, who had marched with his corps to Ringgold, returned and took his proper position. Johnson's and Davis's divisions of McCook's corps moved along the mountain-road from Winston's to Stevens's Gap. Sheridan descended the mountain at Winston's, thence down Lookout Valley to Johnson's Crook, at which point he ascended the mountain. The corps then passed through Stevens's Gap and joined the Fourteenth and Twenty-first.

The position now occupied by the Army of the Cumberland had been reached by long and wearisome marches through the mountains and gorges of Tennessee and Georgia, with ceaseless skirmishing and strategy.

During all the glad spring-time and golden summer the advance kept pace with the feathery fringe of the skirmish smoke, and the thunder of Federal guns rolled southward continuously. And when August had languished into the lap of autumn and the simmering heats of its sultry lingering began to go out with the falling leaves and the fading year, Thomas called upon his flag-bearers to follow him into that death-grapple at Chickamauga. Ah! then

> "The soul of battle was abroad
> And blazed upon the air."

Chickamauga! Who can tell of its horrors, or paint in words its deeds of "high emprise"? Who can portray the wonderful story of that Sabbath-day's valiant work, when Thomas held the outnumbering columns of the foe at bay with his encircled wall of steel?

Minstrelsy and poesy, the inspiration of the painter, and the enchanted numbers of song will give him all his full-flushed meed of glory. History is commonplace and oratory is dumb in the attempt to render him fair measurement and do justice to the superb merit of his achievements. Then back through the dark, bitter night the army, under his control and guidance, filed and pitched its tents at Chattanooga, and there for long, woeful weeks the Army of the Cumberland held its position in the face of the beleaguering enemy without, and griping famine and mortal disease, grim and unsparing, in its very midst.

The War Department became dissatisfied with General Rosecrans, owing to the fact that Bragg had not been defeated and driven out of Northern 'Georgia, and decided upon his removal. It did not take long to decide as to his successor.

Thomas, the "Rock of Chickamauga," was designated, and he issued his orders assuming command on the nineteenth day of October. Here an important and unexpected responsibility was thrust upon him, and that too under the most unfavorable circumstances. The troops were on short rations and with every prospect of being still further reduced, owing to the difficulties of getting supplies from Bridgeport and Stevenson, the enemy commanding the river at one or more points below Chattanooga. This was the state of things when the War Department telegraphed to Thomas to know how long he could hold Chattanooga. His reply, characteristic of the man, was in the strong, terse words, "WE WILL HOLD IT UNTIL WE STARVE." Such was the confidence he had in his troops that he felt sure that they would prefer death, then and there, by starvation in preference to an ignominious abandonment of all the fruits of that campaign.

Thomas's report of the Chickamauga campaign:

"Headquarters Fourteenth Army Corps,
"Chattanooga, Tennessee, September 30, 1863.

"General,—I have the honor to report the operations of my corps from the 1st of September up to date, as follows, viz.:

"General Brannan's division crossed the Tennessee River at Battle Creek; General Baird ordered to cross his first division at Bridgeport, and to move to Taylor's Store; General Negley's second division to cross the river at Caperton's Ferry, and to report at Taylor's Store also.

"*September* 2.—General Baird's division moved to Widow's Creek. General Negley reports having arrived at Moore's Spring, one and a quarter miles from Taylor's Store and two miles from Bridgeport; he was orderd to cross the mountain at that point, it being the most direct route to Trenton, in the vicinity of which place the corps was ordered to concentrate.

"*September* 3.—Headquarters Fourteenth Army Corps moved from Bolivar Springs at 6 A.M. *via* Caperton's Ferry to Moore's Spring, on the road from Bridgeport to Trenton. Baird's division reached Bridgeport, but could not cross in consequence of damage to the bridge; Negley's division marched to Warren's Mills, on the top of Sand Mountain, on the road to Trenton; Brannan's division reached Graham's Store, on the road from Shell Mound to Trenton; Reynolds's division marched six miles on the Trenton road from Shell Mound.

"*September* 4.—Negley's division camped at Brown's Spring, at foot of Sand Mountain, in Lookout Valley; Brannan's division at Gordon's Mill, on Sand Mountain; Reynolds's division at foot of Sand Mountain, two miles from Trenton. Baird's division crossed the river at Bridgeport, and camped at that point. Corps headquarters at Moore's Spring.

"*September* 5.—Baird's division arrived at Moore's Spring; Negley's division still in camp at Brown's Spring. He reports having sent forward a reconnoissance of two regiments of infantry and a section of artillery to scour the country towards Chattanooga and secure some captured stores near Macon Iron-Works. They captured some Confederate army supplies. No report from Brannan's division. Reynolds's division in camp at Trenton; Brannan somewhere in neighborhood. Corps headquarters at Warren's Mill.

"*September* 6.—Baird's division encamped at Warren's Mill; Negley's division reached Johnson's Crook. Beatty's brigade was sent up the road to seize Stevens's Gap; met the enemy's pickets and, it being dark, did not proceed farther. The Eighteenth Ohio, of Negley's division, went to the top of Lookout Mountain, beyond Payne's Mills; met the enemy's pickets and dispersed them. The head of Brannan's column reached Lookout Valley, two miles below Trenton; Reynolds's division in camp at Trenton; rumors of the enemy's design to evacuate Chattanooga. Corps headquarters at Brown's Spring.

"*September* 7.—Baird's division closed up with Negley's in the mouth of Johnson's Crook. Negley's gained possession of the top of the mountain, and secured the forks of the road. Brannan's division reached Trenton; Reynolds remained in camp at that place. Corps headquarters still at Brown's Spring.

"*September* 8.—Baird's division remained in its camp of yesterday, at the junction of Hurricane and Lookout Creeks. Negley's division moved up to the top of Lookout Mountain, at the head of Johnson's Crook, one brigade occupying the pass; another brigade was sent forward and seized Cooper's Gap, sending one regiment to the foot of the gap to occupy and hold it; one regiment was also sent forward to seize

Stevens's Gap, which was heavily obstructed with fallen trees. Brannan's division occupied the same position as last night. Reynolds's division, headquarters at Trenton, with one brigade at Payne's Mills, three miles south of Trenton. Headquarters of the corps still at Brown's Spring.

"*September* 9.—Baird's division moved across Lookout Mountain to the support of Negley. Negley's division moved across the mountain and took up a position in McLamore's Cove, near Rogers's farm, throwing out his skirmishers as far as Bailey's Cross-Roads. Saw the enemy's cavalry in front, drawn up in line; citizens reported a heavy force concentrated in his front at Dug Gap, consisting of infantry, cavalry, and artillery. Brannan's division in same camp as yesterday; Reynolds's division also. The Ninety-second Illinois (mounted infantry) sent on a reconnoissance towards Chattanooga, along the ridge of Lookout Mountain. Colonel Atkins, commanding Ninety-second Illinois, reports: September 9, 11 A.M., entered Chattanooga as the rear of the enemy's column was evacuating the place. Corps headquarters moved from Brown's Spring to Easley's farm, on Trenton and Lebanon road.

"*September* 10.—General Negley's in front of, or one mile west of, Dug Gap, which has been heavily obstructed by the enemy and occupied by a strong picket-line. General Baird ordered to move up to-night to Negley's support; General Reynolds to move at daylight to support Baird's left, and General Brannan to move at 8 A.M. to-morrow morning to support Reynolds. Headquarters and General Reynolds's division camped for the night at foot of the mountain. Brannan's division at Easley's.

"*September* 11.—Baird's division closed up on Negley's at Widow Davis's house about 8 A.M. Soon afterwards, Negley being satisfied, from his own observations and from the reports of officers sent out to reconnoitre, and also from loyal citizens, that the enemy was advancing on him in very superior force, and that this train was in imminent danger of being cut off if we accepted battle at Davis's Cross-Roads, determined to fall back to a strong position in front of Stevens's Gap. His movement he immediately proceeded to put into execution, and by his untiring energy and skill, and with the prompt co-operation of Baird, succeeded in gaining possession of the hills in front of Stevens's Gap, and securing his trains, without losing a single wagon. For a detailed account of this movement, see reports of Generals Negley and Baird, annexed, marked A and B. General Turchin, commanding Third Brigade, Reynolds's division, was pushed forward, by way of Cooper's Gap, to Negley's support on the left, reaching his position about 10 o'clock A.M. Orders were sent to General Brannan to close up as rapidly as possible. Corps headquarters at top of Cooper's Gap.

"*September* 12.—Brannan's division reached Negley's position by 8 A.M., and took post next on the left of Baird. Reynolds's division was posted on the left of Brannan, one brigade covering Cooper's Gap. Reports from citizens go to confirm the impression that a large force of the enemy is concentrated at Lafayette. A report from General McCook confirms that fact. A later despatch from the same source says it is reported that Bragg's whole army, with Johnston's, is at Lafayette. Generals Brannan and Baird, with part of their commands, went out on a reconnoissance towards Dug Gap at 1 o'clock P.M. to-day. General Brannan reports they advanced two miles beyond Davis's Cross-Roads without finding any enemy, with the exception of a few mounted men. Corps headquarters encamped at top of Stevens's Gap.

"*September* 13.—Negley's, Baird's, and Brannan's divisions remained in their camps of yesterday waiting the arrival of McCook's corps, which had been ordered to close to the left.

Reynolds concentrated his division on the road from Cooper's Gap to Catlett's Gap. Two deserters from Eighteenth Tennessee state that they belong to Buckner's corps. Buckner's corps consists of eight brigades and two batteries, six guns each; were in the fight with Negley. Saw a brigade of Forrest's cavalry, commanded by Forrest himself, pass towards the fight on the eleventh. Hill's and Buckner's corps were both engaged. Bragg's army is concentrated at Lafayette. Headquarters moved by way of Cooper's Gap to the foot of the mountain.

"*September* 14.—General Reynolds took up a position at Pond Spring, with his two infantry brigades, and was joined by Wilder at that place. Turchin's brigade, of Reynolds's division, made a reconnoissance to the mouth of Catlett's Gap with the Ninety-second Illinois (mounted infantry). Was opposed by the rebels' mounted pickets from Chickamauga Creek to mouth of Catlett's Gap, at which place he found their reserve drawn up, also a strong line of skirmishers to the right of the road; but having received instructions to avoid bringing on an engagement, he returned to camp with the brigade, leaving two regiments on Chattanooga Valley road, strongly posted on outposts. General Brannan advanced one brigade of his division to Chickamauga Creek, east of Lee's Mills, one mile to the right and south of Reynolds's position at Pond Spring. A mounted reconnoissance was also pushed forward to within a mile of Bluebird Gap without encountering any of the enemy. A negro who had been taken before General Buckner yesterday, and released again, reports that Buckner and his corps are in Catlett's Gap preparing to defend that place. A negro woman, lately from the neighborhood of Dug Gap, reports a large force of rebels between Dug Gap and Lafayette.

"*September* 16.—Corps headquarters and first and second

divisions remained camped, as last reported, at foot of Stevens's Gap. Turchin's brigade, of Reynolds's division, made a reconnoissance towards Catlett's Gap. The enemy fell back as he advanced, until he came upon a force strongly posted, with two pieces of artillery, in the road. He made a second reconnoissance at 2 P.M. that day, with but little further result, as he could advance but a short distance farther, the enemy being in force in his front.

"*September* 17.—First, second, and third divisions changed their positions from their camps of yesterday: Baird's (first) division, with its right resting at Gower's Ford and extending along Chickamauga Creek to Bird's Mill; Negley's (second) division, with its right at Bird's Mill, and its left connecting with Van Cleve's division at Owen's Ford; Brannan's (third) division, on the right of the first, covering four fords between Gower's Ford and Pond Spring; one brigade of the fourth division (Reynolds's) thrown out in front of Pond Spring, on the Catlett's Gap road, covering the pass through the mountains. Wilder's brigade detached and ordered to report to department headquarters. The left of McCook's corps closed in, connecting with our right near Pond Spring.

"*September* 18.—At 4 P.M. the whole corps moved to the left along Chickamauga Creek to Crawfish Springs. On arriving at that place received orders to move on the cross-road leading by Widow Glenn's house to the Chattanooga and Lafayette road, and take up a position near Kelley's farm, on the Lafayette road, connecting with Crittenden on my right at Gordon's Mill. The head of the column reached Kelly's farm about daylight on the 19th, Baird's division in front, and took up a position at the forks of the road, facing towards Reid's and Alexander's bridges over the Chickamauga. Colonel Wilder, commanding the mounted brigade of Reynolds's division, informed me that the enemy had crossed the Chickamauga in force at those two bridges the evening before and driven his brigade across the State road, or Chattanooga and Lafayette road, to the heights east of the Widow Glenn's house. Kelley's house is situated in an opening about three-fourths of a mile long and one-fourth of a mile wide, on the east side of the State road, and stretches along that road in a northerly direction, with a small field of perhaps twenty acres on the west side of the road, directly opposite to the house. From thence to the Chickamauga the surface of the country is undulating and covered with original forest timber, interspersed with undergrowth, in many places so dense that it is difficult to see fifty paces ahead. There is a cleared field near Jay's Mill, and cleared land in the vicinity of Reid's and Alexander's bridges. A narrow field commences at a point about a fourth of a mile south of Kelley's house, on the east side of the State road, and extends perhaps for half a mile along the road towards Gordon's Mill. Between the State road and the foot of Missionary Ridge there is a skirt of timber stretching from the vicinity of Widow Glenn's house, south of the forks of the road, to McDaniel's house, three-fourths of a mile north of Kelley's. The eastern slope of the Missionary Ridge between Glenn's and McDaniel's is cleared and mostly under cultivation. This position of Baird's threw my right in close proximity to Wilder's brigade; the interval I intended to fill up with the two remaining brigades of Reynolds's division on their arrival. General Brannan, closely following Baird's division, was placed in position on his left, on the two roads leading from the State road to Reid's and Alexander's bridges. Colonel Dan McCook, commanding a brigade of the reserve corps, met me at General Baird's headquarters, and reported to me that he had been stationed the previous night on the road leading to Reid's bridge, and that he could discover no force of the enemy except one brigade which had crossed to the west side of Chickamauga at Reid's bridge the day before; and he believed it could be cut off because after it had crossed he had destroyed the bridge, the enemy having retired towards Alexander's bridge. Upon this information I directed General Brannan to post a brigade within supporting distance of Baird, on the road to Alexander's bridge, and with his other two brigades to reconnoitre the road leading to Reid's bridge to see if he could locate the brigade reported by Colonel McCook, and, if a favorable opportunity occurred, to capture it. His dispositions were made according to instructions by 9 A.M. General Baird was directed to throw forward his right wing, so as to get more nearly in line with Brannan, but to watch well on his right flank. Soon after this disposition of these two divisions, a portion of Palmer's division, of Crittenden's corps, took position to the right of General Baird's division. About 10 o'clock Croxton's brigade, of Brannan's division, posted on the road leading to Alexander's bridge, became engaged with the enemy, and I rode forward to his position to ascertain the character of the attack. Colonel Croxton reported to me that he had driven the enemy nearly half a mile, but that he was then meeting with obstinate resistance. I then rode back to Baird's position and directed him to advance to Croxton's support, which he did with his whole division, Starkweather's brigade in reserve, and drove the enemy steadily before him for some distance, taking many prisoners. Croxton's brigade, which had been heavily engaged for over an hour with greatly superior numbers of the enemy, and being nearly exhausted of ammunition, was then moved to the rear to enable the men to fill up their boxes; and Baird and Brannan having united their forces, drove the enemy from their immediate front. General Baird then halted for the purpose of readjusting his line, and learning from prisoners that the enemy were in heavy force on his immediate right, he threw back his right wing in order to be ready for an attack from that quarter. Before his dispositions could be completed the enemy in overwhelming numbers furiously assaulted Scribner's and King's brigades, and drove them in disorder. Fortunately, at this time Johnson's division, of McCook's corps, and Reynolds's division, of my corps, arrived and were immediately placed in position; Johnson preceding Reynolds, his left connecting with Baird's right, and Palmer being immediately on Johnson's right, Reynolds was placed on the right of Palmer, with one brigade of his division in reserve. As soon as formed they advanced upon the enemy, attacking him in flank and driving him in great confusion for a mile and a half, while Brannan's troops met them in front as they were pursuing Baird's retiring brigades, driving the head of his column back and retaking the artillery which had been temporarily lost by Baird's brigades, the Ninth Ohio recovering Battery H, Fifth United States Artillery, at the point of the bayonet. The enemy at this time being hardly pressed by Johnson, Palmer, and Reynolds in flank, fell back in confusion upon his reserves, posted in a strong position on the west side of Chickamauga Creek between Reid's and Alexander's bridges. Brannan and Baird were then ordered to reorganize their commands and take position on commanding ground on the road from McDaniel's to Reid's bridge, and hold it to the last extremity, as I expected the next effort of the enemy would be to gain that road and our rear. This was about 2 P.M. After a lull of about one hour, a furious attack was made upon Reynolds's right, and he having called upon me for reinforcements, I directed Brannan's division to move to his support, leaving King's brigade, of Baird's division, to hold the position at which Baird and Brannan had been posted, the balance of Baird's division closing up to the right of Johnson's division. It will be seen, by General Reynolds's report, Croxton's brigade, of Brannan's division, reached his right just in time to defeat the enemy's efforts to turn Reynolds's right and rear. About 5 P.M., my lines being at that time very much extended in pursuing the enemy, I determined to concentrate them on more commanding ground, as I felt confident that we should have a renewal of the battle the next morning. I rode forward to General Johnson's position and designated to him where to place his division; also to General Baird, who was present with Johnson. I then rode back to the cross-roads to locate Palmer and Reynolds on Johnson's right, and on the crest of the ridge about five hundred yards east of the State road. Soon after, Palmer and Reynolds got their positions; and while Brannan was getting his, on the ridge to the west of the State road, near Dyer's house, to the rear and right of Reynolds, where I had ordered him as a reserve, the enemy assaulted first Johnson and then Baird in a most furious manner, producing some confusion, but order was soon restored and the enemy repulsed in fine style; after which these two divisions took up the positions assigned to them for the night. Before adjusting the line satisfactorily, I received an order to report to department headquarters immediately, and was absent from my command until near midnight. After my return from department headquarters, and about 2 A.M. on the 20th, I received a report from General Baird that the left of his division did not rest on the Reid's bridge road as I had intended, and that he could not reach it without weakening his line too much. I immediately addressed a note to the general commanding requesting that General Negley be sent me to take position on General Baird's left and rear, and thus secure our left from assault. During the night the troops threw up temporary breastworks of logs, and prepared for the encounter which all anticipated would come off the next day. Although informed by note from General Rosecrans's headquarters that Negley's division would be sent immediately to take post on my left, it had not arrived at 7 A.M. on the 20th, and I sent Captain Willard, of my staff, to General Negley to urge him forward as rapidly as possible, and to point out his position to him. General Negley, in his official report, mentions that he received this order through Captain Willard at 8 A.M. on the 20th, and that he immediately commenced withdrawing his division for that purpose, when the enemy was reported to be massing a heavy force in his front, sharply engaging his skirmishers, and that he was directed by General Rosecrans to hold his position until relieved by some other command. General Beatty's brigade, however, was sent under guidance of Captain Willard, who took it to its position, and it went into action immediately. The enemy at that time commenced a furious assault on Baird's left, and partially succeeded in gaining his rear. Beatty, meeting with superior numbers, was compelled to fall back until relieved by the fire of several regiments of Palmer's reserve, which I had ordered to the support of the left, being placed in position by General Baird, and which regiments, with the co-operation of Van Deever's brigade, of Brannan's division, and a portion of Stanley's brigade, of Negley's division, drove the enemy entirely from Baird's left and rear. General Baird being still hardly pressed in front, I ordered General Wood, who had just reported to me in person, to send one of the brigades of his division to General Baird. He replied that his division had been ordered by General Rosecrans to support Reynolds's right, but that if I would take the responsibility of changing his orders, he would cheerfully obey them, and sent Barnes's brigades, the head of which had just reached my position. General Wood then left me to rejoin the remainder of his division, which was still coming up. To prevent a repetition of this attack on the part of the enemy, I directed Captain Gaw, chief topographical officer on my staff, to go to the commanding officer of the troops on the left and rear of Baird's and direct him to mass as much artillery on the slopes of Missionary Ridge, west of the State road, as he could conveniently spare from his lines, supported strongly by infantry, so as to sweep the ground to the left and rear of Baird's position. This order General Negley, in his official report, mentions having received through Captain Gaw, but, from his description of the position he assumed, he must have misunderstood my order, and instead of massing the artillery near Baird's left, it was posted on the right of Brannan's division, nearly in rear of Reynolds's right. At the time the assault just described was made on Baird, the enemy attacked Johnson, Palmer, and Reynolds with equal fierceness, which was continued at least two hours, making assault after assault with fresh troops, which were met by our troops with a most determined coolness and deliberation. The enemy having exhausted his utmost energies to dislodge us, he apparently fell back entirely from our front, and we were not disturbed again until near night, after the withdrawal of the troops to Rossville had commenced. Just before the repulse of the enemy on our left, General Beatty came to me for fresh troops in person, stating that most of those I had sent to him had gone back to the rear and right, and he was anxious to get at least another brigade before they attacked him again. I immediately sent Captain Kellogg to hurry up General Sheridan, whose division I had been informed would be sent to me. About 2 P.M., hearing heavy firing to my right and rear through the woods, very soon after Captain Kellogg left me, I turned in that direction and was riding to the slope of the hill in my rear to ascertain the cause. Just as I passed out of the woods bordering the State road I met Captain Kellogg returning, who reported to me that in attempting to reach General Sheridan he had met a large force in an open cornfield to the rear of Reynolds's position, advancing cautiously, with a strong line of skirmishers thrown out to their front, and that they had fired on him and forced him to return. He had reported this to Colonel Harker, commanding a brigade of Wood's division, posted on a ridge a short distance to the rear of Reynolds's position, who also saw this force advancing, but, with Captain Kellogg, was of the opinion that they might be Sheridan's troops coming to our assistance. I rode forward to Colonel Harker's position and told him that, although I was expecting Sheridan from that direction, if these troops fired on him, seeing his flags, he must return their fire and resist their further advance. He immediately ordered his skirmishers to commence firing, and took up a position with his brigade on the crest of a hill a short distance to his right and rear, placing his right in connection with Brannan's division and portions of Beatty's and Stanley's brigades, of Negley's division, which had been retired to that point from the left, as circumstantially narrated in the report of General John Beatty and Colonel Stanley. I then rode to the east of the hill referred to above. On my way I met General Wood, who confirmed me in the opinion that the troops advancing upon us were the enemy, although we were not then aware of the disaster to the right and centre of our army. I then directed him to place his division on the prolongation of Brannan's, who, I had ascertained from Hood, was on the top of the hill above referred to, and to resist the further advance of the enemy as long as possible. I sent my aide, Captain Kellogg, to notify General Reynolds that our right had been turned, and that the enemy was in his rear and in force. General Wood barely had time to dispose his troops on the left of Brannan before another of those fierce assaults, similar to those made in the morning on my lines, was made on him and Brannan combined, and kept up by the enemy throwing in fresh troops as fast as those in their front were driven back until near nightfall. About the time that Wood took up his position, General Gordon Granger appeared on my left flank at the head of Steedman's division of his corps. I immediately despatched a staff officer, Captain Johnson, Second Indiana Cavalry, of Negley's division, to him with orders to push forward and take position on Brannan's right, which order was complied with with the greatest promptness and alacrity, Steedman moving his division into position with almost as much precision as if on drill, and fighting his way to the crest of the hill on Brannan's right, moved forward his artillery and drove the enemy down the southern slope, inflicting on him a most terrible loss in killed and wounded. This opportune arrival of fresh troops revived the flagging spirits of our men on the right, and inspired them with new ardor for the contest. Every assault of the enemy from that time until nightfall was repulsed in the most gallant style by the whole line. By this time the ammunition in the boxes of the men was reduced, on an average, to two or three rounds per man, and my ammunition-trains having been unfortunately ordered to the rear by some unauthorized person, we should have been entirely without ammunition in a very short time had not a small supply come up with General Steedman's command. This being distributed among the troops, gave them about ten rounds per man. General Garfield, chief of staff of General Rosecrans, reached this position about 4 P.M., in company with Lieutenant-Colonel Thruston, of McCook's staff, and Captains Gaw and Barker, of my staff, who had been sent to the rear to bring back the ammunition, if possible. General Garfield gave me the first reliable information that

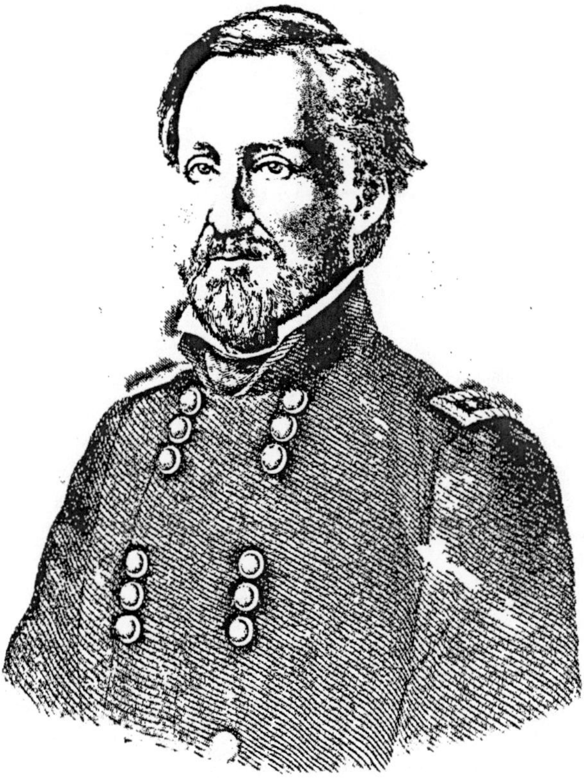

W. S. Rosecrans

the right and centre of our own army had been driven, and of its condition at that time. I soon after received a despatch from General Rosecrans directing me to assume command of all forces and, with Crittenden and McCook, take a strong position and assume a threatening attitude at Rossville, sending the unorganized forces to Chattanooga for reorganization, stating that he would examine the ground at Chattanooga and then join me; also that he had sent out rations and ammunition to meet me at Rossville. I determined to hold the position until nightfall, if possible, in the mean time sending Captains Barker and Kellogg to distribute the ammunition,— Major Lawrence, my chief of artillery, having been previously sent to notify the different commanders that ammunition would be supplied them shortly. As soon as they reported the distribution of the ammunition, I directed Captain Willard to inform the division commanders to prepare to withdraw their commands as soon as they received orders. At 5.30 P.M. Captain Barker, commanding my escort, was sent to notify General Reynolds to commence the movement, and I left the position behind General Wood's command to meet Reynolds and point out to him the position where I wished him to form line to cover the retirement of the other troops on the left. In passing through an open woods bordering on the State road, and between my last and Reynolds's position, I was cautioned by a couple of soldiers, who had been to hunt water, that there was a large rebel force in these woods, drawn up in line and advancing towards me. Just at this time I saw the head of Reynolds's column approaching, and calling to the general himself, directed him to form line perpendicular to the State road, changing the head of his column to the left, with his right resting on that road, and to charge the enemy who were then in his immediate front. This movement was made with the utmost promptitude, and, facing to the right whilst on the march, Turchin threw his brigade upon the rebel force, routing them and driving them in utter confusion entirely beyond Baird's left. In this splendid advance more than two hundred prisoners were captured and sent to the rear. Colonel Robinson, commanding the Twentieth Brigade, Reynolds's division, followed closely upon Turchin, and I posted him on the road leading through the ridge to hold the ground whilst the troops on our right and left passed by. In a few moments General Willich, commanding a brigade of Johnson's division, reported to me that his brigade was in position on a commanding piece of ground to the right of the ridge road. I directed him to report to General Reynolds and assist in covering the retirement of the troops. Turchin's brigade, after driving the enemy a mile and a half, was reassembled, and took its position on the ridge road with Robinson and Willich. These dispositions being made, I sent orders to Generals Wood, Brannan, and Granger to withdraw from their positions. Johnson's and Baird's divisions were attacked at the moment of retiring, but, by being prepared, retired without confusion or any serious losses. General Palmer was also attacked whilst retiring. Gross's brigade was thrown into some confusion, but Cruft's brigade came off in good style, both, however, with little loss. I then proceeded to Rossville, accompanied by Generals Garfield and Gordon Granger, and immediately prepared to place the troops in position at that point. One brigade of Negley's division was posted in the gap, on the Ringgold road, and two brigades on the top of the ridge, to the right of the road, adjoining the brigade in the road; Reynolds's division on the right of Negley's and reaching to the Dry Valley road; Brannan's division, in the rear of Reynolds's right, as a reserve; McCook's corps on the right of the Dry Valley road, and stretching towards the west, his right reaching nearly to

Chattanooga Creek. Crittenden's entire corps was posted on the heights to the left of the Ringgold road, with Steedman's division, of Granger's corps, in reserve behind his left, Baird's division in reserve, and in supporting distance of the brigade in the gap. McCook's brigade, of Granger's corps, was also posted as a reserve to the brigade of Negley's on the top of the ridge, to the right of the road. Minty's brigade of cavalry was on the Ringgold road, about one mile and a half in advance of the gap. About 10 A.M. on the 21st received a message from Minty that the enemy were advancing on him with a strong force of cavalry and infantry. I directed him to retire through the gap and post his command on our left flank, and throw out strong reconnoitring parties across the ridge to observe and report any movements of the enemy on our left front. From information received from citizens, I was convinced that the position was untenable in the face of the odds we had opposed to us, as the enemy could easily concentrate upon our right flank, which, if driven, would expose our centre and left to be cut entirely off from our communications. I therefore advised the commanding general to concentrate the troops at Chattanooga. About the time I made the suggestion to withdraw, the enemy made a demonstration in the direct road, but were soon repulsed. In anticipation of this order to concentrate at Chattanooga, I sent for the corps commanders and gave such general instructions as would enable them to prepare their commands for making the movement without confusion. All wagons, ambulances, and surplus artillery carriages were sent to the rear before night. The order for the withdrawal being received about 6 P.M., the movement commenced at 9 P.M. in the following order: Strong skirmish lines, under the direction of judicious officers, were thrown out to the front of each division to cover this movement, with directions to retire at daylight, deployed and in supporting distance, the whole to be supported by the First Division Fourteenth Army Corps, under the superintendence of Major-General Rousseau, assisted by Minty's brigade of cavalry, which was to follow after the skirmishers. Crittenden's corps was to move from the mills to the left of the road at 9 P.M., followed by Steedman's division. Next, Negley's division was to withdraw at 10 P.M.; then Reynolds, McCook's corps, by divisions from left to right, moving within supporting distance one after the other. Brannan's was posted at 6 P.M., on the road about half-way between Rossville and Chattanooga to cover the movement. The troops were withdrawn in a quiet, orderly manner, without the loss of a single man, and by 7 A.M. on the 22d were in their positions in front of Chattanooga, which had been assigned to them previous to their arrival, and which they now occupy, covered by strong intrenchments thrown up on the day of our arrival, and strengthened from day to day until they were considered sufficiently strong for all defensive purposes. I respectfully refer you to the reports of division, brigade, and regimental commanders for the names of those of their respective commands who distinguished themselves. Among them I am much gratified to find the names of Colonel F. Van Deveer, Thirty-fifth Ohio, commanding Third Brigade, and Colonel John T. Croxton, Fourth Kentucky, commanding Second Brigade, Brannan's division, both of whom I saw on Saturday, and can confirm the reports given of them by their division commander. Colonel B. F. Scribner, Thirty-eighth Indiana, commanding First Brigade, Baird's division, was on the right of that division on Saturday morning when it was attacked in flank by an overwhelming force of the enemy and driven back; yet Colonel Scribner was enabled to rally and reorganize it without the least difficulty as soon as supported by Johnson's division.

All the troops under my immediate command fought most gallantly on battle days, and were ably handled by their respective commanders, viz., Major-Generals Palmer and Reynolds and Brigadier-Generals Brannan, Johnson, and Baird, on Saturday; and on Sunday, in the afternoon, in addition to the above, Major-General Gordon Granger, commanding reserve corps, and Brigadier-General Wood, commanding First Division Twenty-first Army Corps, who with two brigades of his division, under their brave commanders, Colonels Harker and Buell, most nobly sustained Brannan's left, while Brigadier-General Steedman, commanding a division of the reserve corps, as valiantly maintained his right. Colonel Dan McCook, commanding a brigade of the reserve corps, and left by General Granger near McDaniel's house, in a commanding position, kept a large force of the enemy's cavalry at bay while hovering on Baird's left, and with his battery materially aided Turchin's handsome charge on the enemy who had closed in' on our left. Brigadier-General Willich, commanding a brigade of Johnson's division on Saturday, in the attack, and especially on Sunday, nobly sustained his reputation as a soldier. Brigadier-General John Beatty and Colonel F. R. Stanley, commanding brigades of Negley's division, bravely supported Baird's left in the morning of Sunday. Colonel Stanley being struck by the fragments of a shell and disabled in the afternoon, the brigade fought with Brannan's division, under the command of Colonel W. L. Stoughton, Eleventh Michigan. Colonel J. G. Parkhurst, commanding Ninth Michigan Volunteers, and provost-marshal Fourteenth Army Corps, at the head of his regiment, did most valuable service on the 20th in arresting stragglers and reorganizing the troops which had been driven from the field. His report is herewith enclosed, and special reference made thereto for particulars.

"I also tender my thanks to the members of my staff for the services they rendered me; to Lieutenant-Colonel G. E. Flynt, my assistant adjutant-general, Lieutenant-Colonel A. J. Mackey, chief quartermaster, Lieutenant-Colonel J. R. Paul, chief commissary of subsistence, who, although not present on the field of battle, were discharging their duties in their respective departments entirely to my satisfaction. Lieutenant-Colonel A. Von Schrader, Seventy-fourth Ohio, assistant inspector-general, who rendered most efficient service as aide-de-camp during the first day's fight, and who was taken prisoner on the afternoon of the 19th while in discharge of his duty; Major W. E. Lawrence, First Ohio Artillery, my chief of artillery, Captains J. P. Willard and S. C. Kellogg, aides-de-camp; Captain J. D. Barker, First Ohio Cavalry, commanding my escort; Captain W. B. Gaw, chief topographical officer Fourteenth Army Corps, as also the signal officers of the corps, who did duty on the field as aides, were of great assistance in conducting the operations of my command. Surgeons F. H. Grass, medical director, and H. C. Barrell, medical purveyor, were untiring in their efforts to relieve the wants of the wounded. Dr. Grass was wounded early in the engagement, Sunday, but continued in the discharge of his duties. Captain G. C. Moody, Nineteenth United States Infantry, commissary of musters, also rendered efficient service as aide-de-camp. Captain Johnson, Second Indiana Cavalry, of General Negley's staff, and Captain T. C. Williams, Nineteenth United States Infantry, of General Baird's staff, having been cut off from their respective commanders, reported to me for duty, and were of great assistance as aides.

"I submit herewith annexed a consolidated report of the casualties of the Fourteenth Army Corps.

"Very respectfully, your obedient servant,
"GEORGE H. THOMAS,
"Major-General U. S. Vols., Commanding."

ADVANCE TO CHATTANOOGA. 111

The first duty that confronted Thomas on his assuming command was to provision his army, and to do this required the removal of all obstructions to the navigation of the river from Bridgeport to Chattanooga. To effect this he ordered General Hooker to concentrate his entire command at Bridgeport preparatory to advancing along the line of railroad from that point to Chattanooga, and after consulting with General W. F. Smith, his chief engineer, he determined upon other movements, in conjunction with Hooker's advance, which, if successful, would certainly open up the river, and also the main wagon-road from Bridgeport to Brown's Ferry. The army had one road uninterrupted by the enemy, which lay along the north bank of the river, but, owing to the mountainous character of the country over which it passed, it was simply a matter of impossibility to supply the army by that route. Until other avenues were opened, however, all the provisions taken to Chattanooga were hauled over that rough, rocky road. Every wagon that could be spared was loaded with rations for the men, and the poor animals, cooped up in Chattanooga, had to be foraged on tender cane cut from the river bottom, as transportation was too scarce and the pressing necessities of the men too great to permit the use of any wagons for transporting forage.

Thomas directed General W. F. Smith to make a lodgment on the south bank of the Tennessee River at Brown's Ferry, and to seize the range of hills in that vicinity, as they commanded the Kelley's Ferry road. In connection with this movement, Hooker was to cross the river at Bridgeport and advance on Wauhatchie, a station on the line of the railroad. General John M. Palmer, subsequently Governor of the State of Illinois and one of the ablest and best generals in the army, occupied a position on the north bank of the river opposite Chattanooga. He was ordered to move his command along the north side of the river to a point nearly opposite Whitesides; then to cross the river and hold the road passed over by Hooker. On the night of the 27th, General W. F. Smith, with a force of about two thousand men, under the command of General W. B. Hazen, floated down the river in pontoon-boats from Chattanooga, captured the enemy's pickets at Brown's Ferry, and seized the range of hills overlooking the Kelley's Ferry road. General Turchin, with about twelve hundred men, moved along the north bank of the river to Brown's Ferry, and before the dawn of day were ferried across, and by 10 o'clock A.M. a pontoon-bridge spanned the river at that point.

This movement, which originated with Thomas, and which was so admirably executed by those to whom it was entrusted, was attended with great risk. The pontoons, loaded with the command, had to pass under the frowning brow of old Lookout, upon whose summit the enemy was encamped, little dreaming of the movements going on just below. Noiselessly the boats floated down, passing under the guns of the enemy; not a word was said to disturb the quiet of the night until the proper moment arrived, and then, with the suddenness of the thunderbolt, those brave men rushed from their boats, seized the guards, and again all was quiet. Not a single one of the enemy escaped to tell the story, and hence the Federal command had plenty of time to make its lodgment secure. When the enemy awoke to the importance of the advantage gained, a desperate effort was put forth to dislodge Hooker with two divisions of Longstreet's corps, but they were repulsed, and in great confusion driven back some distance.

This little affair has passed into history as the battle of Wauhatchie.

The successful carrying out of Thomas's instructions secured communication with Bridgeport by two routes, one by the way of Wauhatchie and Brown's Ferry, the other by river to Kelley's Ferry, and thence eight miles by wagon along the north bank of the river. Prior to this time Chattanooga was practically invested, the only avenue open being some sixty miles over roads almost impassable, and had the operations previously referred to failed, Chattanooga could not have been held a week longer. The occasion to do something was urgent, and Thomas demonstrated his fitness for the emergency. His plans were well matured, and the discreet and gallant men chosen to carry out his orders did not disappoint him. Just previous to the commencement of the foregoing movement General Grant arrived, to whom Thomas submitted his proposed plans, and, after hearing him through, he gave them his unqualified approval.

From a book published by W. F. G. Shanks, Esq., entitled "Personal Recollections of Distinguished Generals," the following extract relating to General Thomas is taken:

"In the campaign and battle of Chickamauga Thomas was second in command to Rosecrans, but in all its important actions his is the principal figure. The story of Chickamauga has been often and, in one or two instances, well told; but the whole truth about it must be reserved until time shall permit the historian to tell it without fear or favor.

"Thomas stands forth the undisputed hero of that day,—the single spirit upon whom all depends. He is the central figure. There are no heroes beside him. The young and noble ones who died, as Lytle and Burnham, Van Pelt and Jones, and those not less noble spirits who distinguished themselves and lived to be rewarded, as Baird and Dick Johnson, old Steedman and young Johnston, who guided his columns to the assault, Wood and Harker,—all these, surrounding Thomas, but added to his glory as the parhelion adds to the beauty of the sun. On the first day at Chickamauga Thomas did his share toward the destruction of a great rebel army, but it was in vain. The fruits of his victory were frittered away by the incompetency of others. There was no general advance when he advanced. On the second day it was too late; the enemy had succeeded in crossing his whole army over the Chickamauga, and the opportunity to destroy his forces in detail was gone forever. Circumstances then devolved upon Thomas the task of saving a great army, not destroying one. The duty was nobly performed and the army nobly saved; and, though those who were not present, and who judge of the battle from hearsay, may be mystified by the circumlocution and vagueness of official reports, those who stayed at Chickamauga know very well that Thomas alone retrieved that disaster and saved Rosecrans' army."

CHAPTER VI.

Appearance of Chattanooga—Thomas's Staff—General W. D. Whipple, Chief—Who planned Battle of Mission Ridge—Grant's Report—Thomas's Report—Mr. Shanks again—Pursuit of Enemy to Ringgold—Demonstration against Rocky Face and Buzzard Roost—March to Atlanta—Battles—Captain Wells, A. A. G.—General Palmer's Coolness and Gallantry, etc.

PRIOR to the war Chattanooga was a beautiful place, made so by the large number of handsome residences, surrounded by large and beautiful grounds tastefully laid out, with fine growths of shade and ornamental trees, giving the town an aristocratic appearance; but when it became a military camp the trees were cut down for firewood, fences were destroyed, and the shrubbery was eaten up by the half-starved horses and mules belonging to the army. It required only a short time to obliterate all traces of beauty, although Thomas prohibited the wanton destruction of all personal and private property. But the motto of soldiers is, generally, "*Necessitas non habet legend.*"

Thomas gathered around him a splendid staff. He never took to his headquarters an officer for simple ornament. Every member of his military family was selected on account of his peculiar fitness for the particular duty required of him, and no indolent, lazy officer ever found an asylum on his staff.

His chief, General William D. Whipple, a brave, dauntless, and thoroughly-accomplished soldier, was just the man for his place. His gentlemanly conduct towards all those with whom he had business relations made hosts of friends for him, and all who had official business at headquarters saw the genuine soldier and gentleman combined in the gallant chief of staff. It was a noticeable fact that some of the general officers of the army were not so fortunate as Thomas in selecting staff officers.

He had no political friends to reward, and no degenerate kinsmen to fasten themselves, vampire-like, upon his person, and hence he selected none but the best, and consequently was never compelled to apologize for the blunders or omissions of any member of his military family. Preceding the battle of Mission Ridge, Thomas and his staff were not idle. There were many things to be done to counterbalance the demoralization which seized upon his army after the battle of Chickamauga. It was not long, however, before the troops became enthused with the knowledge of his presence and guidance, and when he was ready to engage in the battle his men were in fine spirits and "eager for the fray."

It has been often asserted that the battle of Mission Ridge was planned by some one other than General Grant. The writer remembers very distinctly being at General Thomas's headquarters when an orderly or staff officer arrived and handed him an official communication, which he opened and read and passed over to him for perusal. It was the order for the battle, and was in the handwriting of General Grant himself.

It may be safely stated that General Grant planned all of his own battles. He may have had, and doubtless did, the benefit of the views of many of his subordinate commanders, and he may have been influenced to some extent by their opinions, but it was not necessary for him to call any one to his assistance after he had given a subject mature reflection.

On the 23d day of November the movement against the enemy on Missionary Ridge began. Thomas's command rushed out of the temporary works by which it had been sheltered and drove the enemy beyond Orchard Knob, which was seized and fortified during the night. On the following morning he pushed Howard's corps along the south bank of the Tennessee River and across Citico Creek, where he reported to General Sherman, under whose command he served during the continuance of the battle and the subsequent march to East Tennessee for the relief of the beleaguered garrison of Knoxville. Under Thomas's supervision, Hooker scaled the western slope of Lookout Mountain, driving the enemy from his rifle-pits on the northern extremity and slope of the mountain, aided by Carlin's brigade, which was temporarily detached from Johnson's division for this particular service. During the advance of Hooker's command up the rugged slope of old Lookout, the thin, misty clouds which had enveloped the crest of the mountain lowered so as to obscure his entire force from the view of the main army on the plain below. The rattle and roar of musketry was deafening, and as there was no way by which it could be ascertained how the conflict was going, the anxiety was intense, and all eyes were turned towards Hooker. Suddenly, as if to relieve the army from the painful suspense, a friendly breeze lifted the clouds, revealing Hooker's line, dotted here and there with regimental colors, and all moving steadily onward and upward. The sight was grand and beyond description, being a battle above the clouds in which the Federal army was victorious. During the night the rebel army abandoned its position on his front, and on the following morning Hooker took possession of the top of the mountain with a small force, and with the rest of his command swept across Lookout Valley to Rossville; then, ascending Missionary Ridge, he moved northward towards the centre of the new line. General Sherman assaulted the enemy's right with great determination, and, owing to the advantage of position held by the Confederates, he had a hard and bloody encounter, but he gained a position close up to the rifle-pits of the enemy. General Thomas, with Baird's and Johnson's divisions of Palmer's corps, and Wood's and Sheridan's divisions of Granger's corps, attacked the enemy's centre on Missionary Ridge, and, after fearful fighting, carried its summit. The enemy still resisted Thomas's left, but was speedily overcome, when he abandoned his works at every point, falling back in great confusion. General Grant was in a position from which he could observe the movements of the entire line, and in his report to the War Department he said,—

"The appearance of Hooker's column was at this time anxiously looked for and momentarily expected, moving on the ridge with his left in Chattanooga Valley and his right east of the ridge. His approach was intended as the signal for storming the ridge in the centre with strong columns, but the time necessarily consumed in the construction of the bridge near Chattanooga Creek detained him to a later hour than was expected. Being satisfied, from the latest information from him, that he must by this time be on his way from Rossville, though not yet in sight, and discovering that the enemy, in his desperation to defeat or resist the progress of Sherman, was weakening his centre on Missionary Ridge, determined me to order the advance at once. Thomas was accordingly directed to move forward his troops, constituting our centre, —Baird's division (Fourteenth Corps), Wood's and Sheridan's divisions (Fourth Corps), and Johnson's division (Fourteenth Corps), with a double line of skirmishers thrown out, followed in easy supporting distance by the whole force,—and carry the rifle-pits at the foot of Missionary Ridge, and, when carried, to reform his lines in the rifle-pits with a view to carrying the top of the ridge.

"These troops moved forward, drove the enemy from the rifle-pits at the base of the ridge, like bees from a hive, stopped but a moment until the whole were in line, and commenced the ascent of the mountain from right to left almost simultaneously, following closely the retreating enemy without further orders. They encountered a fearful volley of grape and canister from nearly thirty pieces of artillery, and musketry from well-filled rifle-pits on the summit of the ridge. Not a waver, however, was seen in that long line of brave men; their progress was steadily onward until the summit was in their possession. . . .

"The resistance on Thomas's left being overcome, the enemy abandoned his position near the railroad tunnel in front of Sherman, and by twelve o'clock at night was in full retreat; and the whole of his strong positions on Lookout Mountain, Chattanooga Valley, and Missionary Ridge were in our possession, together with a large number of prisoners, artillery, and small-arms."

The official report of General Thomas of the operations of his troops in the battle of Mission Ridge is as follows:

"Headquarters Department of Cumberland,
Chattanooga, Tennessee, December 7, 1863.

"General,—The following operations of the Army of the Cumberland since the 31st of October are respectfully submitted to the major-general commanding:

"As soon as communication with Bridgeport had been made secure, and the question of supplying the army at this point rendered certain, preparations were at once commenced for driving the enemy from his position in our immediate front on Lookout Mountain and Missionary Ridge, and, if possible, to send a force to the relief of Knoxville. To enable me to dislodge the enemy from the threatening position he had assumed in our front, guns of a heavier calibre than those with the army were needed; also additional means for crossing the Tennessee River. Brigadier-General Brannan, chief of artillery, was directed to send for the necessary number of guns and ammunition, and, after consulting with Brigadier-General W. F. Smith, chief engineer, to prepare the batteries for the guns on their arrival. Whilst awaiting the arrival of the guns and ammunition, work was prosecuted on the fortifications around the town. In addition to his duties of superintending the work on the fortifications, General Smith pushed vigorously the construction of two pontoon-bridges to be used in the execution of the movements which were determined upon as necessary to a successful dislodgment of the enemy.

"Guerillas having become somewhat troublesome to the northeast of McMinnville, and east of the Caney Fork of the Cumberland, Brigadier-General Elliott, chief of cavalry, was ordered, November 14, to establish his headquarters with the first division of cavalry at or near Alexandria, and employ the division in hunting up and exterminating these marauders. General Elliott reached Alexandria on the 18th. On the 27th he reports that his scouts met those of Burnside on Flint Ridge, east of Sparta, and that Lieutenant-Colonel Brownlow, with detachments from the First East Tennessee and Ninth Pennsylvania Cavalry, attacked the rebel Colonel Murry on the 21st, at Sparta, killing 1 and wounding 2, and capturing 10 of the enemy, including a lieutenant of Champ Ferguson's. He also captured a few horses, some ammunition, and destroyed extensive salt-works used by the rebels.

"A company of scouts, under Captain Brixie, also encountered a party of guerillas near Beersheba Springs, capturing 15 or 20 and dispersing the rest.

"Brigadier-General R. S. Granger reports from Nashville, November 2, that a mixed command, under Lieutenant-Colonel Scully, First Middle Tennessee Infantry, sent out from Nashville, attacked Hawkins and other guerilla chiefs, routed and pursued them to Centreville, where Hawkins made another stand, attacking our forces while crossing the river. Hawkins was again routed and pursued until his forces dispersed. Rebel loss, from 15 to 20 killed and 66 prisoners. Our loss, 1 severely and several slightly wounded. Again, on November 4, that Major Fitzgibbon, Fourteenth Michigan Infantry, came upon the combined forces of Cooper, Kirk, Williams, and Scott (guerillas), at Lawrenceburg, thirty-five miles from Columbia, that morning, and after a severe hand-to-hand fight defeated them, killing 8, wounding 7, and capturing 24 prisoners, among the latter 1 captain and 2 lieutenants. Major Fitzgibbon's loss was 3 men slightly wounded and 8 horses killed. He reports the enemy 400 strong, and his force 120.

"*November* 13.—Captain Cutler, with one company of mounted infantry and a portion of Whitmore's battery,—

mounted infantry belonging to the garrison of Clarksville,—had a fight near Palmyra with Captain Grey's company of guerillas, killing 2, wounding 5, and taking 1 prisoner. Cutler's loss was 1 lieutenant and 1 man wounded.

"*November* 16.—A scout was organized by Brigadier-General Payne, and sent out from Gallatin and Lavergne. They report having killed 5 and captured 26 guerillas with horses, sheep, cattle, and hogs in their possession, collected for the use of the rebel army.

"*November* 17.—Brigadier-General Crook was ordered to concentrate his division (Second Cavalry Division) at or near Huntsville, Alabama, to patrol the north side of the Tennessee River from Decatur to Bridgeport, and to hunt up bands of guerillas reported to be roaming about in that region, arresting and robbing Union citizens.

"General Crook reports, on the 21st, that an expedition sent down the Tennessee had destroyed nine boats between Whitesburg and Decatur, some of them sixty feet long.

"The expedition crossed the river and drove off the rebels, taking their boats. From the best information to be obtained, there were two small regiments of cavalry and one battery on the other side doing picket duty. Lee and Roddy reported as having gone to Mississippi.

" Major-General Sherman, commanding Army of the Tennessee, having been ordered with the Fifteenth Corps to this point, to participate in the operations against the enemy, reached Bridgeport with two divisions on the 16th November. He came to the front himself, and, having examined the ground, expressed himself confident of his ability to execute his share of the work. The plan of operations was then written out, substantially as follows: Sherman, with the Fifteenth Corps, strengthened with one division from my command, was to effect a crossing of the Tennessee River, just below the mouth of the South Chickamauga, on Saturday, November 21, at daylight, his crossing to be protected by artillery planted on the heights on the north bank of the river. After crossing his force, he was to carry the heights of Missionary Ridge from their northern extremity to about the railroad tunnel before the enemy could concentrate a force against him. I was to co-operate with Sherman by concentrating my troops in Chattanooga Valley, on my left flank, leaving only the necessary force to defend the fortifications on the right and centre, with a movable column of one division in readiness to move wherever ordered. This division was to show itself as threateningly as possible on the most practicable line for making an attack up the valley. I was then to effect a junction with Sherman, making my advance from the left, well towards the north end of Missionary Ridge, and moving as nearly simultaneously with Sherman as possible. The junction once formed and the ridge carried, communication would be at once established between the two armies by roads on the south bank of the river. Further movements to depend on those of the enemy. Lookout Valley was to be held by Geary's division and the two brigades of the Fourth Corps ordered to co-operate with him, the whole under command of General Hooker. Howard's corps was to be held in readiness to act either with my troops at Chattanooga or with General Sherman's, and was ordered to take up a position on Friday night on the north side of the Tennessee, near the first pontoon-bridge, and there held in readiness for such orders as might become necessary. General Smith commenced at once to collect his pontoons and material for bridges in the North Chickamauga Creek, preparatory to the crossing of Sherman's troops, proper precautions being taken that the enemy should not discover the movement.

"General Sherman then returned to Bridgeport to direct the movements of his troops.

"On the 16th, Colonel Long, commanding Second Brigade Second Division cavalry command, was ordered to report at Chattanooga on Saturday, the 21st, at noon, the intention being for him to follow up the left flank of Sherman's troops, and if not required by General Sherman, he was to cross the Chickamauga, make a raid upon the enemy's communications, and do as much damage as possible. Owing to a heavy rain-storm, commencing on Friday, 20th instant, and lasting all the 21st, General Sherman was not able to get his troops in position in time to commence operations on Saturday morning as he expected. Learning that the enemy had discovered Sherman's movements across Lookout Valley, it was thought best that General Howard should cross over into Chattanooga, thus attracting the attention of the enemy, with the intention of leading him to suppose that the troops he had observed moving were reinforcing Chattanooga, and thereby concealing the real movements of Sherman. Accordingly, Howard's corps was crossed into Chattanooga on Sunday, and took up a position in full view of the enemy. In consequence of the bad condition of the roads, General Sherman's troops were occupied all of Sunday in getting into position. In the mean time, the river having risen, both pontoon-bridges were broken by rafts sent down the river by the enemy, cutting off Osterhaus's division from the balance of Sherman's troops. It was thought that this would delay us another day, but during the night of the 22d two deserters reported Bragg had fallen back, and that there was only a strong picket-line in our front. Early on the morning of the 23d I received a note from the major-general commanding, directing me to ascertain by a demonstration the truth or falsity of this report. Orders were accordingly given to General Granger, commanding the Fourth Corps, to form his troops and to advance directly in front of Fort Wood, and thus develop the strength of the enemy. General Palmer, commanding Fourteenth Corps, was directed to support General Granger's right, with Baird's division refused *en échelon*. Johnson's division to be held in readiness, under arms, in the intrenchments, to reinforce at any point. Howard's corps was formed *en masse* behind the centre of Granger's corps. The two divisions of Granger's corps, Sheridan's and Wood's, were formed in front of Fort Wood, Sheridan on the right, Wood on the left, and his left extending nearly to Citico Creek. The formation being completed, about 2 P.M. the troops were advanced steadily and with rapidity directly to the front, driving before them first the rebel pickets, then their reserves, and falling upon their grand guards, stationed in their first line of rifle-pits, captured something over 200 men, and secured themselves in their new position before the enemy had sufficiently recovered from his surprise to attempt to send reinforcements from his main camp. Orders were then given to General Granger to make his position secure by constructing temporary breastworks and throwing out strong pickets to his front.

"Howard's corps was moved up on his left flank, with the same instructions, and Bridge's Illinois battery was placed in position on Orchard Knob; the troops remained in that position for the night. The Tennessee River having risen considerably from the effect of the previous heavy rain-storm, it was found difficult to rebuild the pontoon-bridge at Brown's Ferry. Therefore it was determined that General Hooker should take Osterhaus's division, which was still in Lookout Valley, Geary's division, Twelfth Corps, and Whittaker's and Grose's brigades, of the First Division Fourth Corps, under Brigadier-General Cruft, and make a strong demonstration on the northern slope of Lookout Mountain, for the purpose of attracting the enemy's attention in that direction, and thus withdrawing him from Sherman whilst crossing the Tennessee at the mouth of the South Chickamauga. General Hooker was instructed that in making this demonstration, if he discovered the position and strength of the enemy would justify him in attempting to carry the point of the mountain, to do so.

"By 4 P.M. on the evening of the 24th, General Hooker reported his troops in position and ready to advance. Finding Lookout Creek so much swollen as to be impassable, he sent Geary's division, Fourth Corps, to cross the creek at Wauhatchie and work down on the right bank, whilst he employed the remainder of his force in constructing temporary bridges across the creek on the main road. The enemy being attracted by the force on the road, did not observe the movements of Geary until his column was directly on his left and threatened his rear. Hooker's movements were facilitated by the heavy mist which overhung the mountain, enabling Geary to get into position without attracting attention. Finding himself vigorously pursued by a strong column on his left and rear, the enemy began to fall back with rapidity, but his resistance was obstinate, and the entire point of the mountain was not gained until about 2 P.M., when General Hooker reported by signal and telegraph that he had carried the mountain as far as the road from Chattanooga Valley to the White House. Soon after, his main column coming up, his line was extended to the foot of the mountain near the mouth of Chattanooga Creek. His right, being still strongly resisted by the enemy, was reinforced by Carlin's brigade, First Division, Fourteenth Corps, which arrived at the White House about 5 P.M., in time to take part in the contest still going on at that point. Continuous and heavy skirmishing was kept up in Hooker's front until ten at night, when there was an unusual quietness along our whole front.

"With the aid of the steamer 'Dunbar,' which had been put in condition and sent up the river at daylight of the 24th, General Sherman by 11 A.M. had crossed three divisions of the Fifteenth Corps, and was ready to advance as soon as Davis's division, Fourteenth Corps, commenced crossing. Colonel Long, commanding Second Brigade, Second Division Cavalry, was then directed to move up at once, follow Sherman's advance closely, and proceed to carry out his instructions of the day before, if not required by General Sherman to support his left flank. Howard's corps moved to the left about 9 A.M., and communicated with Sherman's troops about noon. Instructions were sent to General Hooker to be ready to advance on the morning of the 25th from his position on the point of Lookout Mountain to the Summertown road, and endeavor to intercept the enemy's retreat, if he had not already withdrawn, which he was to ascertain by pushing a reconnoissance to the top of the mountain.

"The reconnoissance was made as directed, and having discovered that the enemy had evacuated during the night, General Hooker was then directed to move on the Rossville road with the troops under his command against Rossville, carry that pass, and operate upon the left and rear of the enemy's position on Mission Ridge. Palmer's and Granger's troops were held in readiness to advance directly on the rifle-pits in their front as soon as Hooker could get into position at Rossville. In retiring, on the night of the 24th, the enemy had destroyed the bridges over Chattanooga Creek, on the road leading from Lookout Mountain to Rossville, and, in consequence, General Hooker was delayed until after 2 o'clock P.M. in effecting the crossing of Chattanooga Creek. About noon, General Sherman becoming heavily engaged with the enemy, they having massed a strong force in his front, orders were given for General Baird to march his division within supporting distance of General Sherman. Moving his command promptly in the direction indicated, he was placed in position to the left of Wood's division of Granger's corps. Owing to the difficulties of the ground, his troops did not get in line with Granger's until about 2.30 p.m.; orders were then given him to move forward on Granger's left, and within supporting distance, against the enemy's rifle-pits on the slope and at the foot of Missionary Ridge. The whole line then advanced against the breastworks and soon became warmly engaged with the enemy's skirmishers. These, giving way, retired upon their reserves, posted within their works, our troops advancing steadily in a continuous line. The enemy, seized with panic, abandoned the works at the foot of the hill and retreated precipitately to the crest, where they were closely followed by our troops, who, apparently inspired by the impulse of victory, carried the hill simultaneously at six different points, and so closely upon the heels of the enemy that many of them were taken prisoners in the trenches.

"We captured all their cannon and ammunition before they could be removed or destroyed. After halting for a few moments to reorganize the troops, who had become somewhat scattered in the assault of the hill, General Sheridan pushed forward in pursuit, and drove those in his front who escaped capture across Chickamauga Creek. Generals Wood and Baird, being obstinately resisted by reinforcements from the enemy's extreme right, continued fighting until darkness set in, slowly but steadily driving the enemy before them.

"In moving upon Rossville, General Hooker encountered Stewart's division and other troops. Finding his left flank threatened, Stewart attempted to escape by retreating towards Graysville, but some of his forces, finding their retreat from that quarter threatened, retired in disorder towards their right along the crest of the ridge, where they were met by another portion of General Hooker's command, and were driven by these troops in the face of Johnson's division of Palmer's corps, by whom they were nearly all made prisoners.

"On the 26th the enemy were pursued by Hooker and Johnson's divisions of Palmer's corps, surprising a portion of their rear-guard near Graysville after nightfall, capturing three pieces of artillery and several hundred prisoners. General Granger's command returned to Chattanooga, with instructions to prepare and hold themselves in readiness for orders to reinforce General Burnside at Knoxville.

"The pursuit was continued on the 27th, capturing an additional piece of artillery at Graysville. Hooker's advance encountered the enemy posted in the pass through Taylor's Ridge, at Ringgold, who, after obstinate resistance of an hour, were driven from the pass, with considerable loss in killed, wounded, and prisoners. Our loss was also heavy. A large quantity of forage and some additional caissons and ammunition were captured at Ringgold.

"Colonel Long returned to Chattanooga from his expedition and reported, verbally, that on the 24th he reached Tyner's Station, destroying the enemy's forage and rations at that place; also some cars, doing considerable injury to the railroad. He then proceeded to Ottowah, where he captured and destroyed some wagons loaded with forage; from thence he proceeded to Cleveland, remaining there one day, destroyed their copper-rolling mill and a large depot of commissary and ordnance stores. Being informed that a train of the enemy's wagons was near Charleston, on the Hiawassee, and was probably unable to cross the river on account of the break in their pontoon-bridge, after a few hours' rest he pushed forward, with a hope of being able to destroy them, but found on reaching Charleston that the enemy had repaired their bridge and had crossed their train safely, and were prepared to defend the crossing with one or two pieces of artillery, supported by an infantry force, on the northern bank. He then returned to Cleveland and damaged the railroad for five or six miles in the direction of Dalton, and then returned to Chattanooga.

"On the 28th General Hooker was ordered by General Grant to remain at Ringgold until the 30th, and so employ his troops as to cover the movements of General Sherman, who had received orders to march his force to the relief of Burnside, by way of Cleveland and Loudon. Palmer's corps was detached from the force under General Hooker and returned to Chattanooga.

"It will be perceived from the foregoing report that the original plan of operations was somewhat modified, to meet and take the best advantage of emergencies which necessitated material modifications of that plan. It is believed, however, that the original plan, had it been carried out, could not possibly have led to more successful results. The alacrity and intelligence displayed by officers in executing their orders, the enthusiasm and spirit displayed by the men who did the work, cannot be too highly appreciated by the nation, for the defence of which they have on so many other memorable occasions nobly and patriotically exposed their lives in battle.

"Howard's (Eleventh) Corps having joined Sherman on the 24th, his operations from that date will be included in Sherman's report. Also those of Brigadier-General J. C. Davis, Second Division, Fourteenth Corps, who reported to Sherman for duty on the 21st.

"I am, general, very respectfully your obedient servant,
"GEO. H. THOMAS,
"Major-General U. S. Vols., Commanding.
"BRIGADIER-GENERAL L. THOMAS,
"Adjutant-General U.S.A., Washington, D. C."

To any one who participated in this battle it was evident that General Bragg, the Confederate commander, concentrated the greater portion of his army against General Sherman on the Federal left, thinking that his was the main attack, and that no effort would be made to carry the works in Thomas's front. This action on the part of Bragg was just what General Grant desired, as it enabled him to storm the heights at all points. Had the rifle-pits on the crest of the hill been well filled, supported as they were by batteries so arranged as to have a direct and a cross-fire upon Thomas's advancing columns, it would have been almost impossible for any body of troops to have breasted the storm of lead and iron which could have been brought to bear upon them. When the Confederate commander in an unguarded moment weakened his line in front of Thomas, the latter took immediate advantage of it, and thus was the summit reached, not, however, without serious loss on the Union side.

On reaching the crest of the ridge the lines were formed and Thomas rode in front, and as he passed each regiment cheer after cheer was sent up in honor of the grand old chieftain. To one regiment he remarked that the men had made a fine race up the hill, and one of the soldiers, who had felt the want of food for weeks, cried out, "Yes, general, you have been training us for this race for several weeks." At that moment, looking around, he observed a steamboat puffing and snorting up the river, and he replied, "That is so; but there comes full rations, and in future the Army of the Cumberland shall have full rations."

The defeat of the enemy and his immediate withdrawal

opened up Chattanooga, and the troops which had been cooped up were enabled to extend their lines, and once more felt themselves masters of the situation. Lookout and Mission Ridge were in the possession of the Federal army, and there had been wiped away every stain of defeat from the shredded and riven banners, and the cloud-capped brows of the mountains had been crested with a halo of triumph. The Army of the Cumberland, under its able leader, had performed a very important part in the battles culminating in the overthrow of Bragg and his well-disciplined army. Thomas was proud of his command, and the members of it idolized their great commander. Ordinarily modest and unassuming, in battle he was grand. Wherever the leaden messengers of death flew the thickest there Thomas could always be found. He was without fear, and, in fact, often exposed himself unnecessarily in his great desire to do his whole duty.

Mr. W. F. G. Shanks, from whose book quotations have been previously made, says, "General Thomas is the purest man I met in the army. He was the Bayard of our army,— 'sans peur, sans reproche,'—and I have endeavored in vain to find a flaw in his character. His character is free from every stain, and he stands forth in the army as above suspicion. He has gone through the war without apparently exciting the jealousy of a single officer. He has so regulated his advancement, so retarded, in fact, his promotion, that when, as the climax to two years' hard service, he fought a great battle and saved a great army, and was hailed and recognized by the whole country as a hero, not one jealous or defeated officer was found to utter dissent to this popular verdict."

The above is strictly true. No officer, either of the regular or volunteer army, ever felt that Thomas owed his advancement to the hard and dangerous work of others. It is true that he was enabled by the courage and devotion of those under him to carry his plans to a successful issue, and these successes passed to his credit and made him a hero, yet there was not a single officer that ever thought him unworthy of the many honors heaped upon him by the Congress of the United States and by the American people. His promotions were due to his skill, ability, and loyal devotion to duty, which ever characterized him in the various grades through which he passed, and each was fought for and won in the great battle movements of the war. It has been said that he was slow, and that he gained the familiar cognomen of "Slow Trot" in consequence thereof. I think that his tardiness was due to the fact that he always calculated the chances of success and defeat, and was unwilling to risk the latter unless he was satisfied that the chances of success were reasonably certain. True it is that he never lost a battle, and his victories were real, on battle-fields, and not on paper alone. General Grant once remarked that in the reports of a certain distinguished general of battles fought two things could be relied on as correct without question, namely, time and place. Such a remark could not be applied to Thomas, as his reports were truthful at all times, and the only complaints ever heard came from officers under him to the effect that his innate modesty and love of truth compelled him to fall a little short of the facts rather than embrace them all in their length and breadth, for fear that it might look like boasting of his own exploits or those of the troops he governed and directed. At the close of the war many new regiments were organized for the regular service, and these regiments were to be officered by those who had distinguished themselves during the war. Each army commander made a number of recommendations and pushed their claims before the authorities at Washington, securing advancement and promotion for those who served under them, but Thomas contented himself with furnishing the list, believing that each case would be decided on its merits. When the announcements were made and he discovered that injustice had been done to many of those who had served long and faithfully under him, he was displeased, but his soldierly training made him scorn the idea of a protest or remonstrance. An officer who had distinguished himself in many battles under the general's eye spoke to him of the humiliation he experienced in being overlooked and left to return to his old place in the regular army. Thomas remarked, "I have taken great pains to educate myself not to feel."

Such was his character in life. He always did the very best he could, and let the consequences take care of themselves. In his entire military life he was never known to ask any favors for himself or to shrink from any responsibility on his own account.

After the battle of Missionary Ridge, Thomas pursued the fleeing enemy, with Palmer's corps and other troops, to Ringgold, returning in a short time to Chattanooga. Having completed his selections for the department staff, the following general orders were issued:

"Headquarters Department of the Cumberland,
"Chattanooga, Tenn., Jan. 9, 1864.
"General Orders No. 9.

"The following-named officers are announced as composing the general staff of this department:

"Brigadier-General William D. Whippple, U.S.V., Assistant Adjutant-General and Chief of Staff.

"Major William McMichael, U.S.V., Assistant Adjutant-General.

"Brigadier-General J. M. Brannan, U.S.V., Chief of Artillery.

"Brigadier-General W. L. Elliott, U.S.V., Chief of Cavalry.

"Lieutenant-Colonel L. C. Easton, Q.M.U.S.A., Chief Quartermaster.

"Lieutenant-Colonel A. P. Porter, Com. U.S.A., Chief Commissary of Subsistence.

"Lieutenant-Colonel Arthur C. Ducat, U.S.V., Assistant Inspector-General.

"Lieutenant-Colonel William M. Wiles, Twenty-second Ind. Vol. Inf., Provost-Marshal-General.

"Surgeon G. Perin, U.S.A., Medical Director.

"Major Oscar A. Mack, Aide-de-Camp.

"Major Ralston Skinner, U.S.V., Judge-Advocate.

"Captain T. G. Baylor, Ordnance Dept. U.S.A., Chief of Ordnance.

"Captain William E. Merrill, Engineers U.S.A., Topographical Engineer.

"Captain John P. Willard, U.S.V., Aide-de-Camp.

"Captain S. C. Kellogg, U.S.V., Aide-de-Camp.

"Captain Jesse Merrill, Signal-Officer U.S.A., Chief of Signal Corps.

"Captain John H. Young, Fifteenth U. S. Inf., Commissary of Musters.

"First Lieutenant Henry M. Cist, Seventy-fourth Ohio Vol. Inf., Acting Assistant Adjutant-General.

"First Lieutenant William L. Porter, Fifty-sixth Ohio Vol. Inf., Acting Aide-de-Camp.

"First Lieutenant James K. Reynolds, Sixth Ohio Vol. Inf., Acting Aide-de-Camp.

"First Lieutenant M. J. Kelly, Fourth U. S. Cav., Chief of Couriers.

"By command of
"MAJOR-GENERAL GEO. H. THOMAS.
"WM. D. WHIPPLE, Assistant Adjutant-General."

In the month of February, 1864, General Thomas thought it advisable to make a demonstration in force against Rocky Face Ridge and Buzzard Roost, behind which the enemy was known to be fortified. Buzzard Roost Gap seemed to be the gateway to Dalton. The enemy's outposts were driven in, and Thomas got near enough to the gap to see that it was too strongly fortified to force his way through it. Standing on the railroad-track, with field-glass in hand, he surveyed the enemy's works. A sharpshooter observing him aimed and fired, the ball passing to the right; again he loaded and fired, the ball passing to the left. Thomas coolly put up his glass and remarked that the next time he would probably hit him, and retired to another place. On the return of the reconnoitring force it was a well-established fact that Dalton could be taken only by a movement through Snake Creek Gap, a pass in the mountain nearly opposite Resaca. General Sherman, when his arrangements were made for a forward movement, ordered McPherson's corps through that pass, thence to Resaca, destroying the bridge, and thus effectually cutting off the Confederates from a retreat by rail. McPherson obeyed, but found himself confronted by a force so large that he could not carry out General Sherman's instructions, and he was compelled to send for additional troops. But when they reached the gap and got within cannon-range of Resaca, Johnston had fallen back from Dalton and confronted our army, disputing its entrance into that village. Thomas formed his line on McPherson's left, and Schofield formed on Thomas's left. Howard moved through Dalton and pressed on to Resaca in close pursuit of Johnston's retreating columns. A heavy battle ensued during the afternoon and evening of the 15th. The enemy retreated south across the Oostanaula during the night, and the next morning the whole army started in pursuit, General Thomas's command in advance. Davis's division of Palmer's corps was sent to Rome, which he captured, driving out of the town quite a large force of cavalry and infantry.

At Adairsville Newton's division had a sharp conflict with the rear-guard, but next morning the enemy was gone. The pursuit was continued, passing through Kingston, and at a point four miles beyond found the enemy in force, but on the approach of the Federal army he again fell back to Cassville, obstinately contesting the ground he was forced to yield. At this point Johnston formed his line of battle and constructed temporary works, apparently intending to offer battle. Had one been fought it would have been one of the most beautiful battle-fields of the war. The grounds were level, and few obstructions presented themselves to the active movement of troops. General Sherman anticipated a battle at or near this place, and made his arrangements accordingly; but when the silver-gray of the morning gradually changed to gold and flooded the field with its soft, mellow light, it revealed the fact that the enemy had fallen back during the night across the Etowah River and occupied Allatoona Pass. General Sherman, who had evinced a longing desire to measure steel with his antagonist, who had avoided a collision, resolved upon trying strategy to see if he could not get the enemy so hemmed in that he would have to fight in order to extricate himself from the meshes thrown around him. To this end Sherman cut loose from the railroad and moved, with twenty days' rations, in the direction of Dallas. On the 25th Hooker fought a hard battle to gain a place known as New Hope Church, situated on a muddy, sluggish stream known as Pumpkin-Vine Creek. This point was of importance, as quite a number of neighboring roads centred there. Hooker drove the enemy from his position, but, night setting in, he did not gain possession of the roads. On the following morning the enemy was well intrenched. McPherson moved to Dallas, Thomas deployed against New Hope Church, and Schofield moved so as to turn the enemy's right flank. This closed the operations for May, which Thomas summarized as follows:

"HEADQUARTERS ARMY OF THE CUMBERLAND,
"IN THE FIELD, NEAR DALLAS, GEORGIA, June 5, 1864.

"COLONEL,—I have the honor to report the operations of my command for the month of May, as follows:

"In obedience to instructions from the major-general commanding the military division, I got my command in readiness for a forward movement on Dalton, Georgia, and was fully prepared to move on the 2d of May as directed. Major-General Hooker, commanding Twentieth Army Corps, was directed to move from Lookout Valley *via* Lee's and Gordon's Mills, on East Chickamauga Creek, to Leet's farm, on the road leading from the mill to Nickojack Gap, the movement to commence on the 2d. Major-General Palmer, commanding the Fourteenth Corps, was to concentrate his command at Ringgold, Georgia, and Major-General Howard, commanding Fourth Army Corps, was to move from Cleveland, East Tennessee, on the 3d, and to concentrate his command in the vicinity of Catoosa Springs, about three miles east of Ringgold; McCook's division of cavalry to move on Howard's left. Kilpatrick's division of cavalry was stationed at Ringgold, picketing towards Tunnel Hill and patrolling on Palmer's right flank. Garrard's division was detached and operating under instructions from Major-General McPherson, commanding the Army of the Tennessee. The army got into position by the 5th, and stood as above, direct communication having been fully established from the right to the left of the whole command.

"According to instructions given on the 6th, the army moved on Tunnel Hill at daylight on the 7th in three columns: Palmer's corps on the direct road from Ringgold, Howard's *via* Lee's house, and Hooker's *via* Nickojack Gap and Trickum. The enemy made some show of resistance in Palmer's front, but evacuated Tunnel Hill on the appearance of Howard's column on his flank, and fled towards Buzzard's Roost, our troops occupying Tunnel Hill ridge. Palmer's command was then moved forward and took position on Howard's right, along the ridge, and both corps remained there for the night. Hooker's column reached Trickum Post-office about 4 P.M., and camped for the night, picketing strongly the roads leading from Buzzard's Roost and Dalton, as well as the approaches from the direction of Villanow. General Kilpatrick's division of cavalry took post at or near Gordon's Springs, to be in readiness to establish communication with the Army of the Tennessee, which was expected at Villanow on the morning of the 8th. Harker's brigade of Newton's division, Howard's corps, was pushed along the crest of Rocky Face Ridge to within half a mile of the rebel signal-station. There it came upon obstructions of too formidable a character to admit of further progress except with very severe loss. It was instructed to hold the position. Wood's division of Fourth Corps, Davis's division of the Fourteenth Corps, and Butterfield's division of the Twentieth Corps then pushed forward a line of skirmishers and drove the enemy to his intrenchments, our men occupying the mouth of Buzzard's Roost. Geary's division of the Twentieth Corps made a reconnoissance well up the side of Chattoogata Mountain, a high and precipitous ridge running due south from Buzzard's Roost. Geary's men fought their way well up to the enemy's intrenchments on the crest, but with considerable loss and without being able to gain possession of Mill Gap. The troops were then withdrawn to a position in the valley out of reach of the enemy's guns. Kilpatrick communicated with General McPherson's command at Villanow, and then returned to Trickum. Brigadier-General Ed McCook was ordered to concentrate his cavalry division and take post on the left of General Schofield until General Stoneman's cavalry could arrive and relieve him. From a prisoner captured at Buzzard's Roost we learned that the force defending the passage of the gap amounted to 11,000 men, comprising Stewart's and Bates's divisions, supported by Hindman's and Stevenson's divisions, numbering 10,000 more. They had considerable artillery, but none heavier than 10-pound calibre. The enemy was fortifying all night of the 7th, and had masked batteries at points all through the pass. Heavy skirmishing was kept up along the whole line during the 9th and 10th, with considerable loss in wounded and but few killed. General Hooker was directed on the 10th to send one division of his command to the support of General McPherson at Snake Creek Gap, to enable the latter to operate more freely from danger to his rear. Kilpatrick's cavalry was also ordered to report to General McPherson. McCook's division of cavalry, posted on the left of General Schofield's command, had a heavy skirmish with three brigades of the enemy's cavalry, on the road leading to Varnell Station, resulting in our driving the rebels to their intrenchments on Poplar Creek Hill, where they opened on McCook's troops with two pieces of artillery. Our loss was 136 men and 15 officers killed, wounded, and missing; among the latter Colonel Lagrange, of the First Wisconsin, who was captured. The enemy's loss was greater than ours. General Hooker was directed to send another division of his command to Snake Creek Gap, with instructions to repair the road through the gap, so as to facilitate the passage of infantry and wagons. On the 11th it was decided to leave one corps, Howard's, supported by Stoneman's and McCook's divisions of cavalry, and move to Snake Creek Gap with the balance of the army, attacking the enemy in force from that quarter, whilst Howard was keeping up the impression of a direct attack on Buzzard's Roost. This movement was to commence on the 12th. Instructions were given to corps commanders to provide their commands with ten days' rations and a good supply of ammunition, sending all surplus wagons back to Ringgold. At 9 A.M. on the 13th General Howard's command occupied Dalton, it having been evacuated by the enemy on the evening of the 12th. Concentrating his troops in Dalton, General Howard pursued the enemy along the railroad in the direction of Resaca, capturing a considerable number of prisoners. The concentration of the balance of the army in Snake Creek Gap having been completed by the night of the 12th, at 8 A.M. on the 13th Hooker's corps, preceded by Kilpatrick's cavalry, moved out on the Resaca road, in support of McPherson's troops, threatening Resaca. Palmer's corps moved out of Snake Creek Gap two miles northeast of Hooker, and then took a course parallel with the Resaca road, with orders to proceed as far as the railroad. On reaching the neighborhood of the railroad his skirmishers encountered those of the enemy strongly posted on the hills immediately west of the railroad, and continued a fierce skirmish with them until nightfall. Butterfield's division of Hooker's corps moved up in support of Palmer's right. About noon of the 14th Schofield's and Palmer's corps attacked the enemy's position on the hills bordering the railroad, meeting with very heavy resistance. General Schofield's left being threatened, and he having called on me for support, I directed Newton's division of Howard's corps, which had just arrived, to move to Schofield's assistance, and subsequently the whole of Howard's corps took post on the left of Schofield. During the afternoon Hooker's corps, which had been acting as support to General McPherson, was shifted to the left of Howard's command; and Williams's division reached the position assigned him just in time to meet and repel a fierce attack of the enemy, who was endeavoring to turn Howard's left flank. McCook's division of cavalry took post on the left of Hooker, to guard against any further attempt of the enemy in that direction. The fighting in Schofield's and Howard's front was very severe, but we drove the enemy from the hills he had occupied and forced him into his intrenchments beyond. From prisoners captured we learned that Johnston's entire army was confronting us.

"At daylight on the morning of the 15th our lines stood nearly as follows: Palmer's corps on the right, connecting with the left of McPherson's line, then Schofield's and Howard's and Hooker's, with McCook's cavalry on our extreme left. Orders were issued during the night of the 14th for the whole line to advance at daylight on the 15th, provision being made for the retirement of Schofield's troops from the position they then occupied, and directions having been given them to take post on the left, where they properly belonged, as soon as crowded out from the centre of my line by the advance of Palmer and Howard. About 11 A.M. General Butterfield's division of Hooker's corps, supported by Williams's and Geary's of the same command, attacked and carried a series of hills strongly occupied by the enemy on the east of the road leading from Tilton to Resaca. The rebels were driven for nearly a mile and a half, our forces capturing four guns and a number of prisoners.

"Information was received by daylight on the 16th that Johnston had evacuated Resaca, and directions were immediately given for the whole army to start in pursuit. Our troops occupied the town about 9 A.M., and commenced repairing the bridge over the Ostanaula, which had been partially burned by the enemy. A pontoon-bridge was also thrown across, above the railroad-bridge, so that by night Howard's corps had got across and marched on Calhoun. Hooker's command crossed the Conasauga at Figlet's Ferry, and at a ford in its vicinity, thence marching south, across the Coosawattie, towards Adairsville. Palmer's command was to follow after Howard's, except Davis's division, which was detached and sent towards Rome, to the support of Garrard's cavalry, then acting under special instructions from the major-general commanding the military division.

"On the 17th our advance skirmished with the enemy nearly the whole distance from Calhoun to within two miles of Adairsville, when a fierce skirmish ensued, completely checking our further progress, and occasioning considerable loss in wounded. Information was brought in about dark that the whole of Johnston's army was at Adairsville. The column was again set in motion on the morning of the 18th, the enemy having left during the night. Howard's and Palmer's commands moved on the direct road and along the railroad towards Kingston, camping at a point three miles north of the latter place. Hooker's corps moved on a road running southeast from Adairsville, his instructions being to proceed as far as Cassville, and there await further orders. General Davis's division of the Fourteenth Corps occupied Rome, capturing a large amount of commissary and quartermaster stores, hospital supplies, and all sorts of ammunition, enough to supply his command for two weeks. The enemy tried to destroy the valuable iron-works at this place, but failed to do much injury. Howard's troops entered Kingston about 8 A.M. on the 19th, skirmishing with the enemy on the southeastern side of the town. The column started again at about 10 A.M., and came up with what was reported to be Cheatham's and another division, in line of battle, on a hill about half-way between Kingston and Cassville. Howard's troops shelled the enemy from this position, pushing on after him to within two miles of Cassville, skirmishing with his rear-guard until dark, when the command halted for the night. Baird's division of Palmer's corps was posted on the right of Howard's corps. Hooker's troops engaged the enemy on the road leading direct from Adairsville to Cassville, skirmishing with him, and driving him into his works at the latter place.

"At 10 P.M. General Howard reported the town in possession of his troops. A deserter came into our lines with the information that Johnston received a reinforcement of 6000 men on the 19th, and that his army was now estimated at 70,000 strong. By direction of the major-general commanding the military division, the whole command rested until the morning of the 23d. In the mean time, the railroad having been placed in running order as far as Cassville depot, twenty days' rations and forage were issued to the troops. Resaca was directed to be strongly held and made a depot of supplies, only such stores and provisions to be brought forward to Kingston and Rome as could be moved by the wagons present with the army. My directions were to move my army at daylight on the morning of the 23d on Dallas, by Euharley and Stilesboro'. The division of Brigadier-General Jeff. C. Davis, at Rome, as soon as relieved by troops from General McPherson's army, to march direct on Dallas by way of Van Wert. The advance-guard of McCook's division of cavalry reached Stilesboro' on the afternoon of the 23d, and found the place occupied by a strong force of the enemy's cavalry, supported by infantry, which resisted his further advance, skirmishing with him until dark. The commands of Major-Generals Hooker, Howard, and Palmer camped on the south side of Euharley Creek, in accordance with my directions. General Hooker was directed to send one division of his command, at daylight on the 24th, to push the enemy across Raccoon Creek towards Allatoona, on the Alabama road, and hold him in that position until relieved by the Army of the Ohio, covering the movements of the balance of the

Twentieth Corps directly through Stilesboro' upon Burnt Hickory, at which latter place his whole command was to encamp. McCook's division of cavalry was to precede the Twentieth Corps in the movement upon Burnt Hickory, and then take up a position towards Allatoona, picketing the roads strongly, and covering the movements of the army. The Fourth Corps followed the Twentieth Corps, camping on its right, and the Fourteenth Corps, not being able to reach Burnt Hickory, on account of the crowded state of the roads and the difficult nature of the ground passed over, camped at a point on Allatoona Ridge, about half-way between Stilesboro' and Burnt Hickory. McCook reached Burnt Hickory about 2 P.M., after skirmishing with the enemy about four miles. He captured a rebel courier bearing a despatch to the rebel General Jackson, commanding a division of cavalry, with instructions from General Johnston to observe our movements towards Burnt Hickory, and stating that Johnston was moving in the direction of Dallas and Powder Springs. General Garrard, commanding Second Cavalry Division, informed me that he was camped on Pumpkin-Vine Creek, about three miles from Dallas, and that in moving on that place, and when within a quarter of a mile from it, he was attacked by what was reported by prisoners to be Bates's division, the advance of Hardee's corps. Garrard repulsed this force and drove it back towards Dallas.

"On the 25th the First Division of cavalry (McCook's) moved on the road leading to Golgotha, preceding Butterfield's division of the Twentieth Corps. The balance of General Hooker's command advanced on the road leading to Dallas, running south of the one used by Butterfield's division. Howard's corps followed Hooker's, and in rear of Howard, Palmer's. About 11 A.M. General Geary's division of the Twentieth Corps, being in advance, came upon the enemy in considerable force at a point about four and a half miles from Dallas. The country on both sides of the road being thickly wooded and covered with undergrowth, Geary skirmished heavily with the enemy, slowly driving him until Butterfield's and Williams's divisions came up and relieved Geary's troops. Soon after the arrival of Williams, about 3 P.M., the column was again put in motion, Williams's division in advance, and, although heavily engaged, drove the enemy steadily before it into his intrenchments. Our loss was heavy, but it is believed that the loss of the enemy was much greater. Shortly after 3 P.M. the head of Howard's column got within supporting distance of Hooker's corps, and Newton's division was placed in position on Hooker's left about 6 P.M., and by morning the whole of Howard's corps was in position on the left of Hooker. The roads were so full of wagons that Palmer's corps could not get into position by the night of the 25th, but on the morning of the 26th Johnson's division of the Fourteenth Corps was moved up to within a short distance of Hooker's and Howard's commands, and was posted in reserve. Davis's division, Fourteenth Corps (which had reported back to its command, it having been relieved at Rome by troops from the Army of Tennessee), was sent by General Palmer to move on Dallas by the most direct road from where he then was, to support General McPherson's command, and communicate with the right of General Hooker. Baird's division of the Fourteenth Corps was left at Burnt Hickory to protect the trains at that point and the rear of the army. McCook's division of cavalry met the enemy's cavalry on the road leading from Burnt Hickory to Marietta, near its intersection with the lower Dallas and Allatoona road. McCook's troops skirmished heavily with the force opposing them, inflicting on them considerable loss and capturing fifty-two prisoners, from whom it was ascertained that the whole of Wheeler's cavalry was posted on the right of the rebel army. The left of General Howard's corps was swung around to the right, occupying a line of hills running nearly perpendicularly to the line occupied by Hooker on the 25th, thereby threatening the enemy's right. The Twenty-third Army Corps, Major-General Schofield commanding, was posted on the left of my command, Schofield's left extending to and covering the road leading from Allatoona to Dallas *via* New Hope Church. There was light skirmishing all day whilst Howard and Schofield were working into position, and at dark on the 26th Howard's left connected with Schofield's right. In the mean time trains were brought up and rations and ammunition issued where practicable. Strong breastworks were thrown up all along the line, the men working cheerfully, and prepared to resist any attack the enemy might see fit to make.

"On the 27th, in accordance with instructions given by the major-general commanding the military division, Hooker's and Howard's corps pressed the enemy, supported by considerable artillery firing. Wood's division of Howard's corps, supported by Johnson's division of Palmer's corps, was moved to the left of Schofield's line and swung round towards the right, attacking the enemy's right flank and driving him to his rifle-pits, with considerable loss, however, to our troops. Our men had to contend with an almost hidden foe, the ground being cut up into ravines and covered by a dense forest filled with undergrowth; but, notwithstanding all the difficulties of the country, officers and men did their work nobly, and having secured a position, were not to be moved from it. The enemy came out of his works in front of Newton's division of Howard's corps, attacking Wagner's and Kimball's brigades, but was driven back after a short and warm contest. General Davis occupied Dallas with his division on the afternoon of the 27th, skirmishing with the enemy and driving him as far as he could without losing his connection with General McPherson. Davis reported that, after skirmishing all the afternoon, he developed the enemy in force and strongly posted in front of his (Davis's) left, with a battery in position on a hill commanding the road between him and General Hooker. Davis had, however, cut a road through the forest to his rear, by which he could communicate safely with Hooker. During the night of the 27th the enemy attacked Davis, and was repulsed after a sharp fight, leaving behind him a few wounded and twenty-seven prisoners, belonging mostly to Polk's corps. By this time it had been ascertained beyond a doubt that Johnston had his whole army with him, strengthened by Polk's command and detachments sent from various points to reinforce him. He had taken up a strong position, which he was steadily strengthening with earthworks, evidently with the determination to make a firm stand where he then was.

"On the 28th our line stood as follows: Hooker's corps (Twentieth) on the right, with Davis's division of Palmer's corps still on his right, but acting as a support to the Army of the Tennessee; two divisions of Howard's corps (Fourth) on the left of Hooker; then the Army of the Ohio, Major-General Schofield commanding; Wood's division of Howard's corps on the left of Schofield's command, with Johnson's division of Palmer's corps on the left of Wood; Stoneman's division of cavalry holding a hill to the left of Johnson; and then McCook's division of cavalry, holding the road leading from Burnt Hickory to Marietta *via* Golgotha, and guarding the left of the army. During the 28th there was considerable artillery firing, with skirmishing at intervals during the day and night.

"During the night of the 29th the enemy felt our line at several points, without making a serious attack at any one place; they found our men vigilant and fully prepared for them.

"Owing to the close proximity of the enemy's lines to the right of ours, neither McPherson nor Davis could withdraw from their positions without being attacked and forced to return, so that the project of using their commands to relieve Hooker, Howard, and Schofield, allowing these latter to take post on the left of the line, could not be carried out, although three attempts at a withdrawal were made by McPherson and Davis on the nights of the 29th, 30th, and 31st. In the mean while the position of the army remained unchanged up to the 31st, our skirmishers and those of the enemy exchanging occasional shots.

"The detailed reports of the subordinate commanders will be forwarded as soon as handed in.

"I have the honor to forward herewith a consolidated return of casualties for the month, as also a return of prisoners captured, and a list of captured property and ammunition expended.

"I am, colonel, very respectfully your obedient servant,

"Geo. H. Thomas,
"Major-General Commanding."

On June 1 Thomas and Schofield moved to the left, covering the roads leading back to Allatoona and Ackworth. The enemy occupied Pine, Lost, and Kenesaw Mountains, covering Marietta and the railroad back to Chattahoochie. General Thomas moved on Pine and Kenesaw Mountains, fighting the bloody battle of Kenesaw. After a short delay the army was again put in motion. Thomas crossed the

Chattahoochie at Powers's and Pace's ferries, and moved to Peach-Tree Creek.

On the morning of July 20, 1864, the author met Colonel McKay, of General Thomas's staff. He remarked that we would have a "big fight" before night. I asked him for his reasons for so believing, and he said that he had just seen an Atlanta paper, and in it was an announcement that General Joseph E. Johnston had been relieved from the command of the Confederate army, and that Hood had been designated as his successor; and, continued McKay, "a man who will bet a thousand dollars without having a pair will fight when he has the troops to do it with."

Sure enough, at four o'clock P.M. he sallied from his works in force, taking his position in line of battle on the right of the Federal centre, in front of Hooker's corps, Newton's division of Howard's corps, and A. G. McCook's brigade of Johnson's division of Palmer's corps. As soon as his lines were formed, the enemy moved forward as if on drill, striking the Federal line with great force, precipitating a bloody engagement, in which Hood was repulsed. His loss was very heavy, and he fell back to his works and began at once to make arrangements for another sortie. Since the death of General Hood his book, "Advance and Retreat," has been published, and he accounts for his defeat through the lukewarm support of one of his corps commanders, General W. J. Hardee.

At the breaking out of the war Hood was a lieutenant in the Second Regiment of Cavalry (now Fifth), and Hardee was major in the same regiment, and doubtless felt a little sore over the fact that Hood had risen so rapidly, and did not give him that cordial support to which he was in all fairness entitled. Hardee was ordered to attack at one o'clock P.M., whereas he delayed doing so until four o'clock P.M. This delay, in Hood's opinion, caused the defeat, but it is thought that the result would have been the same had Hardee complied with his instructions to the letter. Sherman's arrangements were made, based on the army he commanded, with full assurance that victory would perch upon his banners regardless of the time and place of Hood's attack.

Thomas and Palmer were spectators, and their immediate presence inspired the troops to extraordinary endeavor. The Federal army lost heavily, particularly Hooker's corps, against which the heaviest masses were thrown.

Among the severely wounded was Captain E. T. Wells, assistant adjutant-general on the staff of General R. W. Johnson, who was struck with a fragment of a shell which broke several of his ribs. His wound was severe, but he recovered, and after the war closed was appointed United States judge for the Territory of Colorado. It was the writer's good fortune to know him well, and a more gallant officer never drew a sword. He was one of many who was kept in a subordinate position when he had courage and ability eminently fitting him to wear the stars with credit and honor to the nation.

Major-General John M. Palmer, the commander of the Fourteenth Corps, succeeded to that command after the battle of Chickamauga, in recognition of his gallant and faithful services in that engagement. He is a native of Kentucky, though his family removed to Carlinsville, Illinois, when he was quite young. There he studied law and became a prominent member of the bar in that State. In the bleak, dark days of 1861 he entered the volunteer service as colonel of the Fourteenth Illinois Infantry, which he commanded in Fremont's expedition to Springfield.

About the close of the year 1861 he was promoted to the rank of brigadier-general, and for gallant and meritorious services in the battle of Stone River was advanced to the grade of major-general. He commanded a division in the battle of Chickamauga, where his courage and good conduct attracted the attention of General Thomas, upon whose recommendation he was assigned to the command of the Fourteenth Corps.

Palmer was a great favorite with Thomas. His bravery in action, his clear head in council, made him a valuable corps commander, and none appreciated him more highly than his distinguished commander, the hero of Chickamauga, the commander of the Army of the Cumberland. At the close of the war he returned to his adopted State, and was elected governor by an overwhelming majority.

He has been spoken of very favorably as a candidate for the Presidency of the United States, and, if he should ever reach that exalted position, the people of the country can boast of having an honest, clear-headed man to control their affairs so long as he holds in his hands the reins of government.

CHAPTER VII.

Closing in around Atlanta—Hood offers Battle on 20th, 22d, and 28th Days of July—Death of McPherson—Howard succeeds Him—Atlanta captured—Thomas's Report of Operations preceding Battle, etc.

AFTER the battle of the 20th Sherman ordered the closing in of his entire line in semicircular form around Atlanta, and distant therefrom about two miles. Hood, who had issued ammunition, was again ready for another contest, and as he had succeeded Johnston because the latter would not offer battle often enough, he resolved upon fighting as long as he exercised command of the Army of the Tennessee and had a sufficient number of men left to make a reasonable resistance. Accordingly, on the 22d he sallied out, striking our left flank under General J. B. McPherson. This was one of the most terrific struggles of the war. The Federal lines frequently fought on both sides of their rifle-pits, and after a long and desperate battle the Confederates were repulsed. The losses on both sides were very heavy, in consequence of the hand-to-hand character of the engagement. Among the killed on the Federal side was General McPherson, one of the youngest, but one of the ablest, of Sherman's generals. His loss was a severe blow to the Union cause, as it was difficult to supply his place. Had he survived the war, few, if any, would have stood higher on the roll of honor.

General O. O. Howard was assigned to the command of the Army of the Tennessee, succeeding the lamented McPherson. This assignment gave some dissatisfaction, the friends of General John A. Logan claiming that he was entitled to the command of that army by virtue of seniority and previous services. It was a difficult and delicate matter for General Sherman to determine. But, while recognizing the great merits of General Logan, he selected Howard, and directed him to move his army to the right of the line. For several days the opposing armies rested from their labors, with their picket-lines in close proximity to each other, but by general consent there was no firing from either side, and occasionally quite amusing conversations were carried on, and propositions to exchange articles, such as tobacco for coffee, etc., were often made. One of our pickets called over to the picket in his front: "I say, Johnny, when are you going to fight again?" "Well, Yank, I don't know, but I suppose very soon, as we have about men enough left for one more killing." Sure enough they had, and Hood on the 28th moved out against the Federal right, but, owing to the change made in our line, he came in contact with the same troops that he had fought on the 22d. This splendid army seemed to be as fresh as ever. Hood hurled his columns against it, but the advance of the deafening, maddening roar of artillery and musketry told plainly that Howard was advancing.

Time and again the dauntless Hood tried to break the Federal line, but each time failed with heavy loss, when, finally becoming discouraged and disheartened, he withdrew his army within the line of his own defences. The feeling which had been engendered against Howard in consequence of his selection to command the Army of the Tennessee, was forgotten after this battle. There he was in the fore-front directing the details with that cool courage which characterized him in every emergency, and by his skill and bravery he not only won the confidence and esteem of his subordinate commanders, but also of every soldier under his command.

A flank movement to the right against Jonesboro' and Lovejoy's Station resulted in the enemy evacuating Atlanta and the occupation of the city by the troops under General Thomas. In all these movements, resulting in the above capture, Thomas, with his army, had performed a very prominent part; in fact, he had become a necessary part of the army, and General Sherman could not have gotten along very well without him, as "Old Thomas was his wheel-horse," upon whom he could safely rely for loyal co-operation under all circumstances.

Within the three months previous to the capture of Atlanta the army had experienced hard service. After the battle of Mission Ridge only a brief breathing-spell was granted to Thomas and his veterans. Then, without baggage, he pushed down into the very vitals of the Confederacy, and it might be said that during those long months of combat that culminated in the capture of Atlanta and Northern Georgia, like the Israelites of old he followed a cloud by day and a pillar of flame by night; for in that time Dalton, Resaca, Kenesaw, New Hope, Peach-Tree Creek, Jonesboro', and all those crimson names of battle had been traced bloodily into the history of Thomas's devoted Army of the

Cumberland. Every day had the smoke-cloud of battle kissed the heavens, and each night had flamed and flashed with the lambent light of his blazing guns; and he had followed that smoke-cloud and those blazing guns over a hundred fields of strife until the old flag floated in exultation over the great Gate City of the South. It was now that the loyal people of the North could see the beginning of the end of this fearful, this unnatural, struggle, and joy and happiness filled their hearts.

Nearly every officer of high rank had at some time taken a short leave of absence to enable him to return to his home and see his loved ones, but Thomas never left his post of duty, nor had he seen any of the members of his family since he left them several years before to report to General Anderson in Kentucky. Now he began to feel that the war which had called away so many men from their homes and friends would soon terminate for the South amid the black ashes of overthrow and defeat.

Yet he was destined to fight other battles, win other victories, and crown himself with other imperishable honors. His career, which had been one of unbounded success, had to be rounded out by other campaigns and other conflicts, which were destined to stamp him as one of the greatest warriors of the age, one of the wisest and ablest commanders in the great war of the Rebellion.

The following is a report of the operations of Thomas's command in Northern Georgia:

"Headquarters Department of the Cumberland,
"Atlanta, Georgia, September 13, 1864:

"Colonel,—I have the honor to report as follows the operations of my command during the month of August, 1864:

"On the 1st instant the Army of the Cumberland was in position, as heretofore reported,—viz., Palmer's corps (Fourteenth) on the right, posted between the Turner's Ferry road and the Western and Atlantic Railroad, facing a little south of east; Williams's corps (Twentieth) in the centre, extending from the railroad around to the Buck Head road; Stanley's corps (Fourth) on the left, between the Buck Head road and Howard's house, on roads leading from Buck Head and Atlanta. Stanley's left being refused so as to cover the Buck Head road, Garrard's division of cavalry took post on the left of Stanley's corps, with instructions to patrol the approaches to the left of the army from Decatur and Roswell Factory; Kilpatrick's division of cavalry was ordered to take post on the railroad between Marietta and the bridge over the Chattahoochie. The Army of the Cumberland held the left of the grand line investing Atlanta, besides sending two divisions (Ward's, of the Twentieth, and Davis's, of the Fourteenth) to the support of the troops of other commands operating on the extreme right of the grand army.

"Major-General Palmer was directed on the 2d to move with the two remaining divisions of his corps to a position in reserve in rear of the Army of the Ohio, then operating on the extreme right towards East Point; Brigadier-General Williams, commanding the Twentieth Corps, was directed to occupy the works vacated by the troops of General Palmer's command, on his right, by extending his line in that direction; and Ward's division was recalled from the support of the Army of the Ohio to enable General Williams more fully to carry out the above instructions. The withdrawal of

Palmer's corps left me with the Fourth and Twentieth Corps to hold a line of works nearly five miles in length, approaching at some points to within three hundred yards of the enemy's fortifications.

"On the 3d, Major-General Stanley pushed forward a strong line of skirmishers, and succeeded in carrying the enemy's picket-line on the whole corps front, excepting on the extreme right of his line, where his men were met by a very destructive fire of musketry and canister. The enemy opened from at least twenty pieces of artillery. Our loss was about thirty killed and wounded, but we captured quite a number of prisoners, besides gaining considerable information regarding the positions of the enemy's troops and fortifications.

"Both Stanley's and Williams's skirmishers again pressed those of the enemy during the afternoon of the 5th, with a view of diverting his attention from the movements of the Armies of the Tennessee and of the Ohio, on our right. Palmer's corps, which had been placed in position on the right of the Army of the Ohio by direction of Major-General Sherman, pushed out from along Olley's Creek, and pressed close up to the enemy's works, capturing a strong line of rifle-pits, vigorously defended. Our loss was considerable, but we took 150 prisoners and gained an advantageous position. At the close of the engagement the skirmishers of the enemy and our own were only thirty yards apart. Our main line was moved up to within four hundred yards of that of the enemy. On the morning of the 6th the enemy felt our line at various points from right to left, seemingly persistent in his efforts to find a weak point in the latter direction, —on the line of Stanley's corps. From information gained by us through various sources, more or less reliable, we learned the enemy had posted his militia, supported by one division of his veterans, on that part of his line immediately confronting the Fourth and Twentieth Corps, and that he used the balance of his army in extending his line to the left towards East Point, as our movements in the same direction threatened his possession of the railroad. Although this necessitated his holding a large extent of ground, he formed his troops on very advantageous ridges, strengthened by works of a most impregnable character, rendering an assault on our part unjustifiable, from the useless sacrifice of life it would entail. While the enemy was busily engaged fortifying, our troops were not idle. Our position was also soon rendered impregnable to assault, and a constant shelling of the enemy's fortifications and the city of Atlanta was kept up day and night. In the mean while supplies of rations and clothing were being rapidly accumulated at the front, and our men enjoyed a season of rest,—such rest as is to be found in the trenches. On the 6th, Major-General John M. Palmer having been relieved from the command of the Fourteenth Army Corps at his own request, Brigadier-General R. W. Johnson, the senior division commander, took command of the corps.

"On the 7th, under General Johnson's direction, the corps advanced upon the enemy's works in his front, and, moving rapidly, carried the first line of rifle-pits, capturing 172 prisoners, and driving the enemy to their main works. The entire line of the Fourteenth Corps was then advanced and fortified. Our loss during the 6th and 7th, in the Fourteenth Corps, was 70 killed and 413 wounded, including 17 officers.

"Brigadier-General E. M. McCook, commanding Second Cavalry Division, reports as follows the result of his expedition to cut the enemy's railroad communications to Macon and West Point. His instructions are specified in Special Field Order No. 42, of July 26, headquarters Military Division of the Mississippi: 'Two and a half miles of the

Atlanta and West Point Railroad and telegraph-wire destroyed near Lovejoy's Station, eleven thousand wagons burned, two thousand mules killed or disabled, one thousand bales of cotton, one thousand sacks of corn, and three hundred sacks of flour destroyed, besides large quantities of bacon and tobacco.'

"He carried out his orders and accomplished all he was directed to without opposition, and it was only when the command started on its return that General McCook ascertained that the enemy's cavalry was between him and McDonough, at which latter place he had expected to form a junction with General Stoneman's expedition. Finding the enemy across his road in that direction, and being burdened with a good many prisoners and considerable captured property, General McCook turned towards the Chattahoochie River by way of Newman, on the West Point Railroad, and while on his way to that place was attacked by Jackson's division of cavalry, which he repulsed. Near Newman the railroad was cut in three places. Between there and the river he was surrounded by an overwhelming force of the enemy's cavalry, supported by a large infantry force. These troops he attacked in the hope of cutting his way through them, and in doing so broke the whole right of their line, riding over Ross's Texas Cavalry Brigade, and making General Ross and his staff prisoners. The enemy sent fresh troops to supply the place of those shattered by McCook's charge, when the latter, finding he could not break their line permanently, directed his brigade commanders to cut their way out with their commands and endeavor to cross the Chattahoochie by detachments. In this they were successful, but with the loss of their artillery; the latter, however, was *deliberately* destroyed before being abandoned.

"All the prisoners captured by us, about four hundred in number, were also turned loose. General McCook's loss in killed, wounded, and missing, as well as in material, is great, but that of the enemy is much greater proportionately, and is even so acknowledged by themselves. For details I have the honor to refer you to the report of General McCook, accompanying this.

"About the 10th information reached me that the enemy's entire cavalry force was concentrating in the neighborhood of Monticello and on the Ocmulgee River. Refugees and deserters from the enemy stated that it was intended to send this large concentration of cavalry under Wheeler on a raid into Tennessee against our communication.

"On the afternoon of the 14th the enemy's cavalry, said to be six thousand strong, attacked Dalton. Colonel Laibold (Second Missouri Infantry), commanding the post, occupied the fort with a small command, and bravely defended his position until reinforced.

"Early on the morning of the 15th, Major-General Steedman, with two regiments of white and six companies of colored troops, arrived at Dalton from Chattanooga and immediately attacked the enemy, driving him off towards Spring Place after four hours' fighting. The enemy's loss was heavy; he left his dead and wounded on the field. Our loss was 40 killed and 55 wounded; we captured about 50 wounded and 2 surgeons. Before appearing in front of Dalton, Wheeler's men had destroyed about two miles of track on the railroad south of Dalton, but by noon of the 17th the road was again in running order. Believing General Steedman to have sufficient troops at his disposal to beat off any further attack on the railroad, our whole attention was directed to the reduction of Atlanta, and at the same time it was determined to take advantage of the absence of the enemy's cavalry to make one more effort to break the Macon and Western Railroads. Accordingly, on the 18th, Brigadier-

General J. Kilpatrick, commanding Third Cavalry Division, was directed to attack and destroy both railroads, and for this purpose he was reinforced by two brigades taken from Garrard's Cavalry Division, stationed on the left of the army. With this force, numbering in all about four thousand men and two batteries of artillery, General Kilpatrick moved out from Sandtown on the evening of the 18th. He met the enemy's cavalry pickets, when only a short distance out from Sandtown, on the Chattahoochie, and skirmished with them to Jonesboro', on the Macon Railroad, driving them to that place. For six hours the command was engaged destroying the track, etc., until near midnight of the 19th, when part of his command was attacked one mile below the town and driven in, but subsequently the enemy was repulsed. Towards daylight of the 20th he moved in the direction of McDonough, and thence across the country back to the railroad near Lovejoy's Station, reaching that point at about 11 A.M. on the 20th. There he met a brigade of infantry, and, although repulsed at first, finally checked the advantage being gained by the enemy and drove him back with heavy loss. While thus engaged fighting infantry a heavy force of cavalry with artillery came up in his rear, and he found he was completely enveloped. Determining at once to break the enemy's line and extricate his command from its delicate position, he decided to ride over the enemy's cavalry and retire on McDonough. The movement was successfully made, and resulted in a complete rout of Jackson's Cavalry Division, numbering four thousand men, leaving in our hands 4 guns, 3 battle-flags, and all his wagons. Some prisoners were taken, and the enemy's loss in killed and wounded is known to be large. Reforming his command, Kilpatrick fought the enemy's infantry for an hour longer, when, finding his men running out of ammunition, he retired in the direction of Latimer's and Decatur without further molestation, reaching the latter place on the afternoon of the 22d. For details I have the honor to refer you to General Kilpatrick's official report, forwarded herewith, as also to that of Lieutenant G. A. Robinson, commanding Chicago Board of Trade Battery, and to an article in the *Chattanooga Rebel*, published at Griffin, Georgia, August 25.

"Pending the above movements to break the enemy's railroad communication, the troops in front of the city kept up a constant shelling of the fortifications and buildings of Atlanta, and, as refugees informed us, with marked effect.

"The heavy cavalry force under Wheeler still continued to threaten our railroad in Northern Georgia and East Tennessee without seriously interrupting communication with Chattanooga and Nashville. This, however, gave us no uneasiness, as we had a good accumulation of supplies within safe proximity to the main army.

"A considerable force of the enemy under Roddy had made its appearance in Northern Alabama, threatening to cross the Tennessee River near Decatur with a view of destroying the railroad between that place and Nashville. Again, in the vicinity of Clarksville, Tennessee, and Fort Donelson, the enemy had become troublesome, although without doing very material damage. To the discretion and good judgment of Major-Generals Rousseau and Steedman, commanding respectively the District of the Tennessee and of the Etowah, and to Brigadier-General R. S. Granger, commanding the District of Northern Alabama, was left the disposal of the troops and the defence of our communications with our depots at the north.

"In compliance with the directions contained in Special Order No. 57, headquarters Military Division of the Mississippi (appended, marked 'A'), promulgated to my corps commanders on the 16th August, everything was placed in readiness for the execution of the contemplated movements by the time mentioned. The major-general commanding the military division having, however, decided to await the return of General Kilpatrick's expedition, the Army of the Cumberland did not withdraw from its works until after dark on the night of the 25th. Stanley's corps, as directed from my headquarters (see instructions to Generals Stanley, Williams, and Garrard), commenced the movement by withdrawing from the position he then held on the left of the army to a line of ridges and high ground beyond and to the rear of the position where the right of the Twentieth Corps rested. Here he remained and covered the withdrawal of the Twentieth Corps, the latter having been ordered to take post on the Chattahoochie at the railroad-bridge and at Pace's and Turner's Ferries. Garrard's division of cavalry covered the movements of the Fourth and Twentieth Corps, then crossed the Chattahoochie, at Pace's Ferry, on the 26th, and, recrossing at the bridge at Sandtown on the 27th, took post on Stanley's left, picketing Utoy Creek from Utoy Post-office to Sandtown.

"The above movements were successfully executed, both corps being in the positions indicated at an early hour on the morning of the 26th. At 9 A.M. of the same day Stanley withdrew still farther, to a point along Utoy Creek, posting his command on some ridges facing the creek and across the Sandtown road. The Fourteenth Corps, then commanded by Brevet Major-General J. C. Davis, drew out from the position it had last held, on the right of the Army of the Tennessee, and, moving across Utoy Creek, took post on the right of Stanley's corps. Garrard's division of cavalry was directed to operate on the left and rear of the army, while Kilpatrick's division was similarly employed on the right.

"On the 27th, Stanley's corps moved to Mount Gilead

church, and, forming line of battle along the road leading to Fairburn, skirmished lightly with the enemy's cavalry. The Fourteenth Corps (Davis's) moved as far as Holbrook's house, on the Campbelltown road, advancing one brigade to Patterson's house, about a mile beyond, to cover the wagon-trains of the corps. The Twentieth Corps was securely in position on the Chattahoochie River, guarding the crossings and protecting the depots at Marietta. Major-General H. W. Slocum assumed command of the corps by virtue of General Order No. —, War Department.

"At daylight on the 28th, Davis's corps moved from its encampment, near Holbrook's house, to Mount Gilead church, thence past the left of Stanley's corps, taking the road leading from Redwine's house to Red Oak, on the West Point Railroad. Davis reached the railroad at 4 P.M., and posted his corps on the right of it, facing towards East Point. Stanley's command came up immediately after Davis's, and formed line on the left of the road. In this position the command remained for the night. Shortly after dark orders were issued to destroy the road by burning the ties and twisting the rails after heating. The work of destruction was continued throughout the night of the 28th and during part of the 29th, and when completed the railroad had been thoroughly dismantled for a distance of two miles north of my line, and a little over a mile south of it.

"About 6 A.M. on the 30th the Fourteenth and Fourth Corps moved from Red Oak towards the Macon Railroad. The Fourteenth Corps (Davis) concentrated at Flat Shoal church about 9 A.M., and after resting for an hour moved on in an easterly direction towards Couch's house, on the Decatur and Fayetteville road, at which point line was formed and the command went into camp.

"Communication was opened with the Army of the Tennessee at Renfro's house, two miles south of Couch's. The Fourth Corps formed on the left of the Fourteenth, its right extending beyond Mann's house, the line of the corps running in a northwesterly direction from Couch's. The advance divisions of both corps skirmished with the enemy's infantry and cavalry during the day, and by sundown it was ascertained that the enemy was in force at Morrow's Mill, on Crooked Creek, about three-fourths of a mile distant from the left of Stanley's corps. Up to dark no communication had been established with the Army of the Ohio. Garrard's cavalry was in the neighborhood of Red Oak, guarding the left and rear of the army.

"On the morning of the 31st, Stanley's corps moved to Morrow's Mill, where it found the enemy in intrenchments, very well finished, but occupied only by dismounted cavalry; those were driven out.

"The Army of the Ohio having come up, both commanders pushed out for the railroad, which was reached at the Big Bend, between Rough-and-Ready and Jonesboro'. General Stanley posted his corps between the railroad and Crooked Creek, and in that position remained for the night. Part of the Fourteenth Corps, under Brigadier-General Baird, made reconnoissance and demonstration in front of Couch's house, and reached the Macon and Western Railroad about two miles north of Jonesboro', with the advanced brigade, and destroyed about one mile of the track during the afternoon and night, although constantly annoyed by the enemy's cavalry. Whilst in this position a heavy column of the enemy's infantry was seen moving in a southerly direction, on a road still to the eastward of the one held by them. Some stragglers belonging to this column were picked up by our skirmishers, and from them it was ascertained that the troops we saw moving were Hardee's and Lee's corps.

"Up to this period the enemy had evidently been deceived as to the nature and strength of our movement on his communications, and only at this late hour had he detached any considerable force from the army in Atlanta.

"During the afternoon of the 31st, the Army of the Tennessee being heavily attacked in the position it had taken up the night before near Jonesboro', and General Howard having asked for reinforcements, General Davis was instructed to send one division from his corps to its support.

"Kilpatrick's division of cavalry, stationed on the right of the Army of the Tennessee, found a passage across Flint River and drove the enemy's pickets to within one-half mile of Jonesboro'. He was then attacked in turn by a heavy force of infantry and forced to withdraw.

"*September* 1.—At an early hour the remainder of the Fourteenth Corps moved from near Renfro's house, on the Decatur and Fayetteville road, to rejoin that part of the command which had advanced the day before to the Rough-and-Ready and Jonesboro' road. The junction formed, the corps moved south towards Jonesboro', and reached the pickets of the Army of the Tennessee about two and a half miles from the point of concentration. A reconnoissance was then sent out towards the railroad, which drove in the enemy's skirmishers and gained possession of a ridge on the north side of Mill Creek with but small loss. Later in the afternoon two divisions of Davis's corps (Fourteenth) were formed on the ridge, and artillery was opened on the enemy's works with good effect.

"The line of battle being finally adjusted, the command moved forward, attacking the enemy vigorously and driving him several hundred yards to his main works. An assault was then handsomely made on the works, which were carried along the entire line of Davis's command, after very heavy fighting and loss of over 1200 men. Two field-batteries of four guns each were captured in the enemy's fortifications, together with about 1000 prisoners, including one general officer and several field-officers, and a number of small-arms and battle-flags. The enemy's loss in killed and wounded was very severe.

"During this time the Fourth Corps (Stanley's) was moving from Rough-and-Ready towards Jonesboro' along the railroad, destroying it as the troops advanced. Arriving near Jonesboro', the column was deployed with a view to advance against the enemy's right flank, but, it being already quite late, darkness came on and prevented an extensive movement. The line of Stanley's corps was on the left of the railroad, facing southwest; Davis's corps passed the night in the enemy's works, the left of the line connecting with Stanley's right at the railroad.

"During the night the enemy fell back from Jonesboro', retreating towards Lovejoy's Station, where he was followed on the morning of the 2d by the Fourth Corps and the Armies of the Tennessee and of the Ohio. Davis's corps was directed to remain at Jonesboro' to bury the dead and collect captured property.

"Stanley's corps moved along the railroad and to the left of it, coming up with the enemy just north of Lovejoy's Station about noon. Line of battle was formed and preparations made to advance against the enemy in conjunction with the Army of the Tennessee on the right. It was only at a late hour, however, that the assault was made, and darkness prevented any decisive movement. Part of Stanley's troops gained the enemy's works and carried a small portion of them, but could not hold possession of the ground for want of co-operation on the part of the balance of the line.

"During the night information reached us that at 11 A.M. on the 2d the mayor and authorities of Atlanta had surrendered the city to a force of the Twentieth Corps, Major-General Slocum commanding, which, in obedience to instructions previously given, had been sent out from the Chattahoochie to feel the enemy's strength. The city had been evacuated the night previous, the army destroying in its retreat public property of considerable value, including eighty car-loads of ammunition; fourteen pieces of artillery and several thousand stand of small-arms were found.

"On the 3d the major-general commanding the military division issued orders to the effect that the campaign was ended, and that the grand army would return to Atlanta and vicinity until a new plan could be considered regarding future movements. Directions were at the same time given for the withdrawal of the troops. Corps commanders were instructed to send to the rear all surplus wagons and whatever material could obstruct the movements of the troops. The enemy still remained intrenched at Lovejoy's, although he was discovered to be moving his trains towards Griffin, with the supposed intention of withdrawing his main army to that point or still farther.

"At 8 P.M. on the 5th, in conjunction with the rest of the army, the Fourth Corps quietly withdrew from its position and fell back to Jonesboro', reaching that place at daylight on the 6th. The withdrawal was admirably conducted, and executed with complete success, although much impeded by a rain-storm, and consequent bad condition of the roads.

"Both corps, Stanley's and Davis's, remained quietly at Jonesboro' during the 6th, although Davis's rear-guard was attacked by the enemy as it was moving through the town to join the balance of the corps in position north of it. The enemy occupied Jonesboro' during the afternoon, but contented himself with exchanging a few shots with our skirmishers.

"On the 7th, at 7 A.M., the Fourth Corps withdrew from its camp near Jonesboro', moved along the railroad to near Sykes's house, northeast of Rough-and-Ready, and took up a position for the night. The Fourteenth Corps fell back simultaneously with Stanley's command, marching on the main road leading to Rough-and-Ready from Jonesboro', and was posted on the right of the Fourth Corps, north of Rough-and-Ready. The enemy showed no disposition to follow the movements of either command.

"The Army of the Cumberland reached Atlanta on the 8th, and was posted on the outskirts of the town,—Davis's corps on the right of the Campbelltown road, Slocum's corps in the centre, and Stanley's on the left. The pickets of all three corps were thrown out well to the front, and occupied commanding positions.

"For a detailed report of the operations I have the honor to refer you to the reports of the several corps commanders.

"Herewith I have the honor to forward returns of prisoners of war, captured property, ammunition expended, and a consolidated return of casualties.

"In concluding this report I take the greatest pleasure in calling attention to the uniform gallantry displayed by the officers and troops of the Army of the Cumberland in all the battles in which they participated, and to their unwavering constancy and devotion to duty at all times during the entire campaign, commencing with the contests at Rocky Face Ridge and around Dalton, and ending with the operations at Jonesboro' and vicinity which forced the enemy to evacuate Atlanta. During these four months of active campaign hardly a day has passed that some portion of this army was not engaged either in skirmishing or in actual battle with the enemy, and on every occasion behaving with that self-reliance which is the sure prestige of success. All may be justly proud of their participation in the campaign against Atlanta.

"Among the many gallant and lamented dead who have given their lives to sustain and defend the honor of their country and government we must enumerate Brigadier-General C. G. Harker and Colonel Dan McCook, Fifty-second Ohio Volunteer Infantry, who were mortally wounded leading their respective brigades in the assault on the enemy's intrenchments near Kenesaw Mountain, June 27. They were both skilful, brave, and accomplished officers.

"The members of my staff were at all times efficient and active in the discharge of their various duties.

"I enclose herewith the reports of subordinate commanders, which embody the operations of their respective commands, and to which I have the honor to invite the attention of the major-general commanding the Military Division of the Mississippi.

"I am, colonel, very respectfully, your obedient servant,
"GEO. H. THOMAS,
"Major-General U. S. Vols., Commanding."

CHAPTER VIII.

Sherman goes to the Sea—Other Battles to be fought by Thomas in Tennessee—Concentrates his Forces at Nashville—Importuned to attack Enemy before Arrangements were Completed—Despatches from General Grant, etc.—Final Contest and Great Victory—President congratulates Thomas and his Army—Pursuit of Hood—Consequences had Thomas been Defeated—Wilson's Cavalry.

THE Fourteenth and Twentieth Corps, with most of the cavalry of the command, joined General Sherman in that eagle-swoop of his which served in so great a measure to stamp out the expiring embers of the Rebellion, and participated in that storied "March to the Sea." Under that eager, intense, untiring commander who seemed to have comprehended so thoroughly the elements of victory, these two corps went the whole "grand rounds" through Georgia and the Carolinas, and graced with their presence the supreme crisis of that proud triumph when the second great military stay of the Rebellion succumbed to the logic of war and the point of the bayonet in North Carolina. They also joined in that gala-day of glory when two hundred thousand soldiers, in all the splendid pomp and glittering pageantry of their magnificent equipment, tramped up the avenues of the capital city of the land, and the pæans of the great jubilee of the nation's deliverance rang in deep thankfulness from ocean to ocean.

Some one has said that General Sherman is a bundle of nerves,—never still, always in motion. It is true that he was never satisfied unless his army was battering away at the enemy's lines. I remember at one time in Northern Georgia, after several weeks of rain, when it was impossible to move a wagon or a gun-carriage except on old and well-beaten roads, he turned to General Howard and frettingly remarked, "My God, Howard, is not this enough to try your Christian patience?" Howard's reply was characteristic of the Christian soldier: "Not in the least, general,—not in the least! I have confidence in the justice of our cause, and we must succeed regardless of the kind of weather God gives us." Sherman remarked, "I guess you are right, Howard; but I wish God would give us good weather until we can close up this military picnic, and then I will be perfectly willing to endure any amount of bad weather He may have in store for us." If General Sherman ever slept while on the Atlanta campaign no one knows it, and I venture to assert that if telephones had then been discovered the army commanders under him would have had few opportunities for repose.

After the capture of Atlanta the campaign through the South to the coast was considered and decided upon. There has been some dispute in regard to the originator of that movement. It has been claimed by some that Thomas proposed to General Sherman to make that march with the Fourteenth and Twentieth Corps, moving on Savannah or on some point on the coast equally important. It has also been asserted that General Grant claimed the credit of originating it; but my impression is that to Sherman belongs the credit. He was very unjustly criticised in regard to "leaving to the subordinate Thomas, with the lesser half of the army, to fight the main battles and conduct the real campaign, while he, the superior officer, with the greater half of the force, made a *détour* in which no danger was encountered,— no danger, in fact, apprehended,—and which could have been better effected with half the force."

Other critics have expressed themselves to the effect that "Thomas made, at Nashville, Sherman's March to the Sea a success." But this is unfair. Sherman expected Thomas to do just what he did,—that is, defeat the enemy at Nashville, or wheresoever he might meet him. As well might the quartermaster's department claim the success of all campaigns because the army could not live without the supplies which were sent forward to it. Sherman expected Thomas to take care of the rear, just as he expected the supply departments to furnish clothing and camp and garrison-equipage when ordered to do so.

The selection of Thomas for this particular duty was not done unadvisedly, but after much deliberation. Sherman knew that Thomas possessed all the qualifications necessary for the important duty, and, while he disliked to leave his "wheel-horse" behind, yet he knew him to be brave, cool, calm, and deliberate, and just the general to be entrusted with this important duty; and the sequel demonstrated beyond a doubt the correctness of Sherman's selection.

The troops placed under Thomas's command, with which he was to confront Hood if in his rashness he attempted the invasion of Tennessee, were the Fourth and Twenty-third

Corps. These had been greatly depleted by the casualties incident to the summer campaign. Hood had already sent his cavalry to raid upon the railroads, and he expected to be largely reinforced from the "Trans-Mississippi Department," and, with overpowering force, it was his intention to overcome any opposition and push forward to the Ohio. But the Federal movements in the extreme South were such that no troops could be spared for Hood, and hence he was compelled to invade Tennessee and trust to augmenting his command by volunteers, which he hoped would rally under his flag. Few recruits joined him, and he found himself in front of Nashville with a force too small to enable him to carry out his original plans. Before crossing the Tennessee River he divided his mounted force into two columns, one under General Buford, the other under General Forrest, both men of courage and enterprise. The former threatened Huntsville, and the latter Columbia.

General Thomas arrived in Nashville on the 3d day of October, 1864, and took charge of all the Federal troops in Tennessee. The Confederate cavalry raiders were vigorously pursued by Generals Rousseau, Steedman, Morgan, Washburne, and Croxton, and driven across the Tennessee River. While these movements were in progress the position of affairs in Georgia had undergone a change. Hood had crossed the Chattahoochie, and with a portion of his army struck the railroad at Big Shanty and destroyed about twenty miles of the road-bed. On the 5th a Confederate division, under the command of General French, assaulted Allatoona, which was held by a brigade under the command of the gallant General

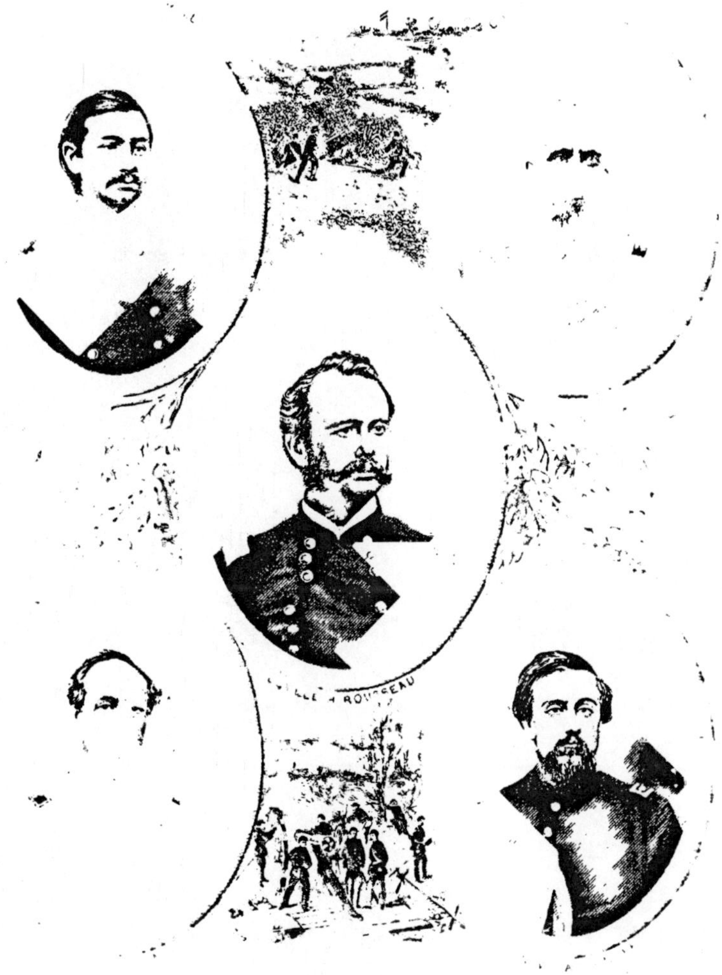
ROUSSEAU

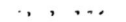

John M. Corse, and was repulsed with heavy loss. Hood then made a demonstration in the direction of Rome, and, crossing the Coosa River below, moved in the direction of Summerville and Lafayette, threatening Chattanooga and Bridgeport. To meet these movements of Hood, General Thomas disposed of his command as follows: General Croxton's cavalry brigade was ordered to watch the line of the Tennessee from Decatur to Eastport, General Morgan's division moved from Athens to Chattanooga, General Steedman's division moved from Decatur to Bridgeport, and General Rousseau's command was concentrated at Athens. On the 12th the enemy's cavalry attacked Resaca and was repulsed. About this time the garrisons at Tunnel Hill, Ringgold, and points intermediate were withdrawn to Chattanooga.

On the 13th, General Hood, with one corps of his army, forced the surrender of Dalton, and after destroying the railroad and telegraph-wires he moved through Nickojack Gap, rejoining his army near Summerville. By the 29th of October, General Sherman had repaired the railroad, and trains commenced running regularly. The Fourth Corps was then ordered to report to General Thomas.

The enemy made a strong feint in the direction of Decatur, Alabama, from the 26th to the 29th, meeting with considerable loss. He then withdrew and commenced crossing the Tennessee River at or near the mouth of Cypress Creek. These movements developed the plans of the enemy and made it evident that he intended the invasion of Middle Tennessee. General Hatch, with his cavalry division, was ordered from Clifton to the support of Croxton at Florence.

On the 30th the Twenty-third Corps was ordered to report to General Thomas, and he was given full control over all the troops in the Military Division of the Mississippi, excepting only those under General Sherman; but it should be remembered that these were scattered over a large district of country, and some held very important points which could not be abandoned to the enemy. General Rousseau, with 5000 at Murfreesboro', could not be called in, for that would turn over to the enemy the strong fortifications at that point; and so Thomas, in calculating the force that he would have available for opposing Hood, had to leave Rousseau out of consideration. General Hood, in "Advance and Retreat," asserts that Thomas had 82,000 men under his command at Nashville. Thomas's infantry force was about 25,000, and his cavalry amounted to less than 8000 effective men.

As soon as Hood had effected a lodgment on the north side of the Tennessee, he forced Croxton back to the east bank of Shoal Creek. With all possible despatch General Stanley proceeded to concentrate the Fourth Corps at Pulaski. Soon Schofield arrived with the Twenty-third Corps and by virtue of seniority assumed command of the whole, and under the direction of General Thomas made such dispositions as were calculated to delay the advance of the enemy as much as possible, so as to allow the concentration of every available man at Nashville, and to give time for the arrival of reinforcements which were ordered from Missouri. As previously stated, Thomas had about 33,000 men, a part of whom were civil employees without experience in military matters. Hood was advancing with his veteran army of 42,000 infantry and 13,000 cavalry, and great anxiety was felt for the final result of such an unequal contest. Thomas was the only one who seemed to have no doubts in regard to the final issue. General Sherman remained with his headquarters at Kingston until November 11, and his uncertain attitude served to hold Hood in check at Florence, where he remained until about the 19th day of November. Then, placing his army in motion, he marched on parallel roads towards Waynesboro', forcing General Hatch's cavalry force from Lawrenceburg. Thomas, whose great brain comprehended the entire movement, directed the various parts of his command to fall back on Nashville, offering such resistance as could be made without bringing on a general engagement. On the 30th, Schofield had his whole command in position at Franklin, with both flanks resting on the Harpeth River, and at once commenced to fortify his front. Hood appeared before the works and rashly ordered an assault. Probably in no battle of the war was better fighting done than at Franklin. There was no cover for the assaulting-party, and the ranks of the enemy were fearfully depleted. The loss among gene al officers was very heavy, as many of the bravest and best of Hood's generals fell on that memorable day.

At one time the Federal line was broken, and had it not been for the coolness and bravery of General D. S. Stanley, who was in the fore-front of the battle, the Federal army would have been routed and driven across the river in the greatest confusion. When he discovered the break in the line, although a corps commander, he placed himself at the head of a brigade, and, leading the charge, drove the enemy back and re-established the continuity of the line. His horse was killed under him, and he was himself severely wounded. Owing to his injuries he had to relinquish his command, and General Thomas J. Wood became the temporary commander of the Fourth Corps, which he handled at all times with consummate ability and to the entire satisfaction of General Thomas.

This signal defeat deeply depressed the enemy, and General Schofield withdrew to Nashville without further molestation, arriving there early on the morning of the 1st day of December, 1864. As the troops arrived in Nashville, General Thomas superintended in person their location in the line of battle. On the morning of December 4, Hood's army marched up to within six hundred yards of the Federal line, with flags flying, deployed as if on drill, and began to fortify their defiant position. The enemy posted his artillery and infantry in the centre and his cavalry on the flanks, resting on the river above and below. His bands were brought out, and the strains of "Dixie" could be heard from a dozen or more points along his line. To those who did not know all the arrangements Thomas had made to defeat Hood and his bold followers, the prospect was anything but bright. Hood had under his command a fine army, commanded by some of the best officers of the South, and he was in front of Nashville, determined to take it all hazards. Under all the circumstances he was a foe worthy of Thomas's serious consideration. The defeat of the Federal army at this place would have delayed, in all probability, the closing scenes of the war for years, and no one knew it so well as George H. Thomas.

Knowing it, he resolved not to measure steel with his adversary without first making his arrangements as complete and perfect as possible. Information reached him from Washington that the authorities were displeased at his delay, and even General Grant was disposed to censure him for not moving against Hood and driving him out of Tennessee.

Thomas expected to be ready for battle by the 7th, but on account of the delay in getting horses for his cavalry he was not ready until the 9th. With the completion of his preparations came a fall of sleet, which rendered the movement of troops for any purpose, and especially for battle, an utter impossibility. The annoyance caused by these vexatious delays led to the following telegrams, which are given to show the great anxiety felt by the commander-in-chief and others for the overthrow of Hood before he could cross the Cumberland and take up his line of march for the Ohio River:

(No. 1.)
"WASHINGTON, December 2, 10.30 A.M.
"LIEUTENANT-GENERAL GRANT, City Point:

"The President feels solicitous about the disposition of Thomas to lay in fortifications for an indefinite period, 'until Wilson gets his equipments.' This looks like the McClellan and Rosecrans strategy of do nothing and let the enemy raid the country. The President wishes you to consider the matter.
"EDWIN M. STANTON,
"Secretary of War."

(No. 2.)
"CITY POINT, VIRGINIA, December 2, 1864, 11 A.M.
"MAJOR-GENERAL GEORGE H. THOMAS, Nashville:

"If Hood is permitted to remain quietly about Nashville

we will lose all the roads back to Chattanooga, and possibly have to abandon the line of the Tennessee River. Should he attack you it is all well, but if he does not you should attack him before he fortifies. . . .

"U. S. GRANT,
"Lieutenant-General."

(No. 3.)
"CITY POINT, VIRGINIA, December 2, 1864, 1.30 P.M.
"MAJOR-GENERAL GEORGE H. THOMAS, Nashville:
. . . "After the repulse of Hood at Franklin, it looks to me that instead of falling back to Nashville we should have taken the offensive against the enemy, but at this distance may err as to the method of dealing with the enemy. You will suffer incalculable injury upon your railroads if Hood is not speedily disposed of. Put forth, therefore, every possible exertion to attain this end. Should you get him to retreating give him no peace.
[Signed] "U. S. GRANT,
"Lieutenant-General."

(No. 4.)
"HEADQUARTERS DEPARTMENT OF THE CUMBERLAND,
"NASHVILLE, TENN., December 2, 1864, 10 P.M.
"GENERAL U. S. GRANT, City Point, Va.:
"Your two telegrams of 11 A.M. and 1.30 P.M. to-day received. At the time Hood was whipped at Franklin, I had at this place but about 5000 men of General Smith's command, which, added to the force under General Schofield, would not have given me more than 25,000 men. Besides, General Schofield felt convinced that he could not hold the enemy at Franklin until the 5000 could reach him. As General Wilson's cavalry force also numbered only about one-

fourth that of Forrest, I thought it best to draw the troops back to Nashville and await the arrival of the remainder of General Smith's force, and also a force of about 5000 commanded by General Steedman, which I had ordered up from Chattanooga. The division of General Smith arrived yesterday morning, and General Steedman's troops arrived last night. I have infantry enough to assume the offensive if I had more cavalry, and will take the field anyhow as soon as the remainder of General McCook's division of cavalry reaches here, which I hope it will in two or three days. We can neither get reinforcements nor equipments at this great distance from the North very easily, and it must be remembered that my command was made up of the two weakest corps of General Sherman's army, and all the dismounted cavalry except one brigade; and the task of reorganizing and equipping has met with many delays, which have enabled Hood to take advantage of my crippled condition. I earnestly hope, however, in a few days more I shall be able to give him a fight.

[Signed] "GEORGE H. THOMAS,
"Major-General U. S. Vols., Commanding."

(No. 5.)
"CITY POINT, VIRGINIA, December 5, 1864, 6.30 P.M.
"MAJOR-GENERAL GEORGE H. THOMAS, Nashville, Tenn.:

"Is there not danger of Forrest's moving down the Tennessee River where he can cross it? It seems to me, while you should be getting up your cavalry as rapidly as possible to look after Forrest, Hood should be attacked where he is. Time strengthens him, in all probability, as much as it does you.

[Signed] "U. S. GRANT,
"Lieutenant-General."

(No. 6.)

"NASHVILLE, December 6, 1864.

"LIEUTENANT-GENERAL U. S. GRANT, City Point:

"Your telegram of 6.30 P.M., December 5th, is just received. As soon as I get up a respectable force of cavalry I will march against Hood. General Wilson has parties out now pressing horses, and I hope to have some six or eight thousand cavalry mounted in three days from this time. General Wilson has just left me, having received instructions to hurry the cavalry to remount as rapidly as possible. I do not think it prudent to attack Hood with less than six thousand cavalry to cover my flanks, because he has under Forrest at least twelve thousand. I have no doubt Forrest will attempt to cross the river, but I am in hopes the gunboats will be able to prevent him. The enemy has made no new developments to-day. Breckinridge is reported at Lebanon with six thousand men, but I cannot believe it possible.

[Signed] "GEORGE H. THOMAS,
"Major-General U. S. Vols., Commanding."

(No. 7.)

"CITY POINT, VIRGINIA, December 6, 1864, 4 P.M.

"MAJOR-GENERAL GEORGE H. THOMAS, Nashville:

"Attack Hood at once, and wait no longer for a remount for your cavalry. There is great danger in delay resulting in a campaign back to the Ohio.

[Signed] "U. S. GRANT,
"Lieutenant-General."

(No. 8.)

"NASHVILLE, December 6, 1864, 9 P.M.

"LIEUTENANT-GENERAL U. S. GRANT, City Point:

"Your despatch of 4 P.M. this day received. I will make

the necessary disposition, and attack Hood at once, agreeably to your orders, though I believe it will be hazardous with the small force of cavalry now at my service.

[Signed] "GEORGE H. THOMAS,
"Major-General U. S. Vols., Commanding."

(No. 9.)
"WAR DEPARTMENT,
"WASHINGTON, December 7, 1864, 10.20 A.M.
"LIEUTENANT-GENERAL GRANT:

* * * * * *

"Thomas seems unwilling to attack because it is hazardous, as if all war was any but hazardous. If he waits for Wilson to get ready, Gabriel will be blowing his last horn.

"EDWIN M. STANTON."

(No. 10.)
"CITY POINT, VIRGINIA, December 8, 1864.

"MAJOR-GENERAL HALLECK, Washington:

"Please direct General Dodge to send all the troops he can spare to General Thomas. With such an order he can be relied on to send all that can properly go. They had probably better be sent to Louisville, for I fear either Hood or Breckinridge will go to the Ohio River. I will submit whether it is not advisable to call on Ohio, Indiana, and Illinois for sixty thousand men for thirty days. If Thomas has not struck yet, he ought to be ordered to hand over his command to Schofield. There is no better man to repel an attack than Thomas; but I fear he is too cautious to take the initiative.

[Signed] "U. S. GRANT,
"Lieutenant-General."

(No. 11.)
"War Department,
"Washington, D. C., December 8, 1864.
"Lieutenant-General Grant, City Point:
"If you wish General Thomas relieved, give the order. No one here will, I think, interfere. The responsibility, however, will be yours, as no one here, so far as I am informed, wishes General Thomas removed.

[Signed] "H. W. Halleck,
"Major-General, Chief of Staff."

(No. 12.)
"Nashville, Tennessee, December 7, 1864, 9 p.m.
"Major-General Halleck, Washington:
"The enemy has not increased his force in our front. Have sent gun-boats up the river above Carthage. One returned to-day, and reported no signs of the enemy on the river bank from forty miles above Carthage to this place. Captain Fitch, United States navy, started down the river yesterday with a convoy of transport steamers, but was unable to get them down, the enemy having planted three batteries on a bend of the river between this and Clarksville. Captain Fitch was unable to silence all three of the batteries yesterday, and will return again to-morrow morning, and, with the assistance of the 'Cincinnati,' now at Clarksville, I am in hopes will now be able to clear them out. So far the enemy has not materially injured the Nashville and Chattanooga Railroad.

[Signed] "George H. Thomas,
"Major-General U. S. Vols., Commanding."

(No. 13.)
"City Point, Virginia, December 8, 1864, 7.30 p.m.
"Major-General George H. Thomas, Nashville:
"Your despatch of yesterday received. It looks to me

evidently the enemy are trying to cross the Cumberland, and are scattered. Why not attack at once? By all means avoid the contingency of a foot-race to see which, you or Hood, can beat to the Ohio. If you think necessary call on the governors of States to send a force into Louisville to meet the enemy if he should cross the river. You clearly never should cross, except in rear of the enemy. Now is one of the fairest opportunities ever presented of destroying one of the three armies of the enemy. If destroyed he can never replace it. Use the means at your command, and you can do this and cause a rejoicing from one end of the land to the other.

[Signed]   "U. S. GRANT,
                        "Lieutenant-General."

(No. 14.)

"CITY POINT, VIRGINIA, December 8, 1864, 10 P.M.

"MAJOR-GENERAL HALLECK, Washington:

"Your despatch of 9 P.M. just received. I want General Thomas reminded of the importance of immediate action. I sent him a despatch this evening, which will probably urge him on. I would not say relieve him until I hear further from him.

[Signed]   "U. S. GRANT,
                        "Lieutenant-General."

(No. 15.)

"NASHVILLE, TENNESSEE, December 8, 1864, 11.30 P.M.

"LIEUTENANT-GENERAL GRANT, City Point:

"Your despatch of 7.30 P.M. is just received. I can only say, in further extenuation why I have not attacked Hood, that I could not concentrate my troops and get their transportation in order in shorter time than it has been done, and am satisfied I have made every effort that was possible to complete the task.

     [Signed] "GEORGE H. THOMAS,
       "Major-General, Commanding."

(No. 16.)
"WASHINGTON, December 9, 1864, 10.30 A.M.

"MAJOR-GENERAL GEORGE H. THOMAS, Nashville, Tenn.:

"Lieutenant-General Grant expresses much dissatisfaction at your delay in attacking the enemy. If you wait till General Wilson mounts all his cavalry, you will wait till doomsday, for the waste equals the supply. Moreover, you will be in the same condition that Rosecrans was last year, with so many animals that you cannot feed them. Reports already come in of a scarcity of forage.

    [Signed] "H. W. HALLECK,
     "Major-General and Chief of Staff."

(No. 17.)
"CITY POINT, VIRGINIA, December 9, 1864, 11 A.M.

"MAJOR-GENERAL HALLECK, Washington, D. C.:

"Despatch of 8 P.M. last evening, from Nashville, shows the enemy scattered for more than seventy miles down the river, and no attack yet made by Thomas. Please telegraph orders relieving him and placing Schofield in command. Thomas should be ordered to turn over all orders and despatches received since the battle of Franklin to Schofield.

    [Signed]   "U. S. GRANT,
      "Lieutenant-General."

"WAR DEPARTMENT, ADJUTANT-GENERAL'S OFFICE,
"WASHINGTON, December 9, 1864.

"GENERAL ORDERS No. —.

"The following despatch having been received from Lieutenant-General Grant, viz.:

"'Please telegraph orders relieving him (General Thomas) at once, and placing (General) Schofield in command,' the President orders:

"I. That Major-General J. M. Schofield relieve at once Major-General G. H. Thomas in command of the Department and Army of the Cumberland.

"II. General Thomas will turn over to General Schofield all orders and instructions received by him since the battle of Franklin.

"E. D. TOWNSEND,
"Assistant Adjutant-General."

(No. 18.)

"NASHVILLE, December 9, 1864, 2 P.M.

"MAJOR-GENERAL H. W. HALLECK, Washington, D. C.:

"Your despatch of 10.30 A.M. this date is received. I regret that General Grant should feel dissatisfaction at my delay in attacking the enemy. I feel conscious that I have done everything in my power to prepare, and that the troops could not have been gotten ready before this. And if he should order me to be relieved, I will submit without a murmur. A terrible storm of freezing rain has come on since daylight, which will render an attack impossible till it breaks.

[Signed] "GEORGE H. THOMAS,
"Major-General U. S. Vols., Commanding."

(No. 19.)

"NASHVILLE, TENNESSEE, December 9, 1864, 1 P.M.

"LIEUTENANT-GENERAL U. S. GRANT, City Point:

"Your despatch of 8.30 P.M. of the 8th is just received. I have nearly completed my preparations to attack the enemy to-morrow morning, but a terrible storm of freezing rain has come on to-day, which will make it impossible for our men to fight to any advantage. I am therefore compelled to wait for the storm to break, and make the attack immediately after. Admiral Lee is patrolling the river above and below the city, and I believe will be able to prevent the enemy from crossing. There is no doubt but Hood's forces are considerably scattered along the river, with the view of attempting a crossing, but it has been impossible for me to organize and equip the troops for an attack at an earlier time. Major-General Halleck informs me that you are very much dissatisfied with my delay in attacking. I can only say I have done all in my power to prepare, and if you should deem it necessary to relieve me, I shall submit without a murmur.

[Signed]   "GEORGE H. THOMAS,
"Major-General U. S. Vols., Commanding."

(No. 20.)

"WAR DEPARTMENT, WASHINGTON, December 9, 1864, 4 P.M.

"LIEUTENANT-GENERAL GRANT, City Point:

"Orders relieving General Thomas had been made out when his telegram of this P.M. was received. If you still wish these orders telegraphed to Nashville they will be forwarded.

[Signed]   "H. W. HALLECK,
"Chief of Staff."

(No. 21.)

"CITY POINT, VIRGINIA, December 9, 1864, 5.30 P.M.

"MAJOR-GENERAL HALLECK, Washington:

"General Thomas has been urged in every possible way

to attack the enemy, even to the giving the positive order. He did say he thought he should be able to attack on the 7th, but he did not do so, nor has he given a reason for not doing it. I am very unwilling to do injustice to an officer who has done so much good service as General Thomas has, however, and will therefore suspend the order relieving him until it is seen whether he will do anything.

[Signed]   "U. S. GRANT,
"Lieutenant-General."

(No. 22.)
"CITY POINT, VIRGINIA, December 9, 1864, 7.30 P.M.
"MAJOR-GENERAL THOMAS, Nashville:

"Your despatch of 1 P.M. to-day is received. I have as much confidence in your conducting the battle rightly as I have in any other officer, but it has seemed to me you have been slow, and I have had no explanation of affairs to convince me otherwise. Receiving your despatch to Major-General Halleck of 2 P.M. before I did the first to me, I telegraphed to suspend the order relieving you until we should hear further. I hope most sincerely that there will be no necessity of repeating the order, and that the facts will show that you have been right all the time.

[Signed]   "U. S. GRANT,
"Lieutenant-General."

(No. 23.)
"CITY POINT, VIRGINIA, December 11, 1864, 4 P.M.
"MAJOR-GENERAL GEORGE H. THOMAS, Nashville:

"If you delay attacking longer, the mortifying spectacle will be witnessed of a rebel army moving for the Ohio, and you will be forced to act, accepting such weather as you find. Let there be no further delay. Hood cannot stand even a drawn battle so far from his supplies of ordnance stores. If he retreats and you follow, he must lose his material and most of his army. I am in hopes of receiving a despatch from you to-day announcing that you have moved. Delay no longer for weather or reinforcements.

[Signed] "U. S. GRANT,
"Lieutenant-General."

(No. 24.)
"NASHVILLE, TENNESSEE, December 12, 1864, 10.30 P.M.
"MAJOR-GENERAL HALLECK, Washington, D. C.:

"I have the troops ready to make the attack on the enemy as soon as the sleet which now covers the ground has melted sufficiently to enable the men to march; as the whole country is now covered with a sheet of ice so hard and slippery it is utterly impossible for troops to ascend the slopes, or even move on level ground in anything like order. It has taken the entire day to place my cavalry in position, and it has only been finally effected with imminent risk and many serious accidents, resulting from the numbers of horses falling with their riders on the road. Under these circumstances, I believe that an attack at this time would only result in a useless sacrifice of life.

[Signed] "GEORGE H. THOMAS,
"Major-General U. S. V., Commanding."

"HEADQUARTERS OF THE ARMIES OF THE UNITED STATES,
"CITY POINT, VIRGINIA, December 13, 1864.
"SPECIAL ORDERS No. 149.

"I. Major-General John A. Logan, United States Volunteers, will proceed immediately to Nashville, Tennessee, report by telegraph to the lieutenant-general his arrival at

Louisville, Kentucky, and also his arrival at Nashville, Tennessee.

* * * * * *

"By command of Lieutenant-General Grant.
   [Signed] "T. S. Bowers,
     "Assistant Adjutant-General."

(No. 25.)

"Major-General George H. Thomas, Nashville:

"It has been seriously apprehended that while Hood, with a part of his forces, held you in check near Nashville, he would have time to co-operate against other important points left only partially protected. Hence Lieutenant-General Grant was anxious that you should attack the rebel forces in your front, and expresses great dissatisfaction that his order had not been carried out. Moreover, so long as Hood occupies a threatening position in Tennessee, General Canby is obliged to keep large forces on the Mississippi River to protect its navigation and to hold Memphis, Vicksburg, etc., although General Grant had directed a part of these forces to co-operate with Sherman. Every day's delay on your part, therefore, seriously interferes with General Grant's plans.
   [Signed] "H. W. Halleck,
   "Major-General and Chief of Staff."

(No. 26.)

"Nashville, December 14, 1864, 8 p.m.

"Major-General H. W. Halleck, Washington, D. C.:

"Your telegram of 12.30 m. to-day is received. The ice having melted away to-day, the enemy will be attacked to-morrow morning. Much as I regret the apparent delay in attacking the enemy, it could not have been done before with any reasonable prospect of success.

[Signed]   "George H. Thomas,
"Major-General U. S. Vols., Commanding."

The foregoing despatches are given to show how a commander may be compelled to fight front and rear at one and the same time. Of course there can be no doubt of the good intentions of those in authority a thousand miles away, but had Thomas rushed madly against Hood in obedience to outside demand his army would have been defeated in all probability, and Hood would have had a clear track and an undisputed march to the Ohio River. That a terrible catastrophe did not befall the Union army at Nashville was due to the fact that Thomas could not be coerced into a movement against the enemy until his arrangements were fully made. It was the outside pressure of "On to Richmond" that gave us such a signal defeat in the first year of the war, and Thomas determined that he would not permit himself to be urged into the commission of a like blunder.

On the night of December 14, 1864, he called around him most of the general officers of his command, not for consultation but to deliver to each his particular instructions, and when they dispersed to join their respective commands they knew just what was expected of them next morning.

At a given signal the whole line was to move forward. Morning came and a dense heavy fog overhung both armies. The line was formed and awaited the disappearance of the

FINAL CONTEST AND GREAT VICTORY. 195

mist, which took place about 9 o'clock, and then with a shout and yell the troops moved forward from right to left. The position in line was as follows: Wilson's cavalry on the right, General A. J. Smith's corps on Wilson's left, General T. J. Wood with the Fourth Corps on Smith's left, and General J. B. Steedman's troops on the extreme left of the Federal line. The Twenty-third Corps, commanded by General J. M. Schofield, was held in reserve; General Wood forced the enemy from his intrenched position, while Smith, Schofield, and Wilson pressed back the rebel left some miles into the hills. Night closed upon the scene and ended the strife for the day. Thomas's plan was without a flaw, and every command performed to the letter the part assigned to it.

The able general whose peerless wisdom projected it had the consummate skill to accomplish it in all its details from the opening volleys on the left, where Steedman's troops bore the national flag up to the very intrenchments of the enemy, and breasted the storm of lead and flame and steel, to the awful tempest of death which rained its torrents of blood upon the quaking breast of Overton's Hill, on the evening of the second day, and shook the forests with its terrific roar. The battle was ended and the Confederates were in full retreat. Thomas with his staff rode to the summit of Overton's Hill, and, scanning the grounds and the results, lifted his hat and said, "Oh, what a grand army I have! God bless each member of it."

Not, perhaps, in all the history of authentic war is there another instance of the besieged, gathered as was this command on the spur of the occasion from every direction, detachments, raw recruits, drafted men, new regiments, with two small corps as the nucleus of organization, throwing down every barrier and laying aside every artificial defence, rushing out upon an outnumbering foe versed in all the strategy of war, and beating him face to face in fair and open contest. What Hannibal failed to do at Carthage and Marc Antony failed to do when he sallied down to meet the young Octavius, was reserved for Major-General George H. Thomas to do at Nashville. Never was victory more complete, or defeat more crushing and overwhelming. Hood's army was literally and actually broken up and destroyed, and its usefulness as an effective military organization ruined effectually and forever. Had this battle terminated differently, the rebellion would have received a new lease of life, and other and bloody campaigns would have been the legitimate consequences. Richmond would have been reinforced, and the rear of Sherman's army would have been endangered, while but a flimsy line of outposts would have intervened between the rich cities of the Northwest and Hood's needy and desperate squadrons. But it was not in the nature of things that it should terminate differently.

During the progress of the first day's fight many prisoners were captured and sent to Thomas's field headquarters to be disposed of by the provost-marshal. The number became so great that it was necessary to send them back to the city under a proper escort. The only troops convenient for the purpose were some colored regiments from which the provost-marshal ordered detachments as they were required. Some of these prisoners were from South Carolina, and, not wishing to be placed under a negro guard, appealed to General Thomas, saying that they would rather die than to enter Nashville in charge of "nigger" soldiers. Thomas remarked, "Well, you may say your prayers, and get ready to die, for these are the only soldiers that I can spare."

It is needless to say that they went into Nashville in charge of the "nigger" guard.

At nine o'clock, December 15, Thomas sent the following despatch:

"Attacked enemy's left this morning; drove it from the river below the city, very nearly to Franklin pike, distance about eight miles."

During the night of the 15th and morning of the 16th the following despatches were received by General Thomas:

"WASHINGTON, December 15, 1864, 11.30 P.M.

"MAJOR-GENERAL GEORGE H. THOMAS, Nashville:

"I was just on my way to Nashville, but receiving a despatch from Van Duzen detailing your splendid success of to-day, I shall go no farther. Push the enemy now, and give him no rest until he is entirely destroyed. Your army will cheerfully suffer many privations to break up Hood's army and make it useless for future operations. Do not stop for trains or supplies, but take them from the country, as the enemy has done. Much is now expected.

[Signed] "U. S. GRANT,
"Lieutenant-General."

"WASHINGTON, December 16, 11.20 A.M.

"To MAJOR-GENERAL THOMAS:

"Please accept for yourself, officers, and men the nation's thanks for your work of yesterday. You made a magnificent beginning. A grand consummation is within your easy reach. Do not let it slip.

[Signed] "A. LINCOLN."

"WASHINGTON, December 15, 1864, 12 Midnight.
"MAJOR-GENERAL THOMAS:

"Your despatch of this evening just received. I congratulate you and the army under your command for to-day's operations, and feel a conviction that to-morrow will add more fruits to your victory.

[Signed] "U. S. GRANT."
"Lieutenant-General."

"WASHINGTON, December 15, 1864, 12 Midnight.
"MAJOR-GENERAL THOMAS:

"I rejoice in tendering to you, and the gallant officers and soldiers of your command, the thanks of this department for the brilliant achievement of this day, and hope that it is the harbinger of a decisive victory that will crown you and your army with honor, and do much toward closing the war. We shall give you a hundred guns in the morning.

[Signed] "E. M. STANTON,
"Secretary of War."

In acknowledgment of these despatches, Thomas replied:

"HEADQUARTERS DEPARTMENT OF THE CUMBERLAND,
"SIX MILES FROM NASHVILLE, December 16, 1864.
"TO THE PRESIDENT OF THE UNITED STATES, HON. E. M. STANTON, AND GENERAL U. S. GRANT, Washington:

"This army thanks you for your approbation of its conduct yesterday, and, to assure you that it is not misplaced, I have the honor to report that the enemy has been pressed at all points to-day on his line of retreat through the Brentwood

Hills, and Brigadier-General Hatch, of Wilson's Corps of Cavalry, on the right, turned the enemy's left and captured a large number of prisoners; number not yet reported. Major-General Schofield's troops, next on the left of cavalry, carried several heights, captured many prisoners and six pieces of artillery. Brevet Major-General Smith, next on the left of Major-General Schofield, carried the salient point of the enemy's line with McWilliams's brigade of McArthur's division, capturing 16 pieces of artillery, 2 brigadier-generals, and about 2000 prisoners. Brigadier-General Garrard's division of Smith's command, next on the left of McArthur's division, carried the enemy's intrenchments, capturing all the artillery and troops on the line. Brigadier-General Wood's, on the Franklin pike, took up the assault, carried the enemy's intrenchments in his front, captured 8 pieces, something over 600 prisoners, and drove the enemy to within one mile of Brentwood Pass. Major-General Steedman, commanding detachments of the Military Division of the Mississippi, most nobly supported General Wood's left, and bore a most honorable part in the operations of the day. I have ordered the pursuit to be continued in the morning at daylight, although the troops are very much fatigued. The greatest enthusiasm prevails. I must not forget to report the operations of Brigadier-General R. W. Johnson in successfully driving the enemy, with co-operation of the gunboats under Lieutenant-Commander Fitch, from their established batteries on the Cumberland River below the city of Nashville, and the services of Brigadier-General Croxton's brigade in covering and relieving our right and rear in the operations of yesterday and to-day. Although I have no report of the number of prisoners captured by Johnson's and Croxton's commands, I know they have made a large number. I am glad to be able to state that the number of prisoners captured yesterday greatly exceeds the number reported by me last evening. The roads, fields, and intrenchments are strewn with the enemy's abandoned small-arms, abandoned in their retreat. In conclusion, I am happy to state that all this has been effected with but a very small loss to us. Our loss does not probably exceed three thousand, very few killed.

[Signed]   "GEORGE H. THOMAS,
"Major-General U. S. Vols., Commanding."

"WASHINGTON, December 18, 1864, 12 M.
"MAJOR-GENERAL THOMAS:

"The armies operating against Richmond have fired two prolonged guns in honor of your great victory. Sherman has fully established his base on Ossabaw Sound, with Savannah fully invested. I hope to be able to fire a salute to-morrow in honor of the fall of Savannah. In all your operations we hear nothing of Forrest.* Great precaution should be taken to prevent him crossing the Cumberland or Tennessee Rivers below Eastport. After Hood is driven as far as possible to follow him, you want to reoccupy Decatur and all other abandoned points.

[Signed]   "U. S. GRANT,
"Lieutenant-General."

"WASHINGTON, December 21, 1864, 12 M.
"MAJOR-GENERAL GEORGE H. THOMAS:

"Permit me, general, to urge the vast importance of a hot pursuit of Hood's army. Every possible sacrifice should be

---

* Forrest was at Murfreesboro' operating against Rousseau, in connection with Bates's division.—*Hood's Advance and Retreat.*

made, and your men for a few days will submit to any hardships and privations to accomplish the great result. If you can capture or destroy Hood's army, General Sherman can entirely crush out the rebel military force in all the Southern States. He begins a new campaign about the 1st of January, which will have the most important results if Hood's army can now be used up. A most vigorous pursuit on your part is therefore of vital importance to General Sherman's plans. No sacrifice must be spared to obtain so important a result.

[Signed]   "H. W. HALLECK,
"Major-General and Chief of Staff."

"IN THE FIELD, December 21, 1864.
"MAJOR-GENERAL HALLECK, Washington, D. C.:

"Your despatch of 12 M. to-day is received. General Hood's army is being pursued as rapidly and as vigorously as it is possible for one army to pursue another. We cannot control the elements, and you must remember that to resist Hood's advance into Tennessee I had to reorganize and almost thoroughly equip the force now under my command. I fought the battles of the 15th and 16th instants with the troops but partially equipped, and, notwithstanding the inclemency of the weather and the partial equipment, have been enabled to drive the enemy beyond Duck River, crossing two streams with my troops, and driving the enemy from position to position without the aid of pontoons, and with but little transportation to bring up supplies of provisions and ammunition. I am doing all in my power to crush Hood's army, and, if it be possible, will destroy it. But pursuing an enemy through an exhausted country, over mud roads completely sogged with heavy rains, is no child's play, and cannot be accomplished as quickly as thought of. I hope, in urging me to push the enemy, the Department remembers that General Sherman took with him the complete organization of the Military Division of the Mississippi, well equipped in every respect as regards ammunition, supplies, and transportation, leaving me only two corps, partially stripped of their transportation to accommodate the force taken with him, to oppose the advance into Tennessee of that army which had resisted the advance of the Army of the Military Division of the Mississippi on Atlanta from the commencement of the campaign till its close, and which is now in addition aided by Forrest's cavalry. Although my progress may appear slow, I feel assured that Hood's army can be driven from Tennessee, and eventually driven to the wall, by the force under my command. But too much must not be expected from troops which have to be reorganized, especially when they have the task of destroying a force in a winter's campaign which was able to make an obstinate resistance to twice its numbers in spring and summer. In conclusion, I can safely state that the army is willing to submit to any sacrifice to oust Hood's army, or to strike any other blow which may contribute to the destruction of the Rebellion.

[Signed] "GEORGE H. THOMAS,
" Major-General."

"CITY POINT, December 22, 1864.
"MAJOR-GENERAL GEORGE H. THOMAS:

"You have the congratulations of the public for the energy with which you are pushing Hood. I hope you will succeed in reaching his pontoon-bridge at Tuscumbia before he gets there. Should you do so, it looks to me that Hood is cut off. If you succeed in destroying Hood's army, there will be but one army left to the so-called Confederacy capable of doing us harm. I will take care of that and try to draw the sting from it, so that in the spring we shall have easy sailing. You have now a big opportunity, which I know you are availing yourself of. Let us push and do all we can before the enemy can derive benefit either from the raising of negro troops on the plantations or white troops now in the field.

[Signed]   "U. S. GRANT,
                                   "Lieutenant-General."

                        "WASHINGTON, December 22, 1864, 9 P.M.

"MAJOR-GENERAL GEORGE H. THOMAS:

"I have seen to-day General Halleck's despatch of yesterday and your reply. It is proper for me to assure you that this Department has the most unbounded confidence in your skill, vigor, and determination to employ to the best advantage all the means in your power to pursue and destroy the enemy. No Department could be inspired with more profound admiration and thankfulness for the great deed which you have already performed, or more confiding faith that human effort could do no more, and no more than will be done by you and the accomplished, gallant officers and soldiers of your command.

[Signed]   "E. M. STANTON."

        "HEADQUARTERS DEPARTMENT OF THE CUMBERLAND,
            "COLUMBIA, December 23, 1864, 8 P.M.

"HON. E. M. STANTON, Secretary of War, Washington, D. C.:

"Your two despatches of 9 P.M. of 22d are received. I am profoundly thankful for the hearty expression of your confidence in my determination and desire to do all in my power to destroy the enemy and put down the Rebellion, and in the name of this army I thank you for the complimentary notice you have taken of all connected with it for the deeds of valor they have performed. . . .

    [Signed]   "GEORGE H. THOMAS,
       "Major-General U. S. Vols., Commanding."

To return to the morning of December 17, 1864. General Thomas continued the pursuit, sending Wood with the Fourth Corps in the direction of Franklin by the direct road. Wilson's cavalry moved out on the Granny White pike to its intersection with the Franklin pike. At that point he took the advance. Johnson's division of cavalry moved on the Hillsboro' pike to the Harpeth River, with instructions to cross it and move by the south bank on Franklin. When he reached the hills overlooking the town he found that the main column of our cavalry was attempting to get possession of the bridge over the Harpeth. Captain Frank G. Smith, a gallant officer of the regular artillery, was instructed to bring his battery into action and open upon the enemy. This was handsomely executed, and as soon as his shot and shell reached the enemy's lines there was a general stampede of the Confederate army. Quick as possible Wilson pushed over the bridge, and was joined at once by Johnson's division, and then a running fight took place for a distance of five miles or more. The cavalry captured a large number of prisoners, artillery, and small-arms. Under the cover of night many of the Confederates who would have been captured had night not intervened were enabled to make good their escape. For several days it had rained in torrents, flooding the creeks, washing away bridges, and rendering many of the streams impassable. Hood had a pontoon-train with him, and was enabled to use it and then take it up before the Federal advance could come up to him. Thomas pushed his columns forward as rapidly as possible, but, notwithstanding his energy and activity, which he seemed to have infused into his commanders and men, the enemy succeeded in reaching the south bank of the Tennessee River and beyond the reach of the victorious pursuers. Thus had Thomas been successful, and thus had the fears of the Lieutenant-General and the Secretary of War that "Hood would march to the Ohio," and that "Gabriel would blow his trumpet before Wilson got his cavalry mounted," proven to have had no foundation in any reasonable possibility.

The great anxiety on the part of General Grant that the third army of the enemy should be broken up and destroyed was natural enough, in order that it might not interfere with other plans on other fields; but the intense anxiety of the Secretary that Thomas should rush into battle unprepared is not so easily understood, unless it was simply the reflection of General Grant's views from Washington instead of City Point. However, any one at all acquainted with Mr. Stanton will give him credit for good intentions and an earnest desire to close out the Rebellion in the very shortest time. If he seemed unreasonably enthusiastic, it was due to his deep-seated loyalty to the old government, which he wished to see restored, and no man labored more faithfully to secure its restoration. His labors as War Secretary during the great Rebellion were overwhelming. For months he slept at his office, working until two or three o'clock in the morning and rising before the sun; and while many of his assistants broke down, he bore the brunt of the burden with inflexible courage and perseverance. He has passed away; so let us forget his faults, but remember his sterling integrity and great services to the nation during the war of the Rebellion and class him among the patriotic great men of that eventful period.

After the last armed enemy had been driven out of the State of Tennessee, Thomas issued the following stirring address to his victorious army:

"HEADQUARTERS DEPARTMENT OF THE CUMBERLAND,
"PULASKI, TENN., December 29, 1864.
"GENERAL ORDERS No. 169.

"SOLDIERS,—The Major-General Commanding announces to you that the rear-guard of the flying and dispirited enemy was driven across the Tennessee River on the night of the 27th instant. The impassable state of the roads and consequent impossibility to supply the army compels a closing of the campaign for the present.

"Although short, it has been brilliant in its achievements and unsurpassed in its results by any other of this war, and is one of which all who participated therein may be justly proud. That veteran army which, though driven from position to position, opposed a stubborn resistance to much superior numbers during the whole of the Atlanta campaign, taking advantage of the largest portion of the army which had been opposed to it in Georgia, invaded Tennessee, buoyant with hope, expecting Nashville, Murfreesboro', and the whole of Tennessee and Kentucky to fall into its power an easy prey, and scarcely fixing a limit to its conquests. After having received at Franklin the most terrible check that

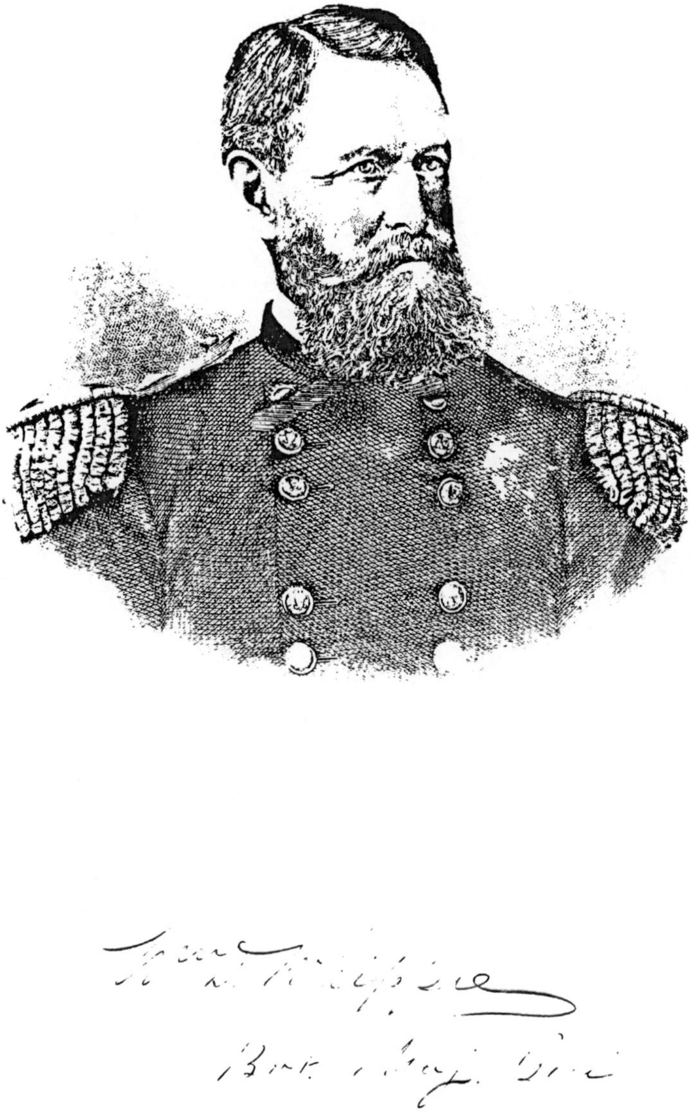

army has received during the war, and later at Murfreesboro', in its attempt to capture that place, it was finally attacked at Nashville, and, although your forces were inferior to it in numbers, was hurled back from the coveted prize on which it had been permitted to look from a distance, and finally sent flying, dismayed, and disordered whence it came, impelled by the instincts of self-preservation, and thinking only of how it could relieve itself for short intervals from your persistent and harassing pursuit by burning the bridges over the swollen streams as it passed them, until finally it had placed the broad waters of the Tennessee River between you and its shattered, diminished, and discomfited columns, leaving its artillery and battle-flags in your victorious hands, lasting trophies of your noble daring and lasting monuments of the enemy's disgrace and defeat.

"You have diminished the forces of the rebel army since it crossed the Tennessee River to invade the State, at the least estimate, fifteen thousand men, among whom were—killed, wounded, and captured—eighteen general officers.

"Your captures from the enemy, as far as reported, amount to sixty-eight pieces of artillery, ten thousand prisoners, as many stand of small-arms,—several thousand of which have been gathered in, and the remainder strew the route of the enemy's retreat,—and between thirty and forty flags, besides compelling him to destroy much ammunition and abandon many wagons; and, unless he is mad, he must forever abandon all hope of bringing Tennessee again within the lines of the accursed rebellion. A short time will now be given you to prepare to continue the work so nobly begun.

"By command of Major-General Thomas.

[Signed] "WILLIAM D. WHIPPLE,
"Assistant Adjutant-General."

General Thomas allowed his men but few days of rest before starting them on that grand swoop over the Southern States. Posting his infantry at various points, the cavalry under General Wilson followed Hood's line of retreat, frequently coming up with the rear-guard, capturing many men, a large number of pieces of artillery, and many stand of small-arms. The capture of Mr. Davis, though not made by General Thomas in person, was made by the cavalry under his general direction. It should be remembered, however, that General Thomas had a very able and skilful cavalry commander, a man young in years, but larger in experience and good judgment, brave, dashing, and ambitious to excel in everything he undertook. When Wilson took charge of the cavalry he made it efficient by infusing his own indomitable spirit into the officers and men composing the corps.

It was a part of Wilson's cavalry at the battle of Nashville which dismounted and charged the enemy's intrenchments, driving their occupants out in great confusion. Wilson organized the cavalry in the Military Division of the Mississippi, and made of it what Sheridan made of the cavalry of the Army of the Potomac,—an effective body of men,—and elevated it from train-guards to form a powerful factor in the fighting force of the army.

The following, taken from a report of Major-General Thomas referring to the battle of Nashville, is inserted as being the best account of the movements preceding and following that conflict attainable, and will prove interesting to the military reader:

"Both armies were ice-bound for a week previous to the 14th December, when the weather moderated. Being prepared to move, I called a meeting of the corps commanders on the afternoon of that day, and having discussed the plan of attack until thoroughly understood, the following Special Field Orders No. 342 were issued:

"'Par. IV. As soon as the state of the weather will admit of offensive operations the troops will move against the enemy's position in the following order: Major-General A. J. Smith, commanding detachment of the Army of the Tennessee, after forming his troops on and near the Hardin pike in front of his present position, will make a vigorous assault on the enemy's left. Major-General Wilson, commanding the Cavalry Corps, Military Division of the Mississippi, with three divisions, will move on and support General Smith's right, assisting as far as possible in carrying the left of the enemy's position, and be in readiness to throw his force upon the enemy the moment a favorable opportunity occurs. Major-General Wilson will also send one division on the Charlotte pike to clear that road of the enemy, and observe in the direction of Bell's Landing to protect our right rear until the enemy's position is fairly turned, when it will rejoin the main force. Brigadier-General T. J. Wood, commanding Fourth Army Corps, after leaving a strong skirmish-line in his works from Lawrens' Hill to his extreme right, will form the remainder of the Fourth Corps on the Hillsboro' pike, to support General Smith's left and operate on the left and rear of the enemy's advanced position on the Montgomery Hill. Major-General Schofield, commanding Twenty-third Army Corps, will replace Brigadier-General Kimball's division of the Fourth Corps with his troops, and occupy the trenches from Fort Negley to Lawrens' Hill with a strong skirmish-line. He will move the remainder of his force in front of the works and co-operate with General Wood, protecting the latter's left flank against an attack by the enemy. Major-General Steedman, commanding District of Etowah, will occupy the interior line in rear of his present position, stretching from the reservoir on the Cumberland River to Fort Negley, with a strong skirmish-line, and mass the remainder of his force in its present position to act according to the exigencies which may arise during these operations. Brigadier-General Miller, with the troops forming the garrison of Nashville, will occupy the interior line from the battery on Hill 210 to the extreme right, including the enclosed work on the Hyde's Ferry road. The quartermaster's troops, under command of Brigadier-General Donaldson, will, if necessary, be posted on the interior line from Fort Morton to the battery on Hill 210. The troops occupying the interior line will be under the direction of Major-General Steedman, who is charged with the immediate defence of Nashville during the operations around the city. Should the weather permit, the troops will be formed to commence operations at 6 A.M. on the 15th, or as soon thereafter as practicable.'

"On the morning of the 15th December, the weather being favorable, the army was formed and ready at an early hour to carry out the plan of battle promulgated in the special field orders of the 14th. The formation of the troops was partially concealed from the enemy by the broken nature of the ground, as also by a dense fog which only lifted towards noon. The enemy was apparently totally unaware of any intention on our part to attack his position, and more especially did he seem not to expect any movement against his left flank. To divert his attention still further from our real intentions, Major-General Steedman had, on the evening of the 14th, received orders to make a heavy demonstration with his command against the enemy's right, east of the Nolensville pike, which he accomplished with great success and some loss, succeeding, however, in attracting the enemy's attention to that part of his line and inducing him to draw reinforcements from towards his centre and left. As soon as General Steedman had completed his movement, the commands of Generals Smith and Wilson moved out along the Hardin pike and commenced the grand movement of the day by wheeling to the left and advancing against the enemy's position across the Hardin and Hillsboro' pikes. A division of cavalry (Johnson's) was sent at the same time to look after a battery of the enemy on the Cumberland River at Bell's Landing, eight miles below Nashville. General Johnson did not get into position until late in the afternoon, when, in conjunction with the gunboats under Lieutenant-Commander Leroy Fitch, the enemy's battery was engaged until after nightfall, and the place was found evacuated on the morning of the 16th. The remainder of General Wilson's command, Hatch's division leading and Knipe's in reserve, moving on the right of General A. J. Smith's troops, first struck the enemy along Richland Creek, near Hardin's house, and drove him back rapidly, capturing a number of prisoners, wagons, etc., and continuing to advance, while slightly swinging to the left, came upon a redoubt containing four guns, which was splendidly carried by assault at 1 P.M. by a portion of Hatch's division dismounted, and the captured guns turned upon the enemy. A second redoubt, stronger than the first, was next assailed and carried by the same troops that captured the first position, taking four more guns and about 300 prisoners. The infantry, McArthur's division of General Smith's command, on the left of the cavalry, participated in both of the assaults, and, indeed, the dismounted cavalry seemed to vie with the infantry who should first gain the works. As they reached the position nearly simultaneously, both lay claim to the artillery and prisoners captured. Finding General Smith had not taken as much distance to the right as I expected he would have done, I directed General Schofield to move his command (the Twenty-third Corps) from the position in reserve to which it had been assigned over to the right of General Smith, enabling the cavalry thereby to operate more freely in the enemy's rear. This was rapidly accomplished by General Schofield, and his troops participated in the closing operations of the day. The Fourth Corps, Brigadier-General T. J. Wood commanding, on the left of General Smith's command, as soon as the latter had struck the enemy's flank, assaulted the Montgomery Hill, Hood's most advanced position, at 1 P.M., which was most gallantly executed by the Third Brigade, Second Division, Colonel P. Sidney Post, Fifty-ninth Illinois, commanding, capturing a considerable number of prisoners. Connecting with the left of Smith's troops (Brigadier-General Garrard's division), the Fourth Corps continued to advance and carried by assault the enemy's entire line in its front, and captured several pieces of artillery, about 500 prisoners, some stands of colors and other materials. The enemy was driven out of his original line of works and forced back to a new position along the base of Harpeth Hills, still holding his line of retreat to Franklin by the main pike through Brentwood and by the Granny White pike. Our line at nightfall was readjusted, running parallel to and east of the Hillsboro' pike, Schofield's command on the right, Smith's in the centre, and Wood's on the left, with the cavalry on the right of Schofield, Steedman holding the position he had gained early in the morning. The total result of the day's operations was the capture of 16 pieces of artillery and 1200 prisoners, besides several hundred stands of small-arms and about 40 wagons. The enemy had been forced back at all points with heavy loss. Our casualties were unusually light. The behavior of the troops was unsurpassed for steadiness and alacrity in every movement, and the original plan of battle, with but few alterations, strictly adhered to. The whole command bivouacked in line of battle during the night on the ground occupied at dark, while preparations were made to renew the battle at an early hour on the morrow.

"At 6 A.M. on the 16th, Wood's corps pressed back the enemy's skirmishers across the Franklin pike to the eastward of it, and then, swinging slightly to the right, advanced due south from Nashville, driving the enemy before him until he came upon his new main line of works, constructed during the night on what is called Overton's Hill, about five miles south of the city and east of the Franklin pike. General Steedman moved out from Nashville by the Nolensville pike and formed his command on the left of General Wood, effectually securing the latter's left flank, and made preparations to co-operate in the operations of the day. General A. J. Smith's command moved on the right of the Fourth Corps (Wood's), and, establishing connection with General Wood's right, completed the new line of battle. General Schofield's troops remained in the position taken up by them at dark on the day previous, facing eastward and towards the enemy's left flank, the line of the corps running perpendicular to General Smith's troops. General Wilson's cavalry, which had rested for the night at the six-mile post on the Hillsboro' pike, was dismounted and formed on the right of Schofield's command, and by noon of the 16th had succeeded in gaining the enemy's rear and stretched across the Granny White pike, one of his two outlets towards Franklin. As soon as the above dispositions were completed, and having visited the different commands, I gave directions that the movement against the enemy's left flank should be continued. Our entire line approached to within six hundred yards of the enemy's at all points. His centre was weak as compared to either his right at Overton's Hill, or his left on the hills bordering the Granny White pike; still, I had hopes of gaining his rear and cutting off his retreat from Franklin. About 3 P.M. Post's brigade of Wood's corps, supported by Streight's brigade of the same command, was ordered by General Wood to assault Overton's Hill. This intention was communicated to General Steedman, who ordered the brigade of colored troops commanded by Colonel C. R. Thompson, Twelfth United States Colored Troops, to co-operate in the movement. The ground on which the two assaulting columns formed being open and exposed to the enemy's view, he readily perceiving our intention, drew reinforcements from his left and centre to the threatened point. This movement of troops on the part of the enemy was communicated along the line from left to right. The assault was made and received by the enemy with tremendous fire of grape and canister and musketry. Our men moved steadily onward up the hill until near the crest, when the reserve of the enemy rose and poured into the assaulting column a most destructive fire, causing the men first to waver and then to fall back, leaving their dead and wounded, black and white indiscriminately mingled, lying amidst the abatis, the gallant Colonel Post among the wounded. General Wood readily reformed his command in the position it had previously occupied, preparatory to a renewal of the assault. Immediately following the effort of the Fourth Corps, Generals Smith's and Schofield's commands moved against the enemy's works in their respective fronts, carrying all before them, irreparably breaking his lines in a dozen places and capturing all his artillery and thousands of prisoners, among the latter four general officers. Our loss was remarkably small, scarcely mentionable. All of the enemy that did escape were pursued over the tops of Brentwood and Harpeth Hills. General Wilson's cavalry, dismounted, attacked the enemy simultaneously with Schofield and Smith, striking him in reserve, and gaining firm possession of Granny White pike, cut off his retreat by that route. Wood's and Steedman's troops hearing the shouts of victory coming from the right, rushed impetuously forward, renewing the assault on Overton's Hill, and although meeting a very heavy fire, the onset was irresistible, artillery and many prisoners falling into our hands. The enemy, hopelessly broken, fled in confusion through the Brentwood Pass, the Fourth Corps in close pursuit, which was continued for several miles, when darkness closed the scene and the troops rested from their labors. As the Fourth Corps pursued the enemy on the Franklin Pike, General Wilson hastily mounted Knipe's and Hatch's divisions of his command and directed them to pursue along the Granny White pike and endeavor to reach Franklin in advance of the enemy. After proceeding about a mile they came upon the enemy's cavalry, under Chalmers, posted across the road and behind barricades. The position was charged by the Twelfth Tennessee Cavalry, Colonel Spaulding commanding, and the enemy's lines broken, scattering him in all directions and capturing quite a number of prisoners, among them Brigadier-General E. W. Rucker. During the two days' operations there were 4462 prisoners captured, including 287 officers of all grades from that of major-general, 53 pieces of artillery, and thousands of small-arms. The enemy abandoned on the field all of his dead and wounded.

"Leaving directions for the collection of the captured property and for the care of the wounded left on the battle-field, the pursuit was continued at daylight on the 17th. The Fourth Corps pushed on towards Franklin by the direct pike, while the cavalry moved by the Granny White pike to its intersection with the Franklin pike, and then took the advance. Johnson's division of cavalry was sent by General Wilson direct to Harpeth River, on the Hillsboro' pike, with directions to cross and move rapidly towards Franklin. The main cavalry column, with Knipe's division in advance, came up with the enemy's rear-guard strongly posted at Hollow-Tree Gap, four miles north of Franklin. The position was charged in front and in flank simultaneously and handsomely carried, capturing 413 prisoners and three colors. The enemy then fell back rapidly to Franklin, and endeavored to defend the crossing of Harpeth River at that place, but Johnson's division coming up from below, on the south side of the stream, forced him to retire from the river bank, and our cavalry took possession of the town, capturing the enemy's hospitals, containing over 2000 wounded, of whom about 200 were our own men. The pursuit was immediately continued by Wilson towards Columbia, the enemy's rear-guard slowly retiring before him to a distance of about five miles south of Franklin, where the enemy made a stand in some open fields just north of West Harpeth River, and seemed to await our coming. Deploying Knipe's division as skirmishers, with Hatch's in close support, General Wilson ordered his body-guard, the Fourth United States Cavalry, Lieutenant Hedges commanding, to charge the enemy. Forming on the pike in columns of fours, the gallant little command charged with sabres drawn, breaking the enemy's centre, while Knipe's and Hatch's men pressed back his flanks, scattering his whole command and causing them to abandon their artillery. Darkness coming on during the engagement enabled a great many to escape, and put an end to the day's operations. The Fourth Corps, under General Wood, followed immediately in rear of the cavalry as far as Harpeth River, where it found the bridges destroyed and too much water on the fords for infantry to cross. A trestle-bridge was hastily constructed from such materials as lay at hand, but could not be made available before nightfall. General Steedman's command moved in rear of General Wood, and camped near him on the banks of the Harpeth. Generals Smith and Schofield marched with their corps along the Granny White pike, and camped for the night at the intersection with the Franklin pike. The trains moved with their respective commands, carrying ten days' supplies and one hundred rounds of ammunition.

"On the 18th the pursuit of the enemy was continued by General Wilson, who pushed on as far as Rutherford's Creek, three miles from Columbia. Wood's corps crossed to the south side of Harpeth River and closed up with the cavalry. The enemy did not offer to make a stand during the day. On arriving at Rutherford's Creek the stream was found to be impassable on account of high water, and running a perfect torrent. A pontoon-bridge, hastily constructed at Nashville during the presence of the army at that place, was on its way to the front, but the bad condition of the roads, together with the incompleteness of the train itself, had retarded its arrival. I would here remark that the splendid pontoon-train properly belonging to my command, with its trained corps of pontoniers, was absent with General Sherman.

"During the 19th several unsuccessful efforts were made by the advance troops to cross Rutherford's Creek, although General Hatch succeeded in lodging a few skirmishers on the south bank. The heavy rains of the preceding few days had inundated the whole country, and rendered the roads almost impassable. Smith's and Schofield's commands crossed to the south side of Harpeth River, General Smith advancing to Spring Hill, while General Schofield encamped at Franklin.

"On the morning of the 20th General Hatch constructed a floating bridge from the *débris* of the old railroad-bridge over Rutherford's Creek, and, crossing his entire division, pushed out for Columbia, but found, on reaching Duck River, the enemy had succeeded the night before in getting everything across, and had already removed his pontoon-bridge. Duck River was very much swollen, and impassable without a bridge. During the day General Wood improvised a foot-bridge over Rutherford's Creek, at the old railroad-bridge, and by nightfall had succeeded in crossing his infantry entire and one or two of his batteries, and moved forward to Duck River. The pontoon-train coming up to Rutherford's Creek about noon of the 21st, a bridge was laid during the afternoon and General Smith's troops were enabled to cross. The weather had changed from dismal rain to bitter cold, very materially retarding the work in laying the bridge, as the regiment of colored troops to whom that duty was entrusted seemed to become unmanned by the cold and totally unequal to the occasion. On the completion of the bridge at Rutherford's Creek, sufficient material for a bridge over Duck River was hastily pushed forward to that point, and the bridge constructed in time to enable Wood to cross late in the afternoon of the 22d and get into position on the Pulaski road, about two miles south of Columbia. The water in the river fell rapidly during the construction of the bridge, necessitating frequent alterations and causing much delay. The enemy, in his hasty retreat, had thrown into the stream several fine pieces of artillery, which were rapidly becoming uncovered and were subsequently removed. Notwithstanding the many delays to which the command had been subject, I determined to continue the pursuit of Hood's shattered forces, and for this purpose decided to use General Wilson's cavalry and General Wood's corps of infantry, directing the infantry to move on the pike, while the cavalry marched on its either flank across the fields, the remainder of the command, Smith's and Schofield's corps, to move along more leisurely, and to be used as the occasion demanded. Forrest and his cavalry, and such other detachments as had been sent off from his main army while besieging Nashville, had rejoined Hood at Columbia. He had formed a powerful rear-guard, made up of detachments from all of his organized force, numbering about 4000 infantry, under General Walthall, and all his available cavalry under Forrest. With the exception of his rear-guard, his army had become a disheartened and disorganized rabble of half-armed and barefooted men, who sought every opportunity to fall out by the wayside and desert their cause to put an end to their sufferings. The rear-guard, however, was undaunted and firm, and did its work bravely to the last.

"During the 23d General Wilson was occupied crossing his command over Duck River, but took the advance on the 24th, supported by General Wood, and came up with the enemy just south of Lynnville, and also at Buford's Station, at both of which places the enemy made a short stand, but was speedily dislodged with some loss in killed, wounded, and prisoners. Our advance was so rapid as to prevent the destruction of the bridges over Richland Creek.

"Christmas morning (the 25th) the enemy, with our cavalry at his heels, evacuated Pulaski and was pursued towards Lamb's Ferry, over an almost impracticable road and through a country devoid of sustenance for man and beast. During the afternoon Harrison's brigade found the enemy strongly intrenched at the head of a heavily wooded and deep ravine, through which ran the road, and into which Colonel Harrison drove the enemy's skirmishers. He then waited for the remainder of the cavalry to close up before attacking; but before this could be accomplished the enemy, with something of his former boldness, sallied from his breastworks and drove back Harrison's skirmishers, capturing and carrying off one gun belonging to Battery I, Fourth United States Artillery, which was not recovered by us, notwithstanding the ground lost was almost immediately regained. By nightfall the enemy was driven from his position with a loss of about 50 prisoners. The cavalry had moved so rapidly as to outdistance the trains, and both men and animals were suffering greatly in consequence, although they continued uncomplainingly to pursue the enemy. General Wood's corps kept well closed up on the cavalry, camping on the night of December 25th six miles out of Pulaski, on the Lamb's Ferry road, and, pursuing the same route as the cavalry, reached Lexington, Alabama, thirty miles from Pulaski, on the 28th, on which date, having definitely ascertained that the enemy had made good his escape across the Tennessee at Bainbridge, I directed further pursuit to cease. At Pulaski the enemy's hospital, containing about two hundred patients, fell into our hands, and four guns were found in Richland Creek. About a mile south of the town he destroyed twenty wagons loaded with ammunition, belonging to Cheatham's corps, taking the animals belonging to the trains to help to pull his pontoons. The road from Pulaski to Bainbridge, and indeed back to Nashville, was strewn with abandoned wagons, limbers, small-arms, blankets, etc., showing most conclusively the disorder of the enemy's retreat. During the foregoing operations with the advance, Smith's and Schofield's troops were in motion towards the front, General Smith's command reaching Pulaski on the 27th, while General Schofield was directed to remain at Columbia for the time being.

"On our arrival at Franklin, on the 18th, I gave directions to General Steedman to move with his command across the country from that point to Murfreesboro', on the Chattanooga Railroad, from whence he was to proceed by rail to Decatur, Alabama, *via* Stevenson, being joined at Stevenson by Brigadier-General R. S. Granger and the troops composing the garrisons of Huntsville, Athens, and Decatur. Taking general direction of the whole force, his instructions were to reoccupy the points in Northern Alabama evacuated at the period of Hood's advance, then cross the Tennessee with the balance of his force and threaten the enemy's railroad communications west of Florence. General Steedman reoccupied Decatur on the 27th, and proceeded to carry out the second portion of his instructions, finding, however, that the enemy had already made good his escape to the south side of the Tennessee, and any movement on his railroad would be useless. On announcing the result of the battles to Rear-Admiral S. P. Lee, commanding Mississippi Squadron, I requested him to send as much of his force as he could spare around to Florence, on the Tennessee River, and endeavor to prevent Hood's army from crossing at that point, which request was most cordially and promptly complied with. He arrived at Chickasaw, Mississippi, on the 24th, destroyed there a rebel battery, and captured two guns, with caissons, at Florence Landing. He also announced the arrival at the latter place of several transports with provisions. Immediately upon learning of the presence at Chickasaw, Mississippi, of the gunboats and transports with provisions, I directed General Smith to march overland from Pulaski to Clifton, *via* Lawrenceburg and Waynesboro', and take post at Eastport, Mississippi. General Smith started for his destination on December 29.

"On the 30th of December I announced to the army the successful completion of the campaign, and gave directions for the disposition of the command, as follows: Smith's corps to take post at Eastport, Mississippi; Wood's corps to be concentrated at Huntsville and Athens, Alabama; Schofield's corps to proceed to Dalton, Georgia; and Wilson's cavalry, after sending one division to Eastport, Mississippi, to concentrate the balance at or near Huntsville. On reaching the several positions assigned them, the different commands were to go into winter quarters and recuperate for the spring campaign. The above not meeting the views of the general-in-chief, and being notified by Major-General Halleck, Chief of Staff, United States Army, that it was not intended for the army in Tennessee to go into winter quarters, orders were issued on the 31st December for Generals Schofield, Smith, and Wilson to concentrate their commands at Eastport, Mississippi, and that of General Wood at Huntsville, Alabama, preparatory to a renewal of the campaign against the enemy in Mississippi and Alabama. During the active operations of the main army in Middle Tennessee, General Stoneman's forces in the northeastern portion of the State were also very actively engaged in operating against Breckenridge, Duke, and Vaughn. Having quickly concentrated the commands of Generals Burbridge and Gillem at Bean's Station, on the 12th of December General Stoneman started for Bristol, his advance, under General Gillem, striking the enemy, under Duke, at Kingsport, on the north fork of the Holston River, killing, capturing, or dispersing the whole command. General Stoneman then sent General Burbridge to Bristol, where he came upon the enemy under Vaughn, and skirmished with him until the remainder of the troops (Gillem's column) came up, when Burbridge was pushed on to Abingdon, with instructions to send a force to cut the railroad at some point between Saltville and Wytheville, in order to prevent reinforcements coming from Lynchburg to the salt-works. Gillem also reached Abingdon on the 15th, the enemy under Vaughn following on a road parallel to the one used by our forces. Having decided merely to make a demonstration against the salt-works, and to push on with the main force after Vaughn, General Gillem struck the enemy at Marion early on the 16th, and after completely routing him, pursued him to Wytheville, Virginia, capturing all his artillery and trains and one hundred and ninety-eight prisoners. Wytheville, with its stores and supplies, was destroyed, and also the extensive lead-works near the town and the railroad-bridge over Reedy Creek. General Stoneman then turned his attention towards Saltville and its important salt-works. The garrison of that place, reinforced by Gittner's, Cosby's, and Witcher's commands, and the remnant of Duke's, all under the command of Breckenridge in person, followed our troops as they moved on Wytheville, and in returning General Stoneman met them at Marion, where he made preparations to give Breckenridge battle, and disposed his command so as to effectually assault the enemy in the morning; but Breckenridge retreated during the night, and was pursued a short distance into North Carolina, our troops capturing some of his wagons and caissons. General Stoneman then moved on Saltville with his entire command, capturing at that place eight pieces of artillery and a large amount of ammunition of all kinds, two locomotives, and quite a number of horses and mules. The extensive salt-works were destroyed by breaking the kettles, filling the wells with rubbish, and burning the buildings. This work accomplished, General Stoneman returned to Knoxville, accompanied by General Gillem's command, General Burbridge proceeding to Kentucky by way of Cumberland Gap. The country marched over was laid waste to prevent its being used again by the enemy; all mills, factories, bridges, etc., being destroyed. The command had everything to contend with as far as the weather and roads were concerned, yet the troops bore up cheerfully throughout, and made each twenty-four hours an average march of forty-two and a half miles. The pursuit of Hood's retreating army was discontinued by my main forces on the 29th December. On reaching the Tennessee River, however, a force of cavalry numbering six hundred men, made up from detachments of the Fifteenth Pennsylvania, Second Michigan, Tenth, Twelfth, and Thirteenth Indiana Regiments, under command of Colonel W. J. Palmer, Fifteenth Pennsylvania, operating with Steedman's column, started from Decatur, Alabama, in the direction of Hood's line of retreat in Mississippi. The enemy's cavalry, under Roddy, was met at Leighton, with whom Colonel Palmer skirmished and pressed back in small squads towards the mountains. Here it was ascertained that Hood's trains passed through Leighton on the 28th of December and moved off towards Columbus, Mississippi. Avoiding the enemy's cavalry, Colonel Palmer left Leighton on the 31st of December, moved rapidly *via* Lagrange and Russellville, and by the Cotton Gin road, and overtook the enemy's pontoon-train, consisting of 200 wagons and 78 pontoon-boats, when ten miles out from Russellville. This he destroyed. Having learned of a large supply-train on its way to Tuscumbia, Colonel Palmer started on the 1st of January towards Aberdeen, Mississippi, with a view of cutting it off, and succeeded in surprising it about 10 P.M. on the same evening, just over the line in Mississippi. The train consisted of one hundred and ten wagons and five hundred mules, the former of which were burned, and the latter sabred and shot. Returning *via* Tall Gate, Alabama, and on the old military and Hackburg roads, the enemy, under Roddy, Biffles, and Russell, was met near Russellville and along Bear Creek, while another force, under Armstrong, was reported to be in pursuit of our forces. Evading the force in his front by moving off to the right under cover of the darkness, Colonel Palmer pushed for Moulton, and coming upon Russell when within twelve miles of Moulton, and near Thorn Hill, attacked him unexpectedly, utterly routing him and capturing some prisoners, besides burning five wagons. The command then proceeded to Decatur without molestation, and reached that place on the 6th of January, after a march of over two hundred and fifty miles. One hundred and fifty prisoners were captured, and nearly one thousand stand of arms destroyed. Colonel Palmer's loss was one killed and two wounded.

"General Hood, while investing Nashville, had sent into Kentucky a force of cavalry numbering about eight hundred men and two guns, under the command of Brigadier-General Lyon, with instructions to operate against our railroad communication with Louisville. McCook's division of cavalry was detached on the 14th of December and sent to Bowling Green and Franklin to protect the road. After capturing Hopkinsville, Lyon was met by La Grange's brigade near Greenbury, and, after a sharp fight, was thrown into confusion, losing one gun, some prisoners and wagons. The enemy succeeded, however, by making a wide detour *via* Elizabethtown and Glasgow, in reaching the Cumberland River and crossing at Burkeville, from whence General Lyon proceeded *via* McMinnville and Winchester, Tennessee, to Larkinsville, Alabama, on the Memphis and Charleston Railroad, and attacked the little garrison at Scottsboro' on the 10th of January. Lyon was here repulsed and his command scattered, our troops pursuing him towards the Tennessee River, which, however, he, with about two hundred of his men and his remaining piece of artillery, succeeded in crossing. The rest of his command scattered in squads among the mountains. Colonel W. J. Palmer, commanding Fifteenth Pennsylvania Cavalry, with one hundred and fifty men, crossed the river at Paint Rock and pursued Lyon to near Red Hill, on the road from Warrenton to Tuscaloosa, at which place he surprised his camp during the night of the

14th of January, capturing Lyon himself, his one piece of artillery, and about one hundred of his men, with their horses. Lyon, being in bed at the time of his capture, asked his guard to permit him to dress himself, which was acceded to, when, watching his opportunity, he seized a pistol, shot the sentinel dead upon the spot, and escaped in the darkness. This was the only casualty during the expedition.

"To Colonel Palmer and his command is accorded the credit of giving Hood's army the last blow of the campaign, at a distance of over two hundred miles from where we first struck the enemy on the 15th of December, near Nashville.

"To all of my sub-commanders, Major-Generals Schofield, Stanley, Rousseau, Steedman, Smith, and Wilson, and Brigadier-General Wood, their officers and men, I give expression of my thanks and gratitude for their generous self-sacrifice and manly endurance under the most trying circumstances, and in all instances. Too much praise cannot be accorded to an army which, hastily made up from the fragments of three separate commands, can successfully contend against a force numerically greater than itself and of more thoroughly solid organization, inflicting on it a most crushing defeat, almost an annihilation. Receiving instructions unexpectedly from General Sherman, in September, to repair to Tennessee and assume general control of the defences of our line of communication in the rear of the Army of the Mississippi, and not anticipating a separation from my immediate command, the greater number of my staff-officers were left behind at Atlanta, and did not have an opportunity to join me. After General Sherman determined on making his march through Georgia before the communications were cut, I had with me Brigadier-General W. D. Whipple, my chief of staff; Surgeon George E. Cooper, medical director; Captains Henry Stone, Henry M. Cist, and Robert H. Ramsey, assistant adjutant-generals; Captain H. C. Beman, acting chief commissary of subsistence; Captains John P. Willard and S. C. Kellogg, aides-de-camp; and Lieutenant M. J. Kelly, chief of couriers, all of whom rendered important service during the battles of the 15th and 16th, and during the pursuit. I cordially commend their services to favorable consideration. There were captured from the enemy during the various actions of which the foregoing report treats 13,189 prisoners of war, including 7 general officers and nearly 1000 other officers of all grades, 72 pieces of serviceable artillery, and —— battle-flags. During the same period over 2000 deserters from the enemy were received, to whom the oath was administered. Our own loss will not exceed 10,000 in killed, wounded, and missing.

"I have the honor to transmit herewith a consolidated return of casualties, the report of Colonel J. G. Parkhurst, provost-marshal-general, and that of Captain A. Mordecai, chief of ordnance.

"I have the honor to be, colonel, very respectfully,
"Your obedient servant,
"GEORGE H. THOMAS,
"Major-General Commanding."

CHAPTER IX.

Thomas careful of those under Him—Never Sacrificed them Uselessly—Votes of Thanks by Congress and Legislature of Tennessee—Medal presented by Latter—Promoted Major-General U.S.A.—Building up Waste Places—Reconstruction—Civil Duties—On Leave of Absence—Headquarters removed to Louisville—Declines a Present from Admirers in Ohio—The Presidency—Brevet Rank Declined—Brevets conferred without much reference to Service—Dyer Court of Inquiry—Transferred to California—Inspects his Command—Visits his Old Post, Fort Yuma—Thomas as a Public Speaker.

IN every calling in life success alone must be the test, and when it is asserted that Thomas never lost a battle nor made any serious mistakes he must be accepted as one of the great leaders of the grand armies of the Union in the late Rebellion. If he was slow he was prudent. He was never known to rush madly into a passage-at-arms without first calculating the chances of success and the resulting consequences in case of defeat. He felt that the soldiers were placed under him not alone to be killed, but to win battles and die if necessary; but the first object was victory, and secondarily to that the preservation of his men, so that he could fight again the next hour if necessary.

There is a popular belief that the importance of a battle is determined by the number of killed and wounded. One of the greatest feats of modern times was the capture of Vera

Cruz and the castle of St. Juan d'Ulloa, which was accomplished by General Winfield Scott without the loss of a man. This brilliant achievement was not applauded with half the enthusiasm that was accorded some of Taylor's battles, which were fought in his "Rough and Ready" style, and always with heavy loss.

On March 3, 1865, the Senate and House of Representatives of the United States of America

"*Resolved*, That the thanks of Congress are due and are hereby tendered to Major-General George H. Thomas, and the officers and soldiers under his command, for their skill and dauntless courage, by which the rebel army under General Hood was signally defeated and driven from the State of Tennessee."

The Legislature of the State of Tennessee on November 2, 1865,

"*Resolved*, That the thanks of the General Assembly, in their own name, and in the name of the people of the State of Tennessee, be presented to Major-General George H. Thomas, and the officers and soldiers under his command, for his wise and spirited and their brave and patriotic conduct in the battle of Nashville, in defence of the capitol of the State, in December, 1864, and that a gold medal be struck in commemoration of the great and decisive event and be presented to him."

This magnificent gold medal, having General Thomas's bust on the adverse and on the reverse the State Capitol, with the motto, "I will hold the town till we starve," was presented to him with imposing ceremonies on the second anniversary of the battle of Nashville, Tennessee.

The result of the battle of Nashville was the complete overthrow of Hood and his army, and the event so pleased the loyal people of the country and the authorities in Washington that Thomas was nominated to fill a vacancy in the grade of major-general in the United States Army. His nomination was confirmed without a dissenting vote, and thus was the faithful, worthy soldier, who came so near being relieved and sent away in disgrace, rewarded for his skill and bravery. What a terrible blow it would have been to him and to the cause had he been relieved! It was a matter of no consequence who might have been designated to supplant him, he could not have filled his place and acquainted himself with the true status of affairs and fought a battle sooner than Thomas did without running a serious risk of complete overthrow and defeat. One can scarce avoid shuddering at the contemplation of the momentous consequences of a defeat instead of a glorious victory at Nashville. True, Sherman's march had been successful, but the capture of Fort McAllister would not have compensated for a lodgment of Hood's army on the Ohio.

Defeat at Nashville would have necessitated new campaigns, and the same bloody fields would have been, as a matter of course, fought over again.

Thomas's success riveted some of the nails in the coffin of the Rebellion, and Sherman's march through Georgia and the Carolinas clinched a few more, while General Grant and General Sheridan, and the gallant officers and men under them, acting as undertakers, completed all other funeral arrangements and decently interred the corpse with military honors under an apple-tree at Appomattox. Thus was closed out one of the most gigantic rebellions ever concocted by the malice and machinations of designing men,—a rebellion which for fierceness and tenacity has no parallel in all the range of modern warfare.

At the close of the war the graves of our dead billowed every battle-field from the Ohio to the ocean, and it was Thomas who conceived the idea of gathering them into national cemeteries. His suggestions were adopted, and the work commenced and continued until all were collected and assigned places in national burying-grounds.

The close of the war imposed upon our commanders civil duties connected with the re-establishment of law and order, and the building up of the waste places which had known no law save military law for so many years.

"Peace hath its victories no less renowned than war."

It now became necessary for Thomas to lay aside in part his warlike garb to enter upon civil military duty. Civil government had to be re-established in all of the Southern States, and to him were assigned the States of Kentucky, Tennessee, Georgia, Alabama, and Mississippi. In the first-mentioned State the civil authority had never been overthrown, but in the mountains and gorges of the State were a number of lawless persons, whose objects were to make forays upon the densely-settled counties, there to set all law at defiance by murder, robbery, and other violations of good order. These men claimed to be returned Confederates, which was not strictly true. They were men who avoided service in either army, preferring to live by robbing those upon whom they could depredate with impunity. Justice to the returned Confederates demands that it should be stated that they were, as a general rule, law-abiding. They had risked all and lost, and their early efforts, after the war, were directed towards providing for themselves and families by some honest industry. True, some were not disposed to accept the results of the war, but this opposition seemed to come from those who did little fighting to speak of when fighting was the order of the day.

Each State under Thomas constituted a separate Military Department, and the five Departments made up the "Military Division of the Tennessee," with headquarters at Nashville. In the exercise of this command his patience and endurance were thoroughly tested. Questions of civil and military character came up for his decision requiring time and labor sufficient for a dozen men, but he proved himself on this, as on all other occasions, equal to the task before him. In Nashville he rented a house for his own occupancy and sent for his wife, who soon joined him. His residence was in a block, and on every pleasant evening he and the other occupants of the same building were in the habit of sitting on the front stoop or porch to enjoy the cool pleasant breezes. On one side of him was a man who had been known as a rebel, but who did not have the courage to fight for the principles which he pretended to hold so dear, and, in order to show his disloyal and unfriendly disposition, was every evening to be seen on his veranda, within handshaking distance of Thomas, of whose presence he affected not to be conscious. This was lost on Thomas, who did not care to be "bored" at that hour of the day when he preferred communion with himself or the members of his family. One evening, after the lapse of six months or more, this high-born Southern gentleman advanced very patronizingly to shake hands, when the general waved him back with the remark, "Too late, too late, sir; you have sinned away your day of grace." The poor fellow withdrew, mortified beyond measure, and was never seen thereafter sitting on his porch or within view of General Thomas.

Slowly the civil law was re-established, and as rapidly as possible all the volunteers were mustered out. When peace was fairly restored, Thomas applied for a leave of absence to enable him to visit his friends in the North, and afterwards to take a trip through Canada. Before leaving, he asked that his headquarters might be transferred to Louisville, Kentucky. His request was granted, and General W. D. Whipple, chief of staff, superintended the transfer of all the different branches of the service connected with the Military Division of the Tennessee, including the voluminous records appertaining to his own office. Suitable accommodations were secured and everything gotten in good running order before the general's return.

About this time his friends and admirers in Cincinnati determined on raising a large sum of money as a present to him, in recognition of his valuable services during the war. As soon as he heard of it he wrote to some one prominent in the movement that he could not think for one moment of accepting a present of that or any other character, that the government had richly rewarded him for all that he had done, and that, in fact, he had already received more than he deserved. He requested that all funds raised on his account, or that might be raised, be turned over, in such manner as the liberal, generous donors might see proper, to the widows and orphans made such by the war.

On his return to Louisville he found everything in order, and he was much pleased with the change.

About the time of his return he was greatly annoyed by the receipt of letters from politicians all over the North asking if he would consent to be a candidate for the Presidency of the United States, and to all of which he replied that under no circumstances would he consent to such a use of his name. The State of Tennessee, through her State Convention, declared unanimously for him, and as this was the first gun of the campaign, it was very apt to be followed by other States.

But Thomas turned a deaf ear to the entreaties of politicians. The writer spoke to him on the subject, and suggested that he had better let public opinion have its own course, that if it was the desire of the loyal people of the country to elevate him to that exalted position he could not well decline to accept. His reply was that he had all he wanted, that he was too young to give up a life position for one of uncertainty, and that his whole life, so far as peace and quiet was concerned, would be broken up by entering into the political arena. Then, becoming somewhat animated, he said, "I will have nothing to do with politics. I am a soldier, and I know my duty; as a politician I would be lost. No, sir; not even if I were elected unanimously would I accept. I want to die with a fair record, and this I will do if I keep out of the sea of politics and cling to my proper profession."

He was determined that there should not be a Thomas

"boom," and his frequent letters declining the honor started the party managers to looking elsewhere for a Presidential aspirant.

President Johnson having some misunderstanding with General Grant, resolved on relieving him from the command of the army. As there was no officer of even grade, it could only be done by conferring the brevet rank upon some one. Thomas was selected and his name forwarded to the Senate. Had the nomination been confirmed he would have been assigned to duty according to his brevet rank, and then, under the law as it stood, he would have been eligible for appointment to the supreme command. It will be remembered that in the early years of the war there were many major-generals appointed before they had earned their promotion, and after it was too late it was ascertained that many of them were inefficient and unworthy of the high commands to which their rank entitled them. To obviate this a law was passed authorizing the assignment of any one major-general to any command the President might desire, even if ranked by those over whom he was placed. Under the operation of that law it was intended to displace General Grant and place Thomas in command of all the land forces of the country. Thomas learned what the programme was, and resolved that he should not be placed in a false position. To prevent it he telegraphed to Senator Chandler, and possibly others, that the government had done enough for him and requested that the Senate refuse to confirm the nomination made by the President. There are few men living who knew what President Johnson's intention was, and this statement may strike many with surprise. Had

Thomas been an avaricious, grasping, ambitious man he would have stepped in and for a season commanded the army, thus placing himself, as well as General Grant, in false positions. Thomas had no such desire to rob General Grant of the honors he had so justly earned. How very few there are in the army, or elsewhere, who would not readily accept promotion by any means it could be obtained without reference to the great injustice it might work upon others! Not so with Thomas; he was too noble and too generous to accept a position rightfully belonging to another. General Grant graduated and entered the army three years after Thomas, and with many officers there would have been unwilling and tardy obedience on account of original seniority; but Thomas was too much of a soldier and the importance of the contest too great for petty squabbling about rank. He served honestly and faithfully under any and all circumstances, and at all times bore true allegiance to his country and to his commander.

If he ever had any feeling that others had been unjustly promoted over his head, certain it was that he never spoke of it to any one. As he once remarked, he "had educated himself not to feel," or, if he did feel, it was so far on the inside of his manly, generous bosom that it never reached the surface. He had no tales of wrongdoing on the part of others to him, or of any want of appreciation on the part of the War Department, but always insisted that he had had more than his share of credit and emoluments. Such a disinterested, unselfish man is rarely to be found in these degenerate days.

As the solution of the problem of reconstruction progressed, new lines were made to bound Military Departments and new names were given to them. On March 11, 1867, Thomas was assigned to the command of the "Third Military District," composed of the States of Georgia, Florida, and Alabama, but was relieved from duty therein, at his own request, on March 16, preferring to remain in command of the Department of the Cumberland.

The return of the officers who had served in the volunteer service to their old places in the regular army produced much confusion, owing to the brevet rank held by some of them. This question seemed fair to lead to unending trouble and dissatisfaction, owing to the indiscriminate manner in which they had been bestowed. Mr. Stanton felt so elated at the downfall of the Rebellion that he thought every officer who had held a commission in the regular or volunteer service should have from two to four brevets, and accordingly these empty honors were conferred as fast as they could be written out. In many instances officers who had not heard the whistle of a hostile bullet were brevetted for faithful services during the war. In some instances captains ranked their colonels by brevet, and it was not an unusual thing for a colonel to address one of his subordinates as general. When these brevetted officers were detailed on courts-martial, a captain or lieutenant might be president of the tribunal and his colonel the junior member. Then, again, there was doubt and uncertainty as to rank among themselves.

To settle this question, and bring order out of chaos and confusion, a board of officers of which Thomas was a member was ordered to convene to decide upon a given date for each general officer by brevet. This board met March

14, 1866, and was in session ten days. The proceedings were approved, but, not having the weight of law on their side, practically failed to accomplish the object intended. Subsequently Congress legislated upon the subject, and to all intents and purposes abolished all laws relating to brevet rank, without substituting some other method by which the services of those who had earned honorable distinction on the battlefield might be made manifest. Some distinctive mark, as a badge, to indicate rank by brevet should be authorized. The private soldier who has served an enlistment is, when he reenlists, permitted to wear a service *chevron* to indicate former faithful service. Why not allow officers who have braved dangers on the battle-field, and who have earned laurels in many bloody conflicts, to wear a badge indicative of such service? Thomas threw the weight of his influence in favor of this, but he failed to have his cherished plan carried out.

General Thomas remained in command of the Department of the Cumberland until January 5, 1869, when he was detailed as a member of the Dyer Court of Inquiry, which occupied his time until about the middle of May. On the conclusion of the business of the court he was ordered to the command of the Military Division of the Pacific, with headquarters in San Francisco. He arrived at his post of duty some time during the month of June, 1869, and at once issued his order assuming command. Only a few years previously he had sailed from that city as a newly-appointed major of cavalry; now he returned as a major-general, having earned his promotion by his gallantry and skill on a score of bloody and hotly-contested battle-fields.

After a short period of rest he determined upon visiting all the posts within the bounds of his command, including the frozen region of Alaska. The government officials knew but little of that remote section of our country until Thomas visited it, and his report, which was minute in detail, established the fact that Mr. Seward had purchased an iceberg for the use and benefit of the United States government. What we are to gain by this purchase has not yet transpired, nor is it at all likely that the present generation will ever have any occasion to use it. Thomas suggested the withdrawal of all the troops from that inhospitable climate, leaving our purchase to the low, degraded Indians who were thrown in when the country was transferred to us. After visiting all other forts he paid a flying visit to his old post, Fort Yuma, where, as a captain, he had been stationed, and where he had suffered so much from the heat and other causes incident to the climate. It filled him with pleasant memories, and those were intensified in a recollection that his rank now would forever exempt him from continuous service there.

It is probable that he paid that post a visit for pretty much the same reason that the old, disabled, and retired English officer employed a drummer and fifer to play *reveille* every morning at five o'clock in front of his house. It was not a fondness for the music, but a satisfaction to turn over, rub his eyes, and say, "Thank heavens! I am no longer compelled to get up and attend morning roll-call." It must have been thus with Thomas. He enjoyed the thought that he would never again be compelled to become a permanent part of the garrison at that point.

Having completed his inspection, he knew the wants of each post, and at once directed his attention to supplying them.

Thomas was not a public speaker, and always avoided, as far as possible, all places where he might be called upon to make extended remarks. He had been trained to act, and the history of the country shows how well he performed the duty that devolved upon him. On one or two occasions he was "cornered" and had to make speeches. The first and only time the writer ever heard him was on the occasion of the meeting of the "Society of the Army of the Cumberland," in the city of Cincinnati, in February, 1867.

He was called on to reply to the toast, "General Thomas." He rose and said,—

"I thank you for the toast. At the same time it is almost too personal for me to attempt to reply. Again, my predecessors have occupied nearly the whole field of discussion to-night, and left me in a pretty bad scrape. I don't know how I shall draw out. Nevertheless I will try to do so; I will make the attempt. I did intend to relate our withdrawal from the front of Atlanta to take up those three lines of march upon the enemy's rear and line of retreat which our illustrious commander, General Sherman, has just now so graphically described. He, you see, has anticipated me. As the president of this Association, I desired also to allude briefly to the services and merits of my predecessors. My immediate predecessor, General Thruston, has ably done that, and I find myself forestalled a second time. Now you see how desperate my condition is. You all know that I am a modest man, and never speak unless I am forced to. I was once offered the command of the Army of the Cumberland when

I thought it should not be taken from a gentleman who had claims for it. I therefore declined it. I would not permit myself to be made use of to do him an injury. At a later day, without any thought of such a position being thrust upon me, the command of the Army of the Cumberland was given to me. You know very well the occasion. It was when we were tied, in a measure, at Chattanooga. We did not have a great deal to eat then, you know, and we economized our rations, and proposed to starve before we gave up that place.

"Gentlemen, you know the Army of the Cumberland expressed that sentiment to the country, and you also know that we would have starved before we gave up Chattanooga. The whole country had confidence in that declaration. Reinforcements came as soon as they could be gotten to us. We waited patiently, diminished our rations from day to day, until they became almost a myth; but the day came when the Army of the Tennessee, on our left, opened the way to relief and final triumph by crossing the Tennessee River and taking a strong position on Mission Ridge. The next day the reinforcements from the Army of the Potomac, which were not then incorporated with the Army of the Cumberland, carried that high point on our right, Lookout Mountain, which opened the eyes of the enemy to the danger of his position.

"That gave us great encouragement. We felt that we could get something to eat before long. The next day was the *grand finale*. The enemy, thinking that he had us entirely in his power, forgot himself and lost Lookout Mountain. To retrieve his disaster he concentrated upon our illustrious friend on my right (General Sherman), the leader of the combined armies afterwards. That concentration gave the corps under my immediate command an opportunity, in soldier parlance, 'to make a straight line for the top of Mission Ridge.'

We carried it; we held it; and we hurled the broken enemy across Chickamauga Creek. Well do I remember when, after the battle was over, right on the top of the hill, I fell among some of our old soldiers, who always took liberties with me, who commenced talking and giving their views of the victory. When I attempted to compliment them for the gallant manner in which they had made the assault, one man very coolly replied, 'Why, general, we know that you have been training us for this race for the last three weeks.'

"Just at that moment, not knowing exactly what to say to him, I looked over my shoulder and saw a steamboat coming into Chattanooga. Said I, 'We have trained you as long as we want to; there comes the rations.'

"Now, gentlemen, my time is very nearly up. I will close by touching on one subject which no gentleman has touched upon to-night. It is this: the civilizing influences of discipline, both in the army and the navy. We have not only broken down one of the most formidable rebellions that ever threatened the existence of any country, but the discipline of the Army of the Cumberland alone has civilized two hundred thousand valuable patriots and citizens. I have travelled a little since the war was over. Wherever I have been, whether on steamboat or rail, I have either seen on the steamboat, engaged in peaceful occupation of merchant sailors, or I have seen in the fields, along the railroads, engaged in peacefully following the plough, and setting an example of industry worthy to be followed by all the country, men innumerable dressed in blue. They did not disdain to wear the uniform; they gloried in it; and I hope that such sentiments, and such civilizing influences as have been produced by this war, will serve for all time to inspire this nation with such a feeling of patriotism that no enemy can ever do us the least harm."

This speech of the general is given in full, as it is believed to be the longest one he ever made. In it his character is revealed such as has been delineated in these pages. How modest! All that his noble army did was due to the courage and good conduct of the officers and men composing that army. He gave them the credit and took none to himself. The writer was present at the delivery of the foregoing speech, and can testify that he, who was a terror to his foe, a thunderbolt on the field of battle, the man who knew no fear, was on that occasion, surrounded by his friends, as modest and diffident as a woman, and seemed to be laboring under a greater degree of excitement than he ever evinced in the heat of battle.

CHAPTER X.

Thomas's Loyalty—Pen-Portrait by William Swinton.

IT has been said that Thomas hesitated in regard to his loyalty to the United States government, and that at one time his mind was made up to cast his fortunes with his native State, turning against the government that had educated him. This is false, without even the shadow of foundation in fact.

He was intensely attached to the cause of the Union, and while the writer was as intimately associated with him as any officer in his regiment, he never heard him express any other views than those of loyalty to the government, first, last, and all the time. He felt that a majority of the people of his native State were for the Union, and that they would have remained in it had not the leaders, by their high-handed and unauthorized conduct, forced the inhabitants into a position of disloyalty by a self-elected, self-constituted convention which dissolved by resolutions the ties that bound them to the Federal government. He never ceased to feel that he was one of the proper representatives of Virginia, that, if the popular voice could be heard, it would unmistakably proclaim that a large majority of the people were in favor of "the Union, the Constitution, and the enforcement of the laws." It was in this way that many of the States were brought into conflict with national authority, not because the people were tired of the old government, not because they had been oppressed or denied any of those rights guaranteed to them by the Constitution, but under the lash of party rulers they were whipped into the traces and made to cry, "Long live the Confederacy! Down with the Stars and Stripes!"

It was the timely arrival of Anderson, Sherman, Thomas, and Buell in Kentucky that restrained the hot-headed people of that State, and prevented the passage of the ordinance of secession. Had their arrival been delayed a few weeks longer Confederate authority would have been established, thus utterly destroying the Union sentiment that pervaded the masses.

It has been said by some one that General Grant, in speaking of the "slowness" of Thomas, remarked that he was slow to decide upon remaining loyal to the Federal government.

The general was doubtless misquoted, as he would not willingly cast such an imputation upon the fair name and fame of one who has passed away and is unable to reply. And, aside from this, General Grant is too magnanimous to have given utterance to any such unjust reflection,—unjust to one who gave evidence of loyalty and devotion to the country before he, General Grant, decided upon entering the service at all for the suppression of the Rebellion.

Long before the bombardment of Fort Sumter it was evident to every rational observer and thinker that we were to have a war, and when the officers of the Second Cavalry assembled, as was their custom, after the arrival of the weekly mail, to discuss the news and probable turn affairs might take, no one ever heard him give forth any uncertain sound in regard to his purpose in the future should war be the legitimate consequence of attempted secession. This matter of Thomas's loyalty is reluctantly referred to, because it is an insult to the memory of a great and good man; and no one would resent it sooner than General Grant if he were to read in the newspapers what the correspondent attributes to him. Thomas was in full accord with that outburst of popular affection, that exhibition of patriotic resolution, that simple, patient, unfaltering adherence to principle and to purpose, which vindicated the authority and assured the existence of the American republic, from the day that war seemed imminent to the close of the unnatural, causeless, and wicked strife, which finally burnt itself out amid the black ashes of overthrow and defeat.

It should be borne in mind that an officer born in one of the Southern States had to antagonize himself to all his kindred, and sever all those endearing ties of friendship and relationship which are so dear to every member of the human family. To place one's self in such a position required patriotism of a high order. Such was Thomas's loyalty to his country that he said, "If these ties can only be preserved on the condition of my abandonment of the government for which my forefathers fought, bled, and died, then let them be severed;" and the resolution was carried out, the government securing the services of a brave and devoted soldier, without a superior and with few equals.

It might just as well be stated here as elsewhere that

DAVID S. STANLEY.

Thomas had offers of advancement from friends in the South if he would leave the Federal army and join the cause of the Southern States, but he spurned the offer and would not permit himself to entertain the overture for a single moment.

Major Frank J. Jones, who served under Thomas and who knew his worth, in a speech recently made in Cincinnati at a dinner-party given to ex-officers of the army and navy, said, in reference to his loyalty,—

"But there is one now at rest with the other dead patriots of the war, the noble General George H. Thomas, whose fidelity and devotion to the old flag meant with him not only war with rebels, but also a severance and permanent destruction of the ties and affections of home and the associations that cluster around the native hearthstone. Yes, gentlemen, he was a Virginian who preferred loyalty to the government which had educated him to treason and its consequent disgrace, which his conscience told him awaited all those who undertook its intended annihilation.

* * * * * * *

"All honor to the precious memory of this noble man, whose deeds of heroism made him the 'Gibraltar of Chickamauga' and the invincible captain of a mighty army at Mission Ridge, Franklin, and Nashville."

What can be more beautiful and, at the same time, truthful than the following tribute to Thomas by William Swinton, published in his book, "Twelve Decisive Battles of the War"?

"The figure of Thomas looms up, in many respects without a superior, in most respects without a rival, even among the Union generals created by the war.

"When the Rebellion opened Major Thomas was a soldier of twenty years' experience, during which he had not only not turned aside to the attractions of civil life, but had accepted only two furloughs. It was during his latter leave of absence that the insurrection broke out, and Thomas received the colonelcy of his regiment, now styled the Fifth Cavalry.

"From this time the fame of General Thomas becomes national. His complete and admirable victory at Mill Spring was the first triumph of magnitude for the North since the disaster at Bull Run, and brought back a needed prestige to the Union arms. As commander of the Fourteenth Army Corps, under Rosecrans, he was conspicuous in the marching and fighting which preceded Murfreesboro', and all-glorious in that decisive battle. Him Rosecrans then portrayed as 'true and prudent, distinguished in council and celebrated on many battle-fields for his courage.' It was he who, alone and unaided, saved the Army of the Cumberland at Chickamauga, when the example of all around him might have excused him for flying from the lost field.

"And again, accordingly, the enthusiastic tribute of praise comes up in the report of Rosecrans: 'To Major-General Thomas, the true soldier, the prudent and undaunted commander, the modest and incorruptible patriot, the thanks and gratitude of the country are due for his conduct at the battle of Chickamauga.' It was Thomas, whose troops, 'forming on the plain below with the precision of parade,' made the wonderful charge on Missionary Ridge which threw Bragg back into Georgia. It was he who in the grand Atlanta campaign commanded, under Sherman, more than three-fifths of that army, and who delivered the opening battle at Buzzard's Roost and the closing battle at Lovejoy's. It was Thomas, in fine, who set the seal of success on the Georgia campaign, three hundred miles away at Nashville.

"Imposing in stature, massive in thew and limb, the face and figure of General Thomas consort well with the impression made by his character,—the firm mouth, the square jaw, the steady blue eye, the grave expression habitual on the impassive countenance being indices to well-known traits. The war showed that his gifts, like his qualities, were, in the main, of that more solid and substantial sort which gain less immediate applause than what is specious and glittering, but which lead on to enduring fame. Yet there was noticeable in him a rare and felicitous union of qualities which do not often appear with full vigor in the same organization. Cautious in undertaking, yet, once resolved, he was bold in execution; deliberate in forming his plan and patiently waiting for events to mature, yet when the fixed hour struck he leaped into great activity. Discretion in him was obviously spurred on by earnestness, and earnestness tempered by discretion. Prudent by nature, not boastful, reticent, he was not the less free from the weakness of will and tameness of spirit which are as fatal to success as rashness. He was, in short, one of those 'whose blood and judgment are so well commingled that they are not a pipe for Fortune's finger to sound what stop she pleases.'

"Of his complete mastery of his profession in all its details, of his consummate skill as a general, the best monument is the story of his battles; for he never lost a campaign or a field, he never met his enemy without giving him cause to grieve for the rencontre, and he culled laurels from fields on which brother-officers were covered with disgrace, and more than once plucked up drowning honor by the locks, as at Chickamauga. As he did not himself fail, so he did not suffer himself to be ruined by incompetency in superiors, much less in subordinates, for he was accustomed to consider beforehand such possibilities and to guard against them. His successes were won by art, not tossed to him by fortune; and whenever victory came to him he was conscious of having earned it. Such successes indicate temperaments at once solid and acute, and in which wisdom and valor concur,—Nestor of the council and Hector of the field.

"He was a soldier who conned his maps before he marched his army, who planned his campaign before he fought it, who would not hurry, who would not learn by thoughtless experiments what study could teach, who believed in the duty of a general to organize victory at each step. He was a lover of system, and was nothing if not systematic. He approved what was regular, and required proof of what was irregular; had that fondness for routine which does not ill become an old army officer; and even in exigencies desired everything to proceed duly and in order. He was not a slave to method, but naturally distrusted what was unmethodical; and that he invariably won battles by virtue of time-honored principles, and in accordance with the rules of the art of war, was, besides its value to the country, a truth invaluable to military science in the land, whose teachings had been somewhat unjustly cast into contempt by the conduct of other successful soldiers. His Nashville campaign gave more than one instance of the trait just noted. Superiors were vexed at his constant retreat from the Tennessee, at his flight behind the parapets of Nashville, at his delay to attack the investing force; but neither this vexation nor the danger of removal which threatened him could avail with Thomas, for that soldier would not be badgered into premature battle. Soon after the wisdom of Thomas in delaying attack in order to mount his cavalry approved itself, for never before in the war had grand victory been so energetically followed by pursuit. In the battle itself, too, spectators fancied that he was pausing too long before engaging his right flank, but he held that wing poised, as it were, in the air till the fit moment, when he swung it like a mighty sledge upon the Confederate and smote him to the dust.

"The best justification of his system was its success, for if discreet he was safe; if slow, sure. He provided for dilemmas and obstacles, he suffered no surprises, made no disastrous experiments at the sacrifice of position, of prestige, or of the lives of his troops, and, indeed, he was wont to make the enemy pay dearly for the privilege of defeat, and usually lost fewer troops in action than his adversary, whether pursuing the offensive or the defensive. Thus, if the processes of his thought were slow of evolution, they at least attained to their goal.

"His natural impulse would seem to be to stand *inébranlable* on the defensive, and, having taken manfully his enemy's blows till the assailant was exhausted, then to turn upon him in furious aggression; so it was with his first national victory at Mill Spring, and so with his latest at Nashville, while his fight at bay at Chickamauga is immortal. A fine analyzer of character might perhaps trace a sympathy between this military method, on the one hand, and the well-known personal traits of the soldier on the other: his modesty, his unassuming, unpretending spirit, his absence of self-assertion and habit of remaining in the background, and, therewith, his vigor when aroused and his bold championship of any cause entrusted to him. At all events, the fame of his persistency, of his firmness, almost amounting to obstinacy, of the unyielding grip with which he held his antagonist, became worldwide. When Grant hurried to the relief of beleaguered Chattanooga, there to supplant Rosecrans, he telegraphed to Thomas, then in command, 'Hold on to Chattanooga at all hazards'; to which message came the sententious response: 'Have no fear. Will hold the town till we starve.' When steadfast he stood in Frick's Gap, on the field of Chickamauga, after the columns on both of his flanks had given way, the torrent of Bragg's onset, the hail of fire that swept the Union ranks moved him not a jot from his firm base, and the billow that swamped the rest of the field recoiled from him. 'The rain descended, and the floods came and beat upon that house, and it fell not: for it was founded upon a rock.' Thereafter the soldiers of the Army of the Cumberland were wont to call him 'The Rock of Chickamauga.'

"Grave and wise at the council board, yet it is on the well-contested field that Thomas shines most conspicuous. In the ordinary tide of battle he is emphatically the imperturbable, calm, poised, entirely cool, self-possessed one, on whom the shifting fortunes of the day have only a subdued effect, and whose equanimity even success cannot dangerously disturb. But he is greatest in extremity, that 'trier of spirits.' In the supreme moment of exigency, which demands a great soul to grasp it,—such an one as came to overtasked Hooker at Chancellorsville,—Thomas shines out pre-eminent and asserts his superiority. Phlegmatic at most hours, the desperate crises of battle are alone sufficient to stir his temperament into fullest action, and then his quiet, steady eyes flame a little with battle-fire.

"He had the great quality of inspiring in his troops perfect confidence and great devotion. Indeed, his soldierly skill was well set off by the air and manner of a soldier: unaffected, manly, far from the pettiness bred by long pampering in the drawing-room, but with a simplicity, robustness, and hardiness of character like that of his own physique, the inheritance of thirty years in field and garrison. Dignified and decorous, his brother-officers found him free from show and pretence, frank, open, and magnanimous; while to his troops he was kindly and amiable. He excited no envy or jealousy in his rivals, who found him straightforward and conscientious; and his men had cause to know that he was observant of merit and rewarded it. His reputation was without reproach, his controlled temper superior to the vicissitudes of camp and battle, and joined to them was a courage which set life at a pin's fee. A Virginian, and of such social ties as might well have made him 'a Pharisee of the Pharisees,' he had proved at the outset the quality of the allegiance he bore to the republic by casting in his lot with the Union arms. His loyalty was disinterested and the result of conviction, not of political aspiration.

"The progress of the war, too, gave him, as it did so many officers, a chance to show the quality and stability of his patriotism. Even while the country resounded with the glories of Chickamauga and Missionary Ridge, Sherman, his junior in experience, in length of service, and in years, and his equal only in rank, was appointed over him to the command vacated by General Grant. Without murmur, perhaps without thought of injury, Thomas took his place under Sherman with the cheerful obedience of a true soldier. On the eve of Nashville he was to have been relieved of command, but desired, for the sake of the country, that he might execute a long-formed plan, after which he would be at such disposal as might seem fit.

"Such was General Thomas, the completely rounded, skilful, judicious, modest soldier,—a man compact, of genuine stuff, a trustworthy man:

"Rich in saving common sense,
And, as the greatest only are,
In his simplicity sublime."

CHAPTER XI.

Nature and Character of Last Illness—Death—General Order of General Sherman announcing the Same—Received with Universal Sadness.

GENERAL THOMAS, having finished the inspection of his command and made such changes as he thought proper, settled down to the office duties devolving upon him. The long strain upon his mind and body had to some extent impaired his health, and he thought that a change to the climate of California would result in great benefit to him. But how uncertain are all human calculations! About noon on the 28th day of March, 1870, while sitting in his office, he was suddenly attacked with faintness and oppression. He walked into an adjoining room to seek fresh air, and fell insensible to the floor. He was taken back into his office and laid upon a lounge. Messengers were immediately sent out for medical aid. Dr. Haggen, a citizen physician, was the first to arrive, and he at once administered a stimulant, which revived him somewhat. Soon after, Surgeons Robert Murray and Charles McCormick, U.S.A., of the general's staff, arrived, accompanied by Surgeon E. J. Bailey, who was temporarily in San Francisco. They found him very faint and weak and suffering from great nervous prostration. Brandy was administered, and he soon became conscious and clear-minded. He got up, and with the assistance of two men walked into an adjoining room and back again. The faintness and prostration, however, soon returned in a much greater degree, and it was soon evident that what was hoped to be merely faintness and exhaustion was a most serious and progressive attack of apoplexy caused by effusion of blood on the brain from a ruptured blood-vessel. In spite of all treatment the symptoms progressed with fatal rapidity. Partial unconsciousness advanced to entire insensibility. The pupils dilated, and his breathing became more and more labored and apoplectic. He was not conscious after 3 o'clock P.M., and at a quarter past seven in the evening he breathed his last. There was no *post-mortem* examination, but in the process of embalming the body the coats of the large artery coming from the heart were found softened from fatty degeneration, so that it is probable that a similarly diseased condition existed in the artery which was ruptured in the brain.

Death is at all times as difficult to chronicle as it is unwelcome and unexpected. We trace the career of a great man with pride and with pleasure, and by the distinctive features that make him great we elevate him above his fellows. He is marked, distinguished, in that he differs from his fellows in the possession of larger faculties or the enjoyment of grander opportunities. But, after all, at last (and just here who would not wish to lay aside the pen?), at last we must record what is the lot of all men: DEATH. In this there is no distinction, all men die. Death is inexorable, and wherever or whenever it comes, it is equally an intruder and unexpected.

We lament the young in death, we mourn the old in death, we would never give up the middle-aged. The rich, the poor, the famous, the obscure,—we weep for them all. There seems to be no time to die in our estimate of life's usefulness. Death is always inopportune. Father, mother, wife, husband, brother, sister, the State, the nation never acquiesce in Death's appointments. "It is appointed unto all men once to die,"—but when? Alas! alas! Scripture gives us no dates in this matter, and if man is indeed slow to imbibe all other divine truth, he certainly has not failed to robe his thoughts with the scriptural indefiniteness as to the approach of death. Shall we wonder then that we recoil from the thought of the death of our hero? When we think of him in the full vigor of manhood, ripe in the experiences of an eventful life, beloved by his countrymen, honored by the nation, might we not wish for him long days to enjoy his laurels and radiate his nobility of character along the path of the generation coming up after him? Such would be our wisdom, such our love. But, " as the heavens are higher than the earth, so are His ways higher than our ways," and our more unfitting time Death appropriates for his. But, while we yield up the mortal to the grim tyrant, we proudly glory in the immortality of his fame.

> And now you, too, Thomas!
> Alas! alas! Death writes again
> Upon the lofty arch of fame,
> Beneath thy emblazoned name,
> "There's no immunity to greatness."
>
> Achieve so much as mortals may,
> Climb so far you see to-morrow's day,

> Battle for the million-freeing truth,
> As angels might be proud to do,
> Clash steel and throat Oppression's hordes,
> Save a race and make them freemen,
> Yet, after all, thrust through by Death!
>
> And yet thou canst not, canst not die
> While earth is canopied with sky;
> Thou didst such fuel add to Freedom's fire
> In all the ages 'twill ne'er expire.
> Thy life roused the ocean depths of thought
> To such great waves against the wrong
> They'll ceaseless lash, nor grow less strong,
> Nor rest on any shore in calm,
> While droops on earth one fettered arm.
>
> Live on, then, brave soldier,
> In the nation's proudest annals,
> In the people's warmest hearts!
> Great in courage, noble in truth,
> Pure as the sunlight in soul,
> Dead, but imperishable!

General William T. Sherman, Commander-in-Chief of the army and a classmate of Thomas, thus feelingly and beautifully announced his death to the army in the following tribute to his memory:

"HEADQUARTERS OF THE ARMY,
"ADJUTANT-GENERAL'S OFFICE,
"WASHINGTON, March 29, 1870.

"GENERAL ORDERS No. 34.

"It has become the painful duty of the general to announce to the army the death of one of our most exalted generals, George H. Thomas, who expired last evening at half-past seven, in San Francisco, California.

"There is no need to turn to the archives to search for his history, for it is recorded in almost every page during the past ten years; but his classmate and comrade owes him a personal tribute, in which he knows every member of the army shares. General Thomas entered the Military Academy in the class of 1836, graduated in 1840, and was commissioned as a second lieutenant, Third Artillery, and sent to Florida. He served with his regiment continuously until December 24, 1853, when he became a captain, having been particularly distinguished at Monterey and Buena Vista, Mexico. On the 12th of May, 1855, he was appointed to the Second Cavalry as major, and served with that regiment continuously until he became its colonel, on the 3d of May, 1861. The great civil war found him at his post, true and firm, amidst the terrible pressure he encountered by reason of his birthplace, Virginia; and President Lincoln commissioned him as a brigadier-general of volunteers and sent him to Kentucky. There, too, his services were constant and eminent in the highest degree. He won the first battle in the West, at Mill Spring, Kentucky, and from first to last, without a day's or an hour's intermission, he was at his post of duty, rising steadily and irresistibly through all the grades to the one he held as major-general of the regular army at the time of his death. At Shiloh, Corinth, Perryville, Stone River, Chickamauga, Chattanooga, Atlanta, and Nashville he fulfilled the proudest hopes of his ardent friends, and at the close of the war General George H. Thomas stood in the very front rank of our war generals.

"The general has known General Thomas intimately since they sat as boys on the same bench, and the quality in him, which he holds up for the admiration and example of the young, is his complete and entire devotion to duty. Though sent to Florida, to Mexico, to Texas, and to Arizona, when duty there was absolute banishment, he went cheerfully, and never asked a personal favor, exemption, or leave of absence. In battle he never wavered. Firm, and of full faith in his cause, he knew it would prevail, and he never sought advancement of rank or honor at the expense of any one. Whatever he earned of these were his own, and no one disputes his fame. The very impersonation of honesty, integrity, and honor, he will stand to us as the *beau ideal* of the soldier and gentleman.

"Though he leaves no child to bear his name, the old Army of the Cumberland, numbered by tens of thousands, called him father, and will weep for him tears of manly grief.

"His wife, who cheered him with her messages of love in the darkest hours of war, will mourn him now in sadness, chastened by the sympathy of a whole country.

"The last sad rites due him as a man and a soldier will be paid at Troy, New York, on the arrival of his remains and of his family, and all his old comrades who can be present are invited there to share in the obsequies.

"At all military posts and stations the flag will be placed at half-staff, and fifteen minute-guns fired on the day after the receipt of this order, and the usual badges of mourning will be worn for thirty days.

"By command of General Sherman.
   [Signed]   "E. D. TOWNSEND,
                              "Adjutant-General."

The foregoing general order, issued the day after the demise of General Thomas, was carried on the wings of lightning to all parts of the world. A mighty man had fallen. Sorrow and sadness filled the hearts of all, and "tears of manly grief" demonstrated the intensity and sincerity of the nation's sorrow.

It being the desire of Mrs. Thomas that the remains of her

husband should be deposited in the family vault at Troy, New York, the same were forwarded by rail in charge of his former personal staff, with a suitable guard, and arrived in Troy on the 7th day of April, 1870. The expressions of respect to the memory of the distinguished dead on the entire route from San Francisco gave unmistakable tokens of the popular grief caused by the demise of one of the noblest of the hero chieftains of our country. The funeral services took place at Troy on the 8th. The following particulars are derived from copies of the *Albany Evening Journal*, kindly furnished by Mr. George C. Bishop.

The train bearing the remains was met at Schenectady by a large delegation of the prominent men of Troy and Albany. The body reposed in the rear car, upon a catafalque erected in the centre, and guarded by ten men belonging to the Second United States Cavalry. An immense throng of people assembled at the Troy depot eager to see the casket that contained the remains of the lamented dead. On the arrival of the train the body was taken to the St. Paul's Episcopal Church, and soon the doors of the edifice were thrown open, and the coffin, draped with flags and trimmed with evergreens, was exposed to view. The sword worn by the gallant soldier on so many gory fields rested upon the casket. A large number of distinguished men were present to show their respect for the memory of the great and good man by participating in the solemn services of the day. Among those present were the President of the United States, members of the Cabinet, representatives from both Houses of Congress, Governors of several States, etc., etc.

The public buildings and many of the private residences were decorated with funeral emblems, and flags at half-mast were seen in all parts of the city.

That there was a deep sense of the loss which the nation had sustained in the death of the lamented hero was evident on all sides.

The funeral exercises at the church were brief. The service was read by Bishop Doane, of Albany.

HYMN.

"Brief life is here our portion,
    Brief sorrow, short-lived care;
The life that knows no ending,
    The tearless life, is there.

"Oh, happy retribution!
    Short toil, eternal rest,
For mortals and for sinners,
    A mansion with the blest.

"And now we fight the battle,
    But then shall wear the crown
Of full and everlasting
    And passionless renown.

"The morning shall awaken,
    The shadows pass away,
And each true-hearted servant
    Shall shine as doth the day.

"Oh, sweet and blessed country,
    The home of God's elect!
Oh, sweet and blessed country,
    That eager hearts expect!

"Jesus, in mercy bring us
    To that dear land of rest,
Who art, with God the Father
    And Spirit, ever blest. AMEN."

Psalms: "Lord, let me know my end, and the number of my days," etc.

Job xix. 25, 26, 27: "I know that my Redeemer liveth, and that he shall stand at the latter day upon the earth. And though after my skin worms destroy this body, yet in my flesh shall I see God: Whom I shall see for myself."

1 Cor. xv. 21, 22: "Since by man came death, by man came also the resurrection of the dead. For as in Adam all die, even so in Christ shall all be made alive."

Dirge from Oratorio of "Samson":

> "Bring the laurels bring the bays,
> Strew the hearse, and strew the ways.
> Glorious hero, may thy grave
> Peace and honor ever have."

HYMN.

> "Jesus lives! no longer now
>   Can thy terrors, Death, appall us;
> Jesus lives! by this we know
>   Thou, O Grave, canst not enthrall us.

> "Jesus lives! for us he died;
>   Then alone to Jesus, living
> Pure in heart, may we abide,
>   Glory to our Saviour giving.

> "Jesus lives! our hearts know well
>   Naught from us His love shall sever;
> Life nor death nor powers of hell
>   Fear us from His keeping ever.

> "Jesus lives! to Him the throne
>   Over all the world is given;
> May we go where He is gone,
>   Rest and reign with Him in heaven."

The pall-bearers were

  Major-General George G. Meade.
  Major-General W. S. Rosecrans.
  Major-General J. M. Schofield.
  Major-General W. B. Hazen.
  Major-General Gordon Granger.
  Major-General John Newton.
  Major-General —— McKay.
  Major-General Joseph Hooker.

At the conclusion of the funeral services the remains were removed to the hearse, and the procession was formed and slowly wended its way through the streets to the cemetery. The thoroughfares along the line of march were literally crowded to suffocation by persons anxious to get a glimpse of the hearse. After the body had been placed in the family vault, the procession was reformed and returned to the city, where it was dismissed, thus closing a pageant which will be long remembered by the citizens of Troy, and which was a fitting tribute to the memory of one of our greatest soldiers. The following article appeared as an editorial in the *Albany Evening Journal* of April 8, 1870:

"The weather is auspicious. Bright skies and a balmy air greet those who to-day, in a neighboring city, are bearing to their last resting-place the remains of a great, a lamented soldier. Our condensed report shows that the ceremonies are of a most imposing character. Comrades of the departed warrior, men whose names, with his, are inseparably linked to the nation's history, and whose fame is world-wide, veterans of many a hard-fought field, battalions of Federal troops, regiments of citizen-soldiery, and multitudes of people escort the dead warrior to his last resting-place. Nor is this a mere hollow pageant. It bespeaks the sincere and general grief of a people who feel that they have suffered no common loss, and is the deserved tribute of his grateful and admiring countrymen to the memory of one who was not only a splendid soldier, but likewise a model man."

At the time of the death of General Thomas he was President of the "Society of the Army of the Cumberland," and at the following meeting General Charles Cruft, in the absence of General Garfield, chairman of the Committee on Memorial, reported the following preamble and resolutions:

"On the 28th of March, 1870, Major-General George H. Thomas, the great soldier, who had presided over this Society from its institution, fell at his post, with all his harness on. His spirit returned to God, who gave it, and the memory of his greatness and goodness is all that is left to us. His death was a national calamity and an irreparable loss to his comrades.

"*Therefore be it Resolved*, That it is vain by words to attempt to express our loss, or to describe the grief which pervades this Society in view of this sad event.

"*Resolved*, That the banners of this Society be draped in mourning, and that an appropriate memorial page be inscribed upon its records.

"*Resolved*, That some fitting monument should be erected by his countrymen to mark the spot where the remains of our beloved commander rests; and that this Society shall take the initiatory steps for its erection; and to that end a committee of one from each State represented in the Society be now appointed to arrange some method to procure the necessary funds, and to provide a design, specifications, and estimates therefor, and to report at the next meeting."

In compliance with the recommendation contained in the last resolution, the Chair appointed the following committee:

General J. D. Cox, Ohio.
General Joseph Hooker, New York.
General O. C. Loomis, Michigan.
General John M. Palmer, Illinois.
General John A. Martin, Kansas.
General William Vandever, Iowa.
General Nathan Kimball, Indiana.
General John T. Croxton, Kentucky.
General Gates P. Thruston, Tennessee.
General John W. Bishop, Minnesota.
General R. H. Ramsey, Pennsylvania.
General N. P. Cogswell, Massachusetts.
General Charles F. Manderson, Nebraska.
General D. S. Stanley, Dakotah Territory.
General Horace Porter, District of Columbia.
Colonel W. H. Sinclair, Texas.
Surgeon J. D. Bromley, New Jersey.
Colonel J. N. Burke, Georgia.
Colonel Joseph Howard, West Virginia.

After ten years of incessant labor the statue was completed, and the eleventh annual reunion of the Society was fixed upon for the time of unveiling the same. An unusually large attendance of the members of the Society, and other kindred societies, attested the high appreciation in which he was held, not only by his old soldiers, but by all those who respected true loyalty, unflinching courage, and true manhood.

It would be interesting to the general reader if the letters accepting the invitations to attend, and those expressing their regret at not being able to meet with their old army friends, could all be given in the body of this work, but this cannot be done. A few are selected as showing the high and exalted position occupied by General Thomas in the hearts and affections of the people of this nation.

FROM LIEUTENANT-GENERAL P. H. SHERIDAN.
"HEADQUARTERS MILITARY DIVISION OF MISSOURI,
"CHICAGO, ILL., November 16, 1879.

"TO THE MEMBERS OF THE SOCIETY OF THE ARMY OF THE CUMBERLAND:

"GENTLEMEN,—To my deep regret I am compelled to state that my physicians have forbidden my attendance at the forthcoming meeting of our Society. I have been confined to my house for nearly two weeks past with an obstinate bronchial trouble, which does not readily yield to medical treatment, and, despite my earnest solicitations, my medical advisers have positively refused to permit me to go to Washington, or, in fact, to leave my room.

"To those who know how deeply I have been interested in the completion of the statue to our old commander, General George H. Thomas, which is to be unveiled on the 19th instant, and how anxiously I have waited to see you all again, after nearly three years of separation, there will be no need of saying how great a disappointment it is to me; but I wish, more especially for the information of those with whom I have not been in immediate correspondence, that they may know that I am not neglectful of the interest of the Society, nor wanting in devotion to the memory of one of our purest and best men. No one among you will appreciate the privileges of our reunion more than I should have done, and none can be more anxious to do honor to the memory of our grand and good general than myself. But for once I am unable to ignore the state of my health, and have had to succumb to the orders of the surgeons. I trust and believe that you will have a happy time, and I know that many hallowed memories will cling around the moment when you first unveil the statue of the man who stood like a rock against the adverse fortunes of the bloody day of Chickamauga.

"With my earnest wishes for the good health and happiness of each and all of you,

"I am, sincerely, your friend,
"P. H. SHERIDAN."

FROM GENERAL U. S. GRANT.

"PALACE HOTEL, SAN FRANCISCO, October 21, 1879.
"GENERAL H. M. CIST, Corresponding Secretary Society Army of the Cumberland.

"DEAR SIR,—On my return from Oregon this A.M. I find your invitation for me to be present at the meeting of the Society of the Army of the Cumberland, on the 19th and 20th of November. I would like specially to be present at your next meeting to testify my profound respect and esteem for the worthy, patriotic, and brave old soldier, General George H. Thomas, whose monument is to be unveiled on that occasion, but I fear I shall not be able to do so. But I do not pronounce yet positively that I will not be there. I have telegraphed to General Sherman to-day on the same subject, saying that I would be able to decide when I meet him in Chicago, one week before your meeting.

"Be assured, if I am not there, my desire to be will be as great as that of any one.

"Very truly yours,
"U. S. Grant."

From General John Pope.

"Headquarters Department of the Missouri,
"Fort Leavenworth, Kansas, November 6, 1879.

"My dear Colonel,—I find myself, greatly to my regret, unable to accept the invitation to be present and participate in the ceremonies at the unveiling of the Thomas statue in Washington, on the 20th inst.

"No one would be more rejoiced than I to embrace any opportunity to show his respect for this great and good man and soldier, and it is a real pain to me to be obliged to decline. The difficulties in progress with the Utes and Apaches in this Department, and the organization and direction of troops moving against them, render it wholly improper and inexpedient that I should be absent from here at such a distance and for such a time, and I beg that you will convey to the Committee my thanks for their consideration, and my great regret at my inability to avail myself of it. Every soldier will readily understand my position.

"Sincerely yours,
"John Pope.
"Colonel H. C. Corbin, U.S.A., etc."

From General T. J. Wood.

"Dayton, Ohio, November 17, 1879.

"My dear Colonel,—I can't tell you how much I regret

that I can't be with you on the 19th and 20th instants. But so it is. Mrs. Wood and my oldest son are prostrated with the typhoid fever, and I must stay with them.

"I have charged our mutual friend, Major Bickham, to express to our assembled comrades how much I regret my inability to participate in rendering this great tribute to our best-loved and most successful commander. I ask you to do the same.

"Your friend and comrade,
"TH. J. WOOD."

FROM U. S. SENATOR MAXEY.

"PARIS, TEXAS, November 8, 1879.
"H. C. CORBIN, ESQ., Secretary, etc., Washington.

"DEAR SIR,—I have the honor to acknowledge the courtesy of an invitation to the eleventh reunion of the Society of the Army of the Cumberland and the unveiling of the Thomas statue, November 19th and 20th insts., and regret that my engagements are such that it will be impracticable for me to reach Washington until after that date.

"I first became acquainted with General Thomas during the Mexican war. He was a massive man. During the late war it was very generally regretted by officers of the Confederate army that his sense of duty led him away from us. No man doubted that he would prove true and invulnerable to the cause he espoused. General Thomas had the good fortune to command the respect of the Union and Confederate armies.

"He made war according to the best usages of modern warfare, and not otherwise. No Confederate doubted honorable treatment at the hands of General Thomas, should he be so unfortunate as to become a prisoner of war.

"General Thomas will go down in history as a prominent

and honorable actor in the grandest and best-fought war recorded in history, and its pages will not, as to him, be blurred by one harsh, unkind, or dishonorable act.

"Most respectfully,
"Your obedient servant,
"S. B. MAXEY."

From U. S. Senator M. C. Butler.

"EDGEFIELD, S. C., November 7, 1879.

"GENTLEMEN,—Your invitation to myself and family to be present at the unveiling of the Thomas statue on the 19th and 20th insts. is just received.

"I shall be compelled to remain at home until after the first Monday in December, on account of urgent professional engagements, and therefore will not be able to accept your invitation; otherwise, I should have great pleasure in being present at your interesting ceremonies, whereby you propose to do honor to the memory of one of the ablest of American soldiers.

"Please accept my thanks for the invitation.
"I have the honor to be,
"Very truly and respectfully,
"Your obedient servant,
"M. C. BUTLER."

From Senator R. E. Withers.

"WYTHEVILLE, VA., November 17, 1879.

"COMMITTEE OF INVITATION, Society of the Army of the Cumberland, Washington, D. C.

"GENTLEMEN,—I find that it will not be in my power to be present at the interesting ceremonies incident to the dedication of the statue of General Thomas. The occasion is one of great interest to all who admire manliness and courage, unselfish devotion to duty, and military genius of the highest order.

"Regretting the necessity which forbids my attendance on the 20th, I am,

"Very respectfully,
"Your obedient servant,
"R. E. WITHERS."

FROM JUSTICE S. F. MILLER.

"SUPREME COURT OF THE UNITED STATES,
"WASHINGTON, November 10, 1879.

"MESSRS. JAMES A. GARFIELD, THOMAS L. YOUNG, A. McD. McCOOK, Committee:

"I accept with pleasure your invitation, in behalf of the Society of the Army of the Cumberland, to be present at the ceremonies of unveiling the statue of General Thomas, the pure man, the noble soldier, and successful general. He well deserves the affection of his comrades and the gratitude of his country bestowed upon his memory.

"I have the honor to be
"Your obedient servant,
"SAM. F. MILLER."

FROM COLONEL B. H. BRISTOW.

"NEW YORK, November 7, 1879.

"MY DEAR COLONEL,—Pray accept my cordial thanks for your kind note conveying a special invitation to the reunion of the Society of the Army of the Cumberland, on the 19th and 20th instants.

"It would give me inexpressible pleasure to join the members of the Society in paying homage to the memory of our grand old commander.

"The survivors of his army cannot perform a better service for the country than the act of unveiling the statue of his manly form, and giving to the public some idea of the life and character of Major-General George H. Thomas, as we saw and knew him in daily intercourse in field and camp. His was a character to be studied and copied. No greater exemplar can be set before the youth of America.

"I knew and loved General Thomas too well to fail, for any ordinary reason, to be present on the occasion to which your note invites me.

"With sincere regard, I am,

"Very truly yours,

"B. H. BRISTOW.

"COLONEL H. C. CORBIN."

FROM GENERAL JOHN M. PALMER.

"SPRINGFIELD, ILL., November 17, 1879.

"GENTLEMEN,—I have until the latest moment withheld my acknowledgment of your invitation to be present at Washington on the 19th instant, to meet with the Army of the Cumberland and participate in the ceremony of unveiling the statue of General George H. Thomas, with the hope that I would be able to accept it; but I am now forced by engagements I am unable to postpone or evade to deny myself the pleasure of doing so.

"I have for months looked forward to the meeting of my comrades at Washington, and the proposed honors to the memory of our great leader, with the greatest satisfaction, and am unable to express the disappointment I feel at finding myself unable to be present. But I beg to assure you that each and every member of 'the Old Army' have a large share of my affectionate regards, and that no one who will look upon the chiselled form and features of the great soldier, the disinterested, pure, patriotic man and citizen, whose statue will stand before you, will then remember him more vividly than I do now, or will more venerate his memory.

"With sentiments of the highest respect for each of you personally, and of affection for all the members of 'the Grand Army' present and those scattered abroad,

"I am, as ever, etc.,

"JOHN M. PALMER."

FROM GENERAL J. H. WILSON.

"BOSTON, November 18, 1879.

"H. C. CORBIN, ESQ., Secretary Local Executive Committee,
"Washington, D. C.:

"DEAR SIR,—I regret more than I can find words to express that I am prevented, by pressure of engagements I cannot defer, from being present at the unveiling of the Thomas statue. My regret is the more profound because I have the greatest respect for the exalted character of General Thomas. He was a true hero, if one ever lived; a great soldier, if one ever died. His patriotism was beyond that of most men, while his devotion to duty was an all-absorbing principle. In every relation of life he was a modest, upright, fearless, self-respecting, stainless gentleman, such as all men and all ages should honor while living and hold in lasting reverence when dead. Of him it may well be said he was

"'Patient in toil, serene in alarms,
Inflexible in faith, invincible in arms!'

"No nobler subject could be found for monumental brass; no purer one be enshrined in the hearts of his admiring and grateful countrymen.

"Again regretting that I cannot be with you, I am

"Very respectfully yours,

"J. H. WILSON."

FROM GENERAL DANIEL BUTTERFIELD.

"UNION CLUB, November 3, 1879.

"GENERAL,—I have the honor to acknowledge the receipt of invitation to be present at the next reunion of the Army of the Cumberland and the ceremony of unveiling of the statue of that noblest of heroes and best of men, our beloved commander, General George H. Thomas. I shall attend with great pleasure and satisfaction.

"Our noble old commander had no superior as a soldier and gentleman in the army, and very few equals. Rather than miss the opportunity to do this deserved honor to his memory, I would walk from here to Washington.

"Very truly yours,

"DANIEL BUTTERFIELD."

"GENERAL J. A. GARFIELD, Chairman, etc."

FROM GENERAL H. W. BENHAM.

"UNITED STATES ENGINEER'S OFFICE,
"NEW YORK CITY, November 7, 1879.

"H. C. CORBIN, ESQ., Secretary, etc., Washington:

"DEAR SIR,—I have the honor to acknowledge your invitation to be present at the unveiling of the Thomas statue at Washington, upon the 19th and 20th of this month; and I regret to fear that I shall not have the pleasure of being able to be present upon that interesting occasion.

"For, in a full knowledge of this most worthily honored officer, from cadet-life upward, in service in Florida and upon the field of Buena Vista, and as commander of a fortress near Boston afterwards, I can say that I have never known any one who combined in a greater degree the highest qualities of the man and the soldier—such iron integrity of principle, such unyielding bravery, and such unsurpassed judgment in action—as the man you now honor.

"Very respectfully,
"Your most obedient servant,
"H. W. BENHAM,
"Brevet Major-General U.S.A."

FROM GENERAL WILLIAM BIRNEY.

"WASHINGTON, November 15, 1879.

"DEAR SIR,—I accept the invitation.

"General Thomas was the ideal of the patriot, soldier, good man, and gentleman, as nearly as any character in history; and his battle of Nashville reflects the highest credit upon him as a general. It was at all points one of the most able and scientific.

"Yours,
"WILLIAM BIRNEY,
"Ex-Brevet Major-General U. S. Vols."

FROM GENERAL GEORGE W. CULLUM.

"315 FIFTH AVENUE, NEW YORK, November 15, 1879.

"GENTLEMEN,—The great pleasure I had promised myself of accepting your invitation to be present at the unveiling of the Thomas statue, I extremely regret I am at the last moment obliged to decline.

"Beside my warm personal regard for Thomas, I had an enthusiastic admiration of him as the unsurpassed soldier of our great civil contest,—the general who had never been defeated, and the leader of armies whose victories had placed him among the greatest heroes of the republic. Thomas was one of those rare men whose 'courage mounteth with the occasion,' who was most conspicuous, coolest, and fertile in invention, and most tremendous in energy, in the exigency of conflict, and who in the day's turning-point, at the white-heat of that furnace-fire of battle which tries the soldier's soul, was the most lustrous.

"Again regretting that I cannot be with you on this most interesting occasion, I have the honor to be,

"Very respectfully and truly,
"Your most obedient,
"GEORGE W. CULLUM,
"Brevet Major-General U.S.A."

FROM GENERAL JOHN GIBBON.

"FORT SNELLING, MINNESOTA, November 11, 1879.

"DEAR MCCOOK,—I am much obliged to you for sending me an invitation to the Army of the Cumberland meeting and the unveiling of the statue of one of the noblest men and soldiers the world has ever known. But I cannot come, I am sorry to say; and as the printed card asks me to signify my acceptance to the secretary of the committee, I consider myself at liberty to address my declination to you.

"Many complimentary things will be said of General Thomas on the occasion, but none will be too good for the man; and I hope he will be long held up to the rising generation as the model soldier and man, whose death was a national calamity. We could ill afford to lose him, and I sincerely wish his type was more common in the army than it is.

"Very truly yours,
"JOHN GIBBON."

From Hon. HAMILTON FISH.

"GLENCLYFFE, GAINSON'S P.-O., N. Y., November 8, 1879.

"H. C. CORBIN, ESQ., Secretary, etc., Washington, D. C.:

"DEAR SIR,—I am in receipt of the invitation, addressed to the president of the Union League Club (New York), inviting myself and the members of the club to participate with the Society of the Army of the Cumberland in the ceremonies incident to the unveiling of the Thomas statue.

"I regret that the state of my health will not allow me to indulge the hope that I may be present on this interesting occasion.

"I am in the country, unable to see any of the members of the Club, but send the invitation to the secretary, confident that the members will appreciate the compliment of the invitation, and that such as can will be glad to unite with your Society in rendering honors to one of the most gallant of the soldiers of his country.

"I am, very respectfully,
"HAMILTON FISH,
"President Union League Club, New York."

From General W. P. CARLIN.

"HEADQUARTERS, FORT YATES, D. T., November 13, 1879.

"COLONEL H. C. CORBIN, Secretary of the Committee Society of the Army of the Cumberland, Washington, D. C.:

"DEAR SIR,—I regret deeply that I shall be unable to

accept the invitation of the committee to attend the eleventh annual reunion of the Society of the Army of the Cumberland and the unveiling of the equestrian statue of our honored commander, Major-General George H. Thomas, on the 19th and 20th instants.

"It would be extremely gratifying to behold the monument to one who so richly deserved to be thus commemorated by his countrymen and his comrades-in-arms. The Society of the Army of the Cumberland has done itself honor by erecting a monument to General Thomas. The memory of such a man should be perpetuated. When future generations seek in history for a character that was perfectly true and perfectly just and perfectly unselfish, they will find it in the life of Major-General George H. Thomas.

"Very respectfully,
"Your obedient servant,
"W. P. CARLIN,
"Brevet Major-General U.S.A."

FROM GOVERNOR R. W. COBB.

"STATE OF ALABAMA, EXECUTIVE DEPARTMENT,
"MONTGOMERY, ALA., November 18, 1879.

"GENERAL A. McD. McCOOK, Washington City, D. C.:

"GENERAL,—I regret that it will not be in my power to accept your invitation to attend the eleventh reunion of the Society of the Army of the Cumberland and participate in the ceremonies attending the unveiling of the Thomas statue. I should be happy to form the acquaintance of your gallant companions-in-arms who will be present on that occasion and join them in homage to the memory of an illustrious citizen, whose valor and achievements are the theme of some of the most brilliant chapters in American history. It was my fortune to fight on the other side, but I none the less appreciate the devotion and sacrifices of the Union soldier, and am none the less proud of his splendid deeds of endurance and daring.

"Very respectfully, general,
"Your obedient servant,
"R. W. COBB."

FROM GOVERNOR GEORGE B. McCLELLAN.

"STATE OF NEW JERSEY, EXECUTIVE DEPARTMENT,
"TRENTON, November 16, 1879.

"COLONEL H. C. CORBIN, Secretary of Committee:

"SIR,—I have deferred acknowledging the committee's very courteous invitation to be present at the unveiling of the statue of General George H. Thomas, with the hope that I might feel myself able to attend. I regret, most sincerely, that a too slow recovery from a severe illness obliges me to absent myself.

"No one could esteem more highly than myself the honor of being permitted to unite in doing honor to the memory of one whose merits as a soldier and a man should secure for him a high and lasting place in the memory of his country. Those who served under his orders—so often the best judges of military merit—have never, I think, failed to do him ample justice.

"Even had he no other title to fame as a soldier and to gratitude as a citizen, the magnificent self-possession with which he disregarded the attempts of men ignorant of the circumstances, or incapable of appreciating them, to force him to give battle prematurely, and the admirable skill and force with which he fought the battle of Nashville when the proper moment arrived, would alone suffice to place him high, very high, on the list of those accomplished generals who have deserved well of America.

"Regretting from my heart that I cannot unite with his immediate comrades of the gallant Army of the Cumberland in laying one more tribute of admiration and respect upon the monument of the man I am proud to regard as a friend and comrade,

"I am, very truly,
"Your obedient servant,
"GEO. B. MCCLELLAN."

FROM GOVERNOR CHARLES M. CROSWELL.

"STATE OF MICHIGAN, EXECUTIVE OFFICE,
"ADRIAN, November 15, 1879.

"SIR,—I am in receipt of your very courteous invitation to attend the eleventh reunion of the Society of the Army of the Cumberland, and to participate in the ceremonies attending the unveiling of the Thomas statue at Washington, on the 19th and 20th days of the present month.

"I would gladly join you on the occasion referred to in doing honor to the memory of one of the truest and noblest of those heroes whose skill and valor saved to us a nation unbroken, but I regret to say that my official engagements are such as to prevent my being present and personally participating in the proceedings.

"Thanking you cordially for your kind invitation,
"I am, your obedient servant,
"CHARLES M. CROSWELL."

FROM EX-GOVERNOR HILIARD HALL.

"NORTH BENNINGTON, VT., November 17, 1879.

"DEAR SIR,—I should be glad to manifest my high admiration of the military services and character of General

Thomas, and my enduring respect for his memory, by being present at the unveiling of his statue in Washington, but the distance from my residence and my great age—nearly eighty-five—must necessarily prevent my attendance.

"I am, dear sir,
"Very respectfully yours,
"HILIARD HALL.
"H. C. CORBIN, ESQ.,
"Secretary of Committee of the General Thomas statue."

FROM HON. ALFRED M. SCALES.

"HON. JAMES A. GARFIELD, AND OTHERS,—The invitation from you to be present at the unveiling of the Thomas statue has been duly received. This is a worthy tribute of a great country to one of her greatest soldiers, and, while I feel honored by the invitation, I regret to say that prior and indispensable engagements will compel my absence.
"Very respectfully,
"A. M. SCALES."

FROM GOVERNOR WM. E. SMITH.

"STATE OF WISCONSIN, EXECUTIVE DEPARTMENT,
"MADISON, November 11, 1879.

"H. C. CORBIN, ESQ., Secretary Local Executive Committee Society of the Army of the Cumberland, 1221 H Street, Washington, D. C.:

"SIR,—I have had the honor to receive, for myself and staff, an invitation to attend the eleventh reunion of the Society of the Army of the Cumberland, November 19th and 20th instants, and participate in the ceremonies attending the unveiling of the Thomas statue, and beg to return to the committee my very sincere thanks therefor, with the assurance that I much regret that official duties will prevent me from leaving Wisconsin at that time. Were my engagements less pressing, I should most assuredly avail myself of the privilege and the honor of attending this reunion, and testifying to the high esteem in which the fame and memory of General Thomas is held by myself and all the patriotic people of Wisconsin.

"Very respectfully,
"Your obedient servant,
"WM. E. SMITH."

FROM COLONEL TOLAND JONES.

"LONDON, OHIO, November 12, 1879.

"COLONEL H. C. CORBIN, Washington, D. C.:

"DEAR SIR,—I have been in receipt of your kind invitation to attend the reunion of the Army of the Cumberland, to be held on the 19th and 20th of this present month, and know not what to say, for I am so anxious to be with you, and dare not say that I will, and cannot say now that I will not.

"But it matters but very little about my presence, in consideration of the great concourse which will assemble to do honor to the greatest hero of the Army of the Cumberland.

"I would like to see the brazen image of our grand old hero unveiled,—that image cast from the brass that under his direction hurled the iron into the soul of the Rebellion, and did so much to perpetuate the Union, which was the pole star of all his actions. That mute statue of that most modest hero, I hope, will stand and speak to untold generations of admiring patriots in all this land while history traces the grandest deeds of earth's noblest men.

"I have the honor, Colonel, to be,
"Yours most truly,
"TOLAND JONES."

From Hon. John Tyler, Jr.

"Washington City, November 15, 1879.

"Colonel H. C. Corbin, Secretary Committee Eleventh Reunion Army of the Cumberland:

"Colonel,—I have received your invitation, on behalf of the Society of the Army of the Cumberland, to the unveiling of the Thomas statue, addressed to myself and daughters, and accept the courtesy.

"United with General Thomas by family ties and those of blood, the honors paid to his memory are more than ordinarily gratifying to us.

"The last private letter that he wrote before his death was most likely to myself, in kindly reference to those of our joint houses, and my reply was on its way to him when the telegraph announced his decease.

"With sincere acknowledgments,

"John Tyler, Jr."

From General William H. Gibson.

"Tiffin, Ohio, October 31, 1879.

"Thomas L. Young:

"Dear General,—I have yours of the 28th instant, urging my attendance at the approaching reunion of the Society of the Army of the Cumberland. It is my purpose to be present on that occasion, and I hope to meet thousands of that grand old organization, gathered from the ends of the earth to honor the memory of the 'grandest Roman of them all,' the immortal General George H. Thomas.

"I shall do all in my power to secure a movement 'in force' upon the capital, to renew old memories and exchange greetings.

"I am, very truly,

"William H. Gibson."

FROM GENERAL M. R. MORGAN.

"ST. PAUL, MINNESOTA, November 10, 1879.
"COLONEL H. C. CORBIN, U. S. Army, Secretary Executive Committee Society of the Army of the Cumberland, Washington, D. C.:

"DEAR COLONEL,—I regret I am so far away from Washington at this time that I find it impracticable to be with you on the 19th and 20th. Although I cannot be there to join in doing honor to the memory of General George H. Thomas, now, as always since my boyhood, I have for him but affectionate remembrances. All demonstrations in honor of such a man are in the interest of those virtues which a nation should delight to foster.

"I am, most sincerely,
"M. R. MORGAN,
"Brigadier-General (by brevet) U.S.A."

FROM COLONEL ALFRED L. HOUGH.

"CAMP ON THE ANIMOS, COL., November 7, 1879.
"H. C. CORBIN, Secretary of Committee.:

"SIR,—I respectfully acknowledge the receipt of request to attend the eleventh reunion of the Society of the Army of the Cumberland. In great disappointment I am compelled to inform the committee that I cannot be present.

"I have long looked forward to the promised pleasure and duty of assisting in unveiling the statue of our loved commander, but fate wills it differently.

"My long and close official connection with General Thomas, ending only with his life, my personal affection for him in life, and my veneration of his memory would seem to make it incumbent that I should be with my comrades in their performance of so pleasant a duty, but a threatened Indian war has hurried me from a comparatively Eastern post to the mountains of Colorado, and duty detains me here.

"I trust you will have a brotherly reunion, as you cannot but have when the memory of our grand hero, whom we all so loved, shall be so vividly brought to your minds and hearts.

"Very truly and affectionately,
"Your comrade,
"A. L. HOUGH."

From Captain E. A. Otis.

"CHICAGO, November 14, 1879.
"GENERAL JAMES A. GARFIELD, Chairman Executive Committee, etc., Washington, D. C. :

"GENERAL,—I have delayed an answer to the invitation to attend the reunion of our Society, hoping to meet with you, but positive engagements prevent it.

"The occasion is one of deep interest, not only to our Society, but to every soldier in the grand old Army of the Cumberland.

"The unveiling of the statue of our glorious leader, General George H. Thomas, is an event of wide significance. The place has been appropriately chosen. At the seat of government of the nation which he served so loyally and well, his monument, raised by the loving hands of his old comrades, will remain to future ages, while his memory will be enshrined forever in the hearts of a grateful and patriotic people. Deeply regretting that I cannot be with you in person, as I am in spirit, I remain,

"Fraternally yours,
"E. A. OTIS."

The foregoing letters, representing all the parts of our republic, include letters from those who were on the opposite side in the great contest of 1861-65. It will be seen that Thomas commanded the admiration not only of his friends, but also of those who were for a short time his enemies.

After the statue was unveiled, various persons were called upon for impromptu speeches, a few of which are here reproduced.

Speech of General W. T. Sherman.

"Mr. President, Comrades of the Army of the Cumberland, Ladies and Gentlemen,—There is a custom in army societies, I think more honored in the breach than in the observance, after the regular exercises are over, to call upon friends to make a few remarks. We call it a 'bummer meeting,' and it generally consists in making a few remarks for the purpose of creating laughter. But on this occasion I disclaim feeling disposed to adhere to that system of making fun. Because we have assembled to-day, and we have all been impressed with the majestic appearance of the statue, and every citizen of Washington, and every member of the Army of the Cumberland, and I, your friend and once your own commander, thank you all for having done a noble work and done it well. The relations between Thomas and myself were more of a social character than of the commander and commanded. You remember that our acquaintance began in boyhood, and it was very hard, after growing up side by side with him, afterwards to believe him to be a hero. But I know that General Thomas had noble qualities. I have listened to him thousands of times before the civil war,—we had been comrades together long before we dreamed of a civil war. You men only saw him in his military dignity; you did not, could not, love him as we did. Here is Van Vliet, the only classmate beside myself who survived his class of '42. Yes, comrades, at West Point, in 1836, we entered almost together, and stayed there till '42, and we afterwards served together fourteen almost consecutive years, long before we thought about the Army of the Cumberland, or cared for it, and I am glad now to be able to add something to the praise to which he is entitled in America's history. I have been on every occasion pleased to hear others speak of George H. Thomas, and when Garfield, in 1870, spoke in Cleveland, Ohio, I thought he had capped the climax and made a picture that would stand forever. The monument which Garfield erected in that reunion held at Cleveland stands high in my memory and will live forever in history. Again, here in your own capital, as the news of the death of Thomas came in on that April day in 1870, there was a memorial service, and Chief Justice Chase, Generals Stark, Garfield, Cox, and Warner all spoke on this noble subject. I said a few words, and, indeed, that day remarks were made that are forever recorded on the pages of history. The orator this morning made several points that remained deeply fixed in my mind. The fact that Thomas began at the bottom as a soldier,—a cadet, a second lieutenant and first lieutenant, and captain, and major, lieutenant-colonel, brigadier-general, and major-general,—outlines his noble character, and nothing could prevail against that powerful element in his character that forbade him to jump over intermediate grades of command. There is another point which Matthews spoke of to-day, and I want to impress it on the Virginians. The day is coming, gentlemen of Virginia, of North Carolina, of South Carolina, of Alabama, when you and your fellow-citizens will be making their pilgrimage to this magnificent monument, just as all have done to that of Washington, and say that there was a man who, under the tumult and excitement of the times, stood true and firm to his country, and he is the hero, and that brave George Thomas will become the idol of the South. I predict it, gentlemen; I won't be alive then, nor I don't want to live long enough to see it. There is one other point, gentlemen, and I will give place to some one else. There is a point of history which I wish to mention, and which seems to me to have been entirely forgotten. George Thomas was indebted for his first commission as brigadier-general to Robert Anderson, and to him alone. I was present myself, and I heard him ask Mr. Lincoln to appoint Thomas a brigadier-general, to allow him to go with him into Kentucky. I know that the promise was fulfilled, for I went with him to Kentucky to Robert Anderson. Gentlemen of the Army of the Cumberland, you owe the fact that you had such a man as Thomas, from the first to the last days of his glorious career, to Anderson. Yet there are men now living who write and publish that Robert Anderson was not true. If George Washington was a traitor, then Anderson was a traitor; but if Washington was a patriot, then so was Robert Anderson. That man could not bear even to think of anything wrong, and any man that talks about Robert Anderson—well, I had better not say anything more about that man. George Thomas and Robert Anderson, your first commanders: they were the first in Kentucky to organize the Army of the Cumberland,—not the great aggressive army itself, but the grand nucleus of that army. You have the right to look to that army, for it has acquired its reputation through your courage and loyalty, and your reputation is dear to me as it is to all of you. Yes, friends and fellow-soldiers, I wish I had you all in one compass, so that there wouldn't be ladies and gentlemen and citizens to hear us. I wish that I could have a few hours' talk with you, and I could explain to you a great many things which you don't understand."

Speech of Secretary McCrary.

"Mr. President, Ladies and Gentlemen,—I know not what I, a civilian, can say to you upon this occasion. It appears to me to be an occasion when you desire and expect to hear from those heroes of the great war who are here to-night in such large numbers. Perhaps, however, it may not be inappropriate for me to extend to the Society of the Army of the Cumberland, upon this most interesting occasion, hearty greeting from the people of my own State of Iowa, and to say to you in their name that I know they all, both soldiers and citizens, feel a deep interest in these proceedings, and earnestly desire, in common with the people of the entire country, to join with you in giving all honor to the memory of that brave, patient, patriotic soldier, George H. Thomas.

"The people of the State of Iowa will yield to none in rendering all honor, all praise, all glory, not only to the officers, but to the men who stood in the ranks and fought the battles of the Constitution and Union. Upon the block of granite which that State contributed to the Washington monument there is this inscription: "Iowa—her affections, like the rivers of her borders, flow to an inseparable Union." When these words were written, in the first years of the State's existence, they were regarded as a beautiful and somewhat poetic sentiment. Neither the author of the words nor the people, at that time, imagined how soon they were to be verified and written in shining letters of light upon history's page by the heroism of Iowa's soldiers, in common with the soldiers of all the loyal States, upon the field of battle.

"When the war of the Rebellion commenced the State of Iowa was but fifteen years old, and yet before the close of the war she had sent to the front seventy-five thousand men,—an army far larger than the entire army of the Revolution at its maximum, and composed of men as brave as ever drew a sabre or shouldered a musket.

"These men went forth, under the lead of Grant, Sherman, Thomas, and other illustrious patriots-in-arms, to make good the motto of their noble young State, and to show to the world that the Union of these States can no more be severed than can the mingled waters of the Mississippi and the Missouri as they united flow on to the sea. The soldiers of Iowa upheld by their deeds of valor the motto which Iowa had inscribed upon the monument erected to the memory of the Father of His Country and of the Union. They maintained the principle that the Union was then, and forever should be, inseparable. Because of this fact, established by the heroism of the great armies of the republic, we may reasonably hope and believe that this great nation is just entering upon a career of greatness, grandeur, and beneficence without a parallel in the history of the world.

"We owe it all to the noble men who stood in the ranks, and the noble commanders who led them on, to fight the battles and win the victories of the Union. Ladies and gentlemen, look upon this picture. What a debt of gratitude we owe to those brave men who imperilled their lives that the Union might live! To such heroes as General Thomas, who went forth to fight the great battles and win the great victories of the Union, we cannot pay too much homage. In the history of coming ages their names will be recorded, and coming peoples, enjoying the fruits of their labor and bravery, will bless them."

General Anson G. McCook, the orator of the occasion, delivered a beautiful address to the Society, in the course of which he referred to General Thomas as follows:

* * * * * *

"My Comrades,—Very briefly, and I fear very imperfectly, I have discharged the duty assigned me. To-day, with appropriate ceremonies, we unveiled the statue of our old commander. By it we show to this and succeeding generations our reverence for his memory, our appreciation of his great and invaluable services. Made of enduring bronze, it will stand for all time, teaching daily the lesson of his life: that love of country and obedience to its laws are the first and paramount duties of an American citizen. His patriotism was not circumscribed by the narrow limits of his native State, but it was as broad and catholic as his own great nature. Virginia, the mother of States and of statesmen, has been the birthplace of many whose fame and virtues are the common heritage of the republic; but the State of Washington, of Jefferson, of Madison, of Marshall, and of Scott, never brought forth a nobler son, a better citizen, a truer soldier, or a more unselfish patriot than George H. Thomas."

CONCLUSION.

In the foregoing pages it has been the aim of the writer to give not only his own opinion of General Thomas, but also to embody the opinions of those who were acquainted with him personally, and who were cognizant of his services as a soldier. The record of such a man is full of the highest incentives to virtue, and to all those noble traits which beautify, adorn, and ennoble human character.

It is hoped that this tribute may serve not only to perpetuate his memory, but to present his illustrious example for the imitation of the young men of the army, as also those in civil pursuits all over the land. No more beautiful character ever lived. He was indeed a leader in whom was no guile. Unselfish, pure in mind and heart, noble, generous, and forgiving, these were the characteristic attributes of George Henry Thomas.

APPENDIX.

COLONEL STANLEY MATTHEWS, who had been selected to deliver an address on the occasion of the unveiling of the statue, spoke as follows :

"According to the mythology of the ancient Greeks, Memory was the mother of the Muses; so that, as Plutarch tells, the completed sisterhood of nine was included under the common name of Remembrances.

"The truth in the fiction is that history is the parent of art. And as nature is the art whereby God constitutes and governs the world, because it is the revelation of the invisible and eternal, in forms of sublimity and beauty, to the mind of man, so human art, in all its varied forms,—poetry, eloquence, music, painting, sculpture, architecture,—is but the interpreter and expounder of the divine art, and fixes in its express and admirable forms whatsoever that is divine which it discovers in nature or in man. The heroic in action and suffering must precede, because it inspires, the heroic in representation. Man must become conscious of the noble and the good before he can express it; and he can become conscious of it only in his experience. Gods and heroes walked the earth, and wrought their wonders in action and suffering, before Phidias and Praxiteles could embody them.

"Achilles, first; afterward Homer. And art is therefore, if a prophecy, nevertheless, only because it is a memorial; for it is on the prepared and receptive background of the past that it paints or carves visions of the glory it foretells. Lord Bacon said, 'As statues and pictures are dumb histories, so histories are speaking pictures.'

"The name of George Henry Thomas, soldier and patriot, has already been inscribed on that scroll of honorable fame which posterity will reverently guard in the archives of our national history. To-day art, summoned to its proper work, lifts aloft the dignity and majesty of his person, as the Society of the Army of the Cumberland, by these public acts and solemn ceremonials, dedicates to the people of the United States the form and presence of its beloved commander.

"Surely this was a noble subject for the modeller's plastic hand. What dignity and power, what firmness and self-possession, what immobility, and yet what quiet graciousness, what gravity, and what benignity were set together in the manly proportions of his physical frame! A presence to inspire respect, but winning confidence and trust. He was large, firm-planted, and paternal, like a sturdy oak, striking its roots deep in the earth, but with outspreading branches offering protection and shelter from fierce heats or fiercer storms. Large and weighty, his movements were easy and quiet, his postures and gestures unobtrusive, so that his port and mien suggested a reserve of strength not called into action. Thus his physical power seemed to be magnified, and yet there was nothing in him ponderous, overwhelming, or boisterous, and he breathed and spoke gently and in soft tones, like a woman or a child. In fine, he was

> "'A combination and a form, indeed,
> Where every god did seem to set his seal
> To give the world assurance of a man.'

"The proportions of his physical frame were in harmony with those of the spiritual body which inhabited and animated it. The internal, as well as the external, man was statuesque, massive, monumental. Vigor and endurance were qualities alike of his material and his mental constitution. Strength was the base and pediment on which was grounded and built up the lofty structure of his character, capped and crowned with simplicity,—'whole in himself,'—a shaft and column of Doric style and beauty:

> "'Rich in saving common sense,
> And, as the greatest only are,
> In his simplicity sublime.'
>
> "'O good gray head, which all men knew,
> O iron nerve to true occasion true,
> O fall'n at length that tower of strength
> Which stood four-square to all the winds that blew!'

"There was nothing in him fluctuating, mercurial, or eccentric. He was set, inflexible, undeviating, steering steadily by the stars, upon the arc of a great circle. He was resolute, unyielding, with a fortitude incapable of intimidation or dismay, and yet without pretension, boasting, self-assertion, or noisy demonstration. He was conspicuous for modesty and dignity, and was altogether free from affectation or envy.

"He did not lack in proper self-esteem; but did not think more highly of himself than he ought. Better than any other man could, he took the measure of his own dimensions, and never worried lest he might be overlooked or neglected, not doubting that sooner or later he would gravitate by his own weight and power to his predestined place, over all opposition and contradiction.

"But he was not coarse, vulgar, and impassive, careless of the good opinion of good men; rather, on the contrary, he was quick in his sensibilities, keen to detect the selfishness of others, and smarted under a sense of injustice when inflicted upon himself. Yet no personal consideration ever warped his judgment or clouded his sense of duty. He was genial and frank in his communications, yet reticent and self-contained as to all that related to himself, neither inviting nor volunteering confidences. As he had nothing to conceal, his whole character was so transparent that he never opened himself to misconstructions. He did not take refuge from suspicions of ignorance in an affectation of the mystery of silence; for he was as a living epistle, known and read of all men. No conspicuous man in our recent history is better known as to his inmost character, more thoroughly understood, or more correctly appreciated; so that there is no reason to believe that the judgment of posterity as to his place in history will be other than a record of contemporary opinion. There lies buried with him in his grave no mystery, to pluck the heart out of which will require that he should ever be disturbed in his resting-place.

"It is not too much to say of General Thomas that he was a model soldier. Arms was his chosen profession. The whole period of his life, from youth to his untimely death, was spent in its study and practice. He had no ambition outside of it. His only ambition in it was to attain the rewards it held out to merit. He envied no superior his rank. He was in no haste to rise upon the misfortunes of others. He recognized but one way to glory: the path of duty.

"He perfected himself by patient painstaking in all its details. He carefully learned the duties of high command by a thorough practical experience of those of every inferior and subordinate responsibility. He became thus an adept in the knowledge and use of every arm of the service, and learned as an apprentice to handle and work every part of the great machinery and enginery of war.

"At the age of twenty, in 1836, he entered the Military Academy. In 1840, having graduated, he was commissioned as a second lieutenant, and rose successively through every intermediate grade until, on December 15, 1864, the date of the first day's battle at Nashville, he was promoted to be a major-general in the army of the United States.

"In each stage in his military history he saw active service appropriate to his rank, receiving his first brevet while a second lieutenant, for gallantry and good conduct, in 1841, in the war against the Florida Indians; in the war against Mexico, in 1846–48, at Fort Brown, Monterey, and Buena Vista; again, in Florida, in 1849–50, against the Seminoles; as an instructor of artillery and cavalry in the Military Academy, from 1851 to 1854; on frontier duty in California and in Texas; until the breaking out of the civil war, in 1861, found him a lieutenant-colonel of the Second Cavalry, of which he then became colonel.

"These were the days and years of preparation, of the study and practice of military art, the formation of military habits, the education and training of the military character, the development and cultivation of the military instinct. And the seed sown during this season bore its ample fruits in due time.

"At the beginning of the Rebellion, in 1861, he had attained the forty-fifth year of his age, the full age of a matured and ripened manhood. He was no longer in the flush and hey-day of impetuous youth. He had grown to his stature gradually and slowly, as always grows timber close-grained and of fine fibre. What he was capable of doing he had learned to do in the usual exercise and natural processes of his understanding. He was neither a genius, accomplishing results without apparent means by lightning-strokes of magic and mere will, nor was he a favorite child of fortune, winning success by accident and chance against odds, plucking the flower safely out of the nettle danger when, by the common laws of human conduct, he ought to have suffered the penalty of rashness and improvidence. One of the valuable lessons of his military career is that every success rests upon the rational basis of a thorough organization of the means necessary to insure it,—that valor is nothing better than blind and bloody persistence unless supported on either flank by knowledge and prudence.

"This was the secret of one of the chief characteristics of his work: its thoroughness. He did nothing by halves. He wasted no material or time in experiments, the issue of which were indeterminate. He did not worry and wear out his ranks in purposeless marches and countermarches, to make them believe he was doing something when he was not. He carefully nursed and provided for them, so as to bring his troops to the highest point in spirit and efficiency, and kept them well in hand. He determined what most important end was reasonably practicable; he matured the plan best adapted to secure its accomplishment, and carefully gathered and organized the means necessary for its execution; and then, when all things were ready, he launched the dread thunderbolt of power, and with one stroke dealt the destruction he had devised. Mill Spring and Nashville—his first and last battles in the West—are capital illustrations of this feature of his military character. In reference to this last memorable and decisive battle of Nashville, the importunity and impatience of his superiors, at a distance too great to appreciate the difficulties of his situation, provoked from him no complaint. He telegraphed to the then Lieutenant-General, 'I can only say I have done all in my power to prepare, and if you should deem it necessary to relieve me, I shall submit without a murmur.' When the time arrived for the delivery of the meditated blow, and its complete and thorough success was known, he received ample compensation for this temporary distrust in hearty and ungrudging congratulations from President, Secretary of War, and Lieutenant-General, as creditable to them as they were gratifying and just to him, confirmed as they were by the thanks of Congress, for the skill and dauntless courage by which the rebel army under General Hood was signally defeated and driven from the State of Tennessee.

"Speaking of the circumstances of that occasion, General J. D. Cox, a most competent judge, himself a most honorable participant in its trials and its triumphs, in his oration at Chicago in 1868 said,—

"'Fortunately our commander at Nashville was a man of Washingtonian character and will, and, knowing that his country's cause depended upon his *being* right, and not upon his merely *seeming* so, he waited with immovable firmness for the right hour to come. It came, and with it a justification of both his military skill and his own self-forgetful patriotism, so complete and glorious that it would be a mere waste of words for me to talk about it.'

"This episode finely illustrates not only the temper of that crisis in our public affairs, but the best characteristics of its chief figure.

"It was the dictate of a sound and prudent judgment, and became the habit of his life, to assume no important responsibility which he did not feel well prepared to meet. We have seen that at Nashville, with the experience of more than three years of constant and active service, he was willing rather to be relieved from his command than to accept the responsibility of a movement he believed to be premature. In an earlier stage of his service, he resisted the temptation of ambition by declining what amounted to promotion because he was able to prefer the public good to his personal advancement. In the fall of 1862 the circumstances, as related by General Buell himself in a private, unpublished note, were as follows:

"'The army was to move on the 30th of September against Bragg, who occupied Bardstown, Frankfort, and, in fact, the whole of Central Kentucky. On the morning of the 29th an order was received from Washington assigning General Thomas to the command in my stead. He very soon came to my room and stated his intention to ask the revocation of the order; that he was not prepared by information and study for the responsibility of the command. I tried to dissuade him, told him that I would give him all of my information and plans, and assured him of my confidence in his success. Finding him determined, I said that I could under no circumstances consent to his sending a despatch which could imply that I had any wish or influence in the matter. He promised that much, went away, and after a while returned with the message which he had prepared for General Halleck. I thought that he was actuated in his course by a generous confidence in me and a modest distrust of himself with so little warning; and I considered that both motives did honor to his sterling character.'

"His language in the despatch referred to was this:

"'General Buell's preparations have been completed to move against the enemy, and I therefore respectfully ask that he may be retained in command. My position is very embarrassing, not being as well informed as I should be as the commander of this army, and on the assumption of such responsibility.'

"But the quality which more than all others specifically and constitutionally distinguished General Thomas was his invincibility, his heroic faculty for enduring, unwearied, and successful obstinacy in defence. It was not mere brute courage nor insensibility to danger. Neither was it mere resoluteness and stoutness of heart, nor a certain sullen defiance, which in some cases has seemed to await an expected adversity. It was cheerful and sweet tempered, although of supreme seriousness and intensity. But its chief faculty was its contagion, by which it propagated its fearlessness and hopefulness to the whole body of his support; so that every soldier in his company felt an assurance of security and success in his presence and authority. The latent heat of his passion grew into a glow under heavy hammering, and spread through all the particles that adhered and gathered to it, until the fused and molten mass, red hot with its combustion, consumed everything that approached it. It was the sympathy of confidence and self-devotion that indissolubly bound together commander and men, and made them jointly invincible. It was a shield which quenched the fiery darts of the adversary, an armor of tempered steel which none of his arrows could pierce.

"A signal illustration of this power of resistance is furnished by the course of battle at Stone River, where he stayed the tide of rebel success with his immovable front. But its most conspicuous example is seen on the last day's fighting at Chickamauga. In his memorial oration at Cleveland in 1870, General Garfield—himself soldier, scholar, and statesman—in a tribute of which the highest praise is to say that it is worthy both of himself and of its theme, in most felicitous phrase, has drawn his picture as he appeared in that scene. He says,—

"'While men shall read the history of battles, they will never fail to study and admire the work of Thomas during that afternoon. With but twenty-five thousand men, formed in a semicircle, of which he himself was the centre and soul, he successfully resisted for more than five hours the repeated assaults of an army of sixty-five thousand men flushed with victory and bent on his annihilation. . . . When night had closed over the combatants, the last sound of battle was the booming of Thomas's shells bursting among his baffled and retreating assailants. He was indeed the "Rock of Chickamauga," against which the wild waves of battle dashed in vain. It will stand written forever in the annals of his country that there he saved from destruction the Army of the Cumberland,—

> "'A day of onsets of despair!
> Dash'd on every rocky square,
> Their surging charges foamed themselves away.'

"Speaking of him in the general order announcing his death, the general of the army, in terms both just and warm, recorded and published his estimate of the character and career of General Thomas. He said,—

"'The general has known General Thomas intimately since they sat, as boys, on the same bench, and the quality in him which he holds up for the admiration and example of the young is his complete and entire devotion to duty. Though sent to Florida, to Mexico, to Texas, to Arizona, when duty there was absolute banishment, he went cheerfully, and never asked a personal favor, exemption, or leave of absence. In battle he never wavered. Firm, and of full faith in his cause, he knew it would prevail, and he never sought advancement of rank or honor at the expense of any one. Whatever he earned of these was his own, and no one disputes his fame. The very impersonation of honesty, integrity, and honor, he will stand to us as the *beau ideal* of the soldier and gentleman.'

"General Thomas, in his simple and modest way, has left

on record a statement concerning himself, which will be accepted now without question. In a letter of November 26, 1869, expressing his regret that he would not be able to attend the reunion of the Society of the Army of the Cumberland that year, at Indianapolis, he said,—

"'It was my hearty desire, from the beginning to the end of the late war, to accept with cheerfulness and perform with zeal and honesty whatever duties devolved upon me. At the same time it was my constant endeavor to impress those who were with me and under my command with a sense of the importance of the services they had undertaken to perform.'

"These sentences show that George H. Thomas was something more and better than merely a soldier. He was a patriot. He had a country and a cause, and in their defence he drew his sword. The principles and interests for which he perilled his life and staked his fame, more even than the gallant service he performed in their behalf, great and distinguished as it was, justify the celebration of this day. The occasion seems appropriate for a statement and vindication of the grounds on which they are established and now securely rest.

"The reason and religion of all ages and races have recognized the love of country as a nobler passion than the love of life. The pleasure-loving Greek identified piety with patriotism; and Pericles, when he pronounced the panegyric over the slain heroes of the Peloponnesian war, knew not how to eulogize them better than to praise the institutions of their country, which was capable of producing citizens willing to die in their defence. The Latin poet framed a phrase of Roman devotedness for all times and lands when he sang, 'Dulce et decorum est pro patria mori.' The Christian religion, although its founder is the Prince of Peace, and its advent was heralded by heavenly voices, proclaiming, 'Peace on earth, good will to men,' nevertheless has sanctioned and sanctified, by the example of its Divine Author, that spirit of self-sacrifice which is the essence of all disinterested service which man can render to mankind; and teaches that as the only true life is not the life of the body, but the life of God in the human soul, so the ends for which life was given are of more value than mere living. Reason and instinct combine to uphold the private law of self-defence; and the preservation of the State, at the expense of individual life, is but an extension and enlargement of the same principle in the domain of public law. For the maintenance of the social and political state is essential to the development of the individual destiny, and its life is part of the life of every citizen.

"The law of all civil society, and under every form of government, has classed treason and rebellion with capital crimes, worthy of death; too often when the sovereignty defied was embodied in the person of the monarch, perverting the presumptions of guilt and magnifying the unrealized imaginations and intentions of the accused into overt acts of crime. Our own constitution, jealous of liberty and yet mindful of the obligations of a loyal citizenship to a form of government founded on popular assent and essential to the preservation of public and private rights, limited the offence to overt acts of war against its existence or authority, or adhering to its armed enemies, giving them aid and comfort.

"The mythology of the ancients represented the enormity and hideousness of rebellion under the figure of the monster Typhon. Lord Bacon, interpreting the fable, says,—

"'And now the disaffected, uniting their force, at length break out into open rebellion, which, producing infinite mischiefs, . . . is represented by the horrid and multiplied deformity of Typhon, with his hundred heads, denoting the divided powers; his flaming mouths, denoting fire and devastation; his girdles of snakes, denoting sieges and destruction; his iron hands, slaughter and cruelty; his eagle's talons, rapine and plunder; his plumed body, perpetual rumors, contradictory accounts,' etc., and able for a time to strip from the majesty of the state the sinews of its power.

"As patriotism is then both a duty and a delight, and treason and rebellion condemned as equally sinful and shameful, by every system of religion and every system of law, by the reason and instincts of mankind, whence are *civil wars*, and whence especially came *ours?*

"Oftener, in governments where the sovereignty is hereditary in the line of family descent, disputed successions divide the allegiance of the people and are settled by the arbitrament of arms. In despotisms, oppressed and burdened populations revolt against tyrannies, too severe and painful for longer endurance; and revolution becomes the last resort and remedy for men who love liberty better than life.

"But the rebellion of the Confederate States, in 1861, was of a different class. It was not a war of factions, supporting rival claimants to an official succession, both acknowledging the legitimacy of the institutions of government; nor was it an attempted revolution in behalf of right against power. It was, on the contrary, a determined and desperate struggle not merely to overthrow a *government*, but to destroy the *nationality* represented by it.

"The conspiracy which found in it its culmination was an old one, and at first unconscious of its true nature and direction. Its germ appeared in the opposition developed to the original adoption of national institutions as formulated in the Federal constitution. It appeared soon after in the Virginia and Kentucky resolutions of '98, imputed to Jefferson, but which were hardly consistent with that theory of national sovereignty upon which he must have relied for a conviction of treason against Aaron Burr; it was revived in the doctrine of nullification, as defended by Calhoun and his school, leading logically to secession and civil war.

"It was founded on a complete and fundamental misconception of the character of the political institutions of the country, and of the relation of the governments of the States to that of the United States, and a failure to realize the truth, that behind and below both these instrumentalities of political action there was a constituency that was their originating and supporting cause, the unity of which made one *nation* of all the people. The false doctrine which embodied these misconceptions was styled the doctrine of State rights; but erroneously, for there had been no denial that the States had indestructible rights. The only controversy had been to define what they were and who were the judges of their limits. The real meaning and mischief of the false dogma was State supremacy, for it taught that to the States, and not to the United States, was committed the right to decide the boundary of their respective jurisdictions. Each in respect to the powers delegated or reserved was, of course, independent of the other, and in that sense sovereign; but inasmuch as the constitution and laws of the United States made in pursuance thereof, and all treaties made under their authority, it is declared, shall be the supreme law of the land, and the judges in every State shall be bound thereby, anything in the constitution or laws of any State to the contrary notwithstanding; and inasmuch as it is further declared that the judicial power of the United States shall extend to all cases in law and equity, arising under the constitution, the laws of the United States, and the treaties made under their authority, it is apparent that by the very frame of the fundamental and organic structure of the national authority, the supreme sovereignty, in all its relations to individuals, to domestic States and foreign nations, belongs to that constituency which is rightly designated as the people of the United States, and is exercised by that government which represents and effectuates their collective and national will. It is this supremacy of jurisdiction and authority that constitutes our nationality, and is essential to it. In this view the unit of power and dignity is the nation; the States are significant merely as its parts and fractions. The national government is the centre and circumference that encloses and unites within its complete circle the entire aggregate of our political institutions, and integrates them into one harmonious, co-operating whole.

"Abroad, it establishes our place as one in the world's family of independent, equal, and sovereign nations. At home, within the sphere of its prescribed powers, and determining their limits and applications, without responsibility to any superior, it acts upon the individual people whose allegiance it commands, with the irresistible energy and limitless resources of the supreme and sovereign will of an indivisible people. It is the result and exponent—the consequence, rather than the cause—of those common features and characteristics which belong to us as one people living in one land, which, in the aggregate, constitute a national character, the development of which, in social and political action, represents in history our national life and spirit. It is the ideal of all patriotic aspiration; the inspiration and object of our public hopes; the shield of our security; the guardian of our persons and rights; the defender of our interests; our present help in every time of earthly need. The sway of its law is the bond of our peace and the pledge of our prosperity; the supremacy of its authority, the condition and cause of order, harmony, and co-operation among all the possible conflicts and jealousies of subordinate political agencies; its flag— 'the banner of beauty and glory,'—the symbol of our power and pride, the emblem of our unity, the imperial standard of our loyal and reverent devotion.

"It is not inconsistent with this spirit to value and cherish the local attachments which connect us with the States of our nativity and abode; but only in an inferior and subordinate degree. Our first duty and our chief love are due to the nation, which alone constitutes our country. For the principal value of our citizenship of the State is that it confers upon us the dignity and privilege of our nationality.

"In contempt of this view of our constitutional organization as a nation, the opposing theory was taught of the supremacy of the States, the subordination of the Union. According to this doctrine, the only sources and supports of political authority, known in our system, were the States, while the Federal Government, under its constitution, was merely a mode of their agency. Of course, upon such a construction of our political relations, the only patriotism of which, as citizens, we were capable, consisted in allegiance to the State of our domicil; for loyalty is the expression of fealty to a person, either natural or political; it cannot be exacted or yielded to an inanimate parchment or compact. So that the obligations of the Federal constitution ceased to bind individuals who were released from the duty of obedience by the sovereign authority of their States; and the States themselves could not be made responsible, for they had no political superiors. Hence it was thought, at the time, by some public men, that there was no constitutional warrant to attempt the coercion of the States, and writers, in that interest, denominate the rebellion against the national government as a war between States.

"And founding upon this false interpretation of the constitutional facts of our history, the national life was assailed in organized and bloody war.

"It is not to be supposed, however, that the inspiring purpose and main motive of the rebellion was to establish the abstract theory of the supremacy of the States. That theory was used as the legal excuse and justification of the asserted right to renounce the authority of the Federal constitution; but the right was not exercised merely to assert its existence. There were ulterior objects and purposes which enlisted the sympathies and united the efforts, not merely of *States*, but of a *section*, and that without regard to State lines, and even in disobedience of State authority. Such was notably the case of some distinguished public men, and thousands of others, in States which never by any act of secession sanctioned or justified their course, who broke their allegiance to both State and nation to swell the ranks of the rebellion, to adhere to the Confederate government, or to give it aid and comfort.

"Accordingly, we find powerful interests, partly pecuniary, partly political, pervading a section of the country, which organized and arrayed its public sentiment to eradicate every seed of dissent within it, and to defend itself against every hostility from without. These interests, it is needless to say, all grew out of the institution of negro slavery. They intrenched themselves early behind the ramparts of State sovereignty and supremacy. Upon this basis was founded the political power of the slaveholding interest, known in our history as the slave-power.

"One of its most signal struggles with the national spirit was upon the question of tariff duties, levied with a discrimination in favor of American manufactures. It was supposed that, as to all its principal products, except sugar, slave-labor would be rendered more profitable to its owners, by free access to the markets of the world, in direct exchange for foreign manufactures, and that a discriminating duty against foreign fabrics was a tax levied on their produce for the benefit of the home manufacture. But instead of resting satisfied with an appeal to the general intelligence and the common sense of justice of the whole country, the cotton-producing interest threatened forcible resistance to the execution of the revenue laws, through State authority, and, under the banner of nullification, denied and defied the national authority.

"This, however, was a mere episode. It was an incidental illustration of a more general fact, which soon began to become manifest, and which eventuated in civil war. It was that *the continued existence of slavery was incompatible with the permanence of national institutions.* The exigencies of the slaveholding interest demanded sacrifices which could only be made at the expense and by the ultimate extinction of all the ideas which lay at the foundation of our existence as a nation. Slavery was rapidly making of us two peoples in place of one, and separating us so widely in thought, feeling, culture, and every constituent of character and motive of conduct, as to make any mere political bond of union a name without reality. It was more disintegrating than if it had succeeded in teaching the two sections different languages; because, with apparent continued use of but one, it had introduced such a confusion of thought as to make their communication incomprehensible. Their ideas were not capable of mutual translation. What to one was good was to the other evil; and contradiction and mutual exclusion was substituted for the fellowship of sympathy and a community of aims and purposes. The immortal Declaration of our National Independence, which had been supposed to be founded upon eternal, unchangeable, and indestructible truths of reason, and to formulate the justification of human right for all mankind, had become the subject of derision as a series of sophisms and glittering generalities; while the national constitution, with the glosses which had been imposed upon its practical construction, was denounced, on the other hand, as a 'covenant with death and a league with hell.' The right freely to speak and write, and peaceably to assemble for the consideration and discussion of public questions, was denied, wherever its exercise threatened the safety of slaveholding or disturbed the consciences of those who practised it; while, on their part, their teachers and leaders sedulously inculcated the belief that it was the mission of their situation, laid upon them by a necessity both human and divine, to extend, strengthen, and perpetuate the system.

"The sole condition on which it tolerated political association was the recognition of its right of a domination. Its alternative was *rule* or *ruin*. So that when it was driven from the seat of national power by a political revolution, wrought by public sentiment and in strict accordance with law, without waiting for any overt act of hostility, with desperate foresight of its inevitable doom, it plunged into the dread abyss,—

> 'Hurled headlong flaming from the ethereal sky,
> With hideous ruin and combustion, down
> To bottomless perdition.'

"Under the mocking banner of State rights it opened its cannon upon the national power, and when Sumter fell it buried forever under its ruins the lost cause of a Confederacy of which slavery was proclaimed to be the corner-stone.

"It was a victory, not only for the nation but for mankind, and marks a step in the progress of the race that cannot and will not be reversed. The evils of the war—and they are many that follow always in its train—will be forgotten and effaced; but the good will remain forever. Nationality restored upon the basis of universal freedom, and the political and civil equality of all the citizens of the commonwealth, is a result that vindicates itself, needing neither apology nor defence. Those who were overcome in the conflict, as well as those who overcame them, can unite, without bitterness or hypocrisy, in a triumph that divides the trophies of its good equally with both. And when those who were our brethren and became our enemies, but not more ours than their own, are able and willing, as they ought, to join with us in grateful and joyous thanksgiving to the gracious God who turned the scales of battle not against them, but against their cause, we too, can, without humiliation or self-contempt, join with them in solemn celebrations and funeral rites over the graves of Confederate as well as Federal dead, as sacrifices and expiations not made in vain.

"The sum of the whole matter is, that the life of the nation is essential to the life of the people; that its authority and power are supreme, and not subordinate; that its integrity is vital to the growth and perfection of that rational and orderly, but impartial and benevolent liberty, which constitutes the sacred deposit intrusted to its keeping, and contained within the forms of its constitution; that neither sectional strife nor party contention must ever invade its sphere or draw in question its essential jurisdiction; that it shall be cherished as an ally and friend of all legitimate powers of the States, and not as an alien and enemy of the liberties of its people; that the sentiment of nationality shall be cherished as the spirit of patriotism, and our love of country made, in good faith, to embrace not the locality bounded by our personal or party horizon, but the whole galaxy and constellation of fixed and immutable stars that fill the heaven of our hopes; and that no spirit of faction shall be allowed to confuse the boundaries that divide and separate the allotments of authority and jurisdiction which have been wisely made to embody and enforce the constitutional will of the people.

"In this unnatural contest George H. Thomas adhered to

the government to which he had sworn allegiance, and not to its enemies in arms. He was born, it is true, in Virginia, but his home and country was the United States of America. He had been educated at the expense of its government at a national military academy upon the condition, if not express, at least honorably implied, that he should devote his military knowledge and skill in support of its authority and in obedience to its laws. He had chosen the military profession as the pursuit of his life, and had served for twenty-one years in its armies, receiving his reward in the honors and emoluments of its service. He had performed the duties of his successive ranks, at posts and stations to which he had from time to time been assigned, without regard to the boundaries of States. He had stood guard at the outposts and picketed the frontiers of the vast area of national domain, scarcely less than the continent, and thought he was defending the homes of his countrymen. He had followed the flag of the nation into a foreign territory and participated in a war that extended our national border to the Pacific Ocean. He knew that it was the duty of the army to uphold the civil power of the government, the President of which was, by the constitution, its commander-in-chief, and that that instrument made no distinction between foreign and domestic enemies. He knew that Washington had employed the national military force for the suppression of insurrection and the enforcement of the laws of Congress, and that Marshall lent no countenance to a doctrine that would seduce him from his military allegiance. His reason told him where his duty lay; his conscience bade him follow it. In the uniform of an officer of the army of the United States he followed its flag across the Potomac, at the head of its troops and in obedience to its lawful commands, upon the soil of his native State, sacred to him only as it was consecrated to the constitution and the Union. And if his conduct and career was in contrast with that of others of her sons whom on that account she has preferred to honor, nevertheless a generation in Virginia will yet arise who will learn and confess the truth that George H. Thomas, when he lifted his sword to bar the pathway of her secession, loved her as well as these and served her better.

"This monument, consecrated to-day to him whose fame we celebrate, is also sacred to the memory of that invisible host without whom he was nothing,—the unrecorded dead, the untitled soldiers of the Union, the vanished and nameless Army of the Republic, who were not merely willing to die, but to be forgotten, so that the memory of the good their death should bring might live after them. As long as the love of country shall survive among the generations of this people, or liberty makes its home under the protection of our National institutions, the example of their patriotic devotion will not die for lack of honorable remembrance or worthy imitation. We stand with uncovered heads and hearts laid bare, to-day, in the presence of an innumerable company of these heroic spirits,—witnesses, sympathizing with us in these solemn and patriotic ceremonials, honoring the memory of our great soldier and patriot. The listening ear of fancy catches their choral song as it floats and dies away upon the air,—

> 'Yea, let all good things await
> Him who cares not to be great
> But as he saves or serves the State!'

(To the President of the United States:)

"And now, Mr. President, it only remains for me, in the name and on behalf of the Society of the Army of the Cumberland, to present and deliver, through you, to the people of the United States, whose chosen representative you are, this statue of George H. Thomas. Protected and preserved by their care, in this seat and capital of their national power, may it long stand as a token of the honor which a grateful people bestow upon conspicuous and unselfish devotion to public duty! And when marble shall have crumbled to decay, and brass become corroded by the rust of time, may the liberties of the people which he defended still survive, illustrated and supported by successive generations, inspired to deeds of virtue and heroic duty by the memory of his example!"

INDEX.

A.

Abercrombie, Col. J. J., 13, 44.
Advance on Lookout Mountain, 118.
Allen, Lieut. J. W., 62.
Anderson, Gen. Robert, 46, 50-52, 157.
Atkins, Col., 92d Ills. Vols., 93.

B.

Bailey, Surgeon E. J., 254.
Baird, Gen. Absalom, 86, 87, 91-94, 97-101, 106, 108-110, 114, 118, 119, 128, 147, 167, etc.
Banks, Gen. N. P., 45.
Barker, Lieut. J. D., 82.
Barker, Capt. J. D., 104, 110.
Barnes, Col., 101.
Barrel, Surgeon H. C., 110.
"Battle above the Clouds," 118.
Battle of Franklin, 179.
Battle of Mill Spring, 57.
Battle of Mission Ridge, 120.
Battle of Nashville, 194.
Battle of Stone River, 73.
Baylor, Capt. T. G., 135.
Beatty, Col., 79-81, 92.
Beatty, Gen., 101, 103, 109.
Beauregard, Gen. P. G. T., 42, 43, 67.
Beebe, Surgeon G. D., 82.
Birney, Gen. William, 275.
Bishop, Mr. George C., 260.
Bowers, Maj. T. S., 193.
Boyle, Gen. J. T., 47.
Brackett, Col. A. G., 30.
Bradley, Col. E. D., 53.

Bramlette, Gen. T. E., 49.
Brannan, Gen. J. M., 86, 87, 91-96, 98-101, 103, 104, 109, 120, 135, etc.
Breckinridge, Gen. J. C., 49.
Breckinridge, Lieut. J. C., 62.
Bristow, Gen. B. H., 271.
Brownlow, Lieut.-Col., 121.
Buckner, Col., 79th Ills. Vols., 83.
Buckner, Gen. S. B., 65.
Buell, Gen. D. C., 53, 55, 64-66, 69, 71, 72.
Buell, Col. George P., 109.
Buford, Gen. A., 176.
Bunker Hill, Va., movement on, 45.
Burnside, Gen. A. E., 129, 130.
Burt, Lieut. A. S., 61, 63.
Butler, Senator M. C., 270.
Butterfield, Gen. D., 140, 142, 147, 274.
Buzzard Roost, Ga., examined, 212.
Byrd, Col. R. R., 54.

C.

Camp Dick Robinson, 47.
Captures at Nashville, 227.
Carlin, Gen. W. P., 84, 117, 126, 277.
Carrington, Col. H. B., 53.
Carter, Col. J. P. S., 54.
Carter, Lieut.-Col. M. B., 62.
Carter, Gen. S. P., 54.
Cavalry at Franklin, Tenn., 204.
Cavalry regiments consolidated, 46.
Chattanooga, appearance of, 115.
Chickamauga campaign, 85.
Chickamauga, report of battle, 91.
Childs, Maj., 20.

318   INDEX.

Cist, Capt. H. M., 226.
Cist, Lieut. H. M., 136.
Closing around Atlanta, 154.
Cobb, Gov. R. W., 278.
Coburn, Gen. John, 53.
Committee on equestrian statue, 265.
Conclusion, 292.
Confidence of Secretary of War in Gen. Thomas, 203.
Connell, Col. J. M., 53.
Cooper, Surgeon George E., 226.
Corinth, advance on, 67.
Corinth, siege and capture of, 67.
Corse, Gen. J. M., 177.
Cosby, Gen. George B., 30.
Crab Orchard, battle of, 56.
Crittenden, Gen. George B., 55, 56.
Crittenden, Gen. T. L., 66, 72-74, 76, 86-88, 98, 105, 107, 108.
Crook, Gen. George, 122.
Croswell, Gov. C. M., 280.
Croxton, Gen. J. T., 98, 100, 108, 176, 177, 199.
Cruft, Gen. Charles, 106, 126, 264.
Cullum, Gen. G. W., 275.
Cumberland Ford, 49.
Cutler, Capt., 122.

D.

Dalton, battle of, 137.
Davis, Gen. J. C., 76, 86-88, 127, 130, 137, 140, 145, 149, 150, 158, 165, 166, 168-171, etc.
Davis, Jefferson, 208.
Destruction of Macon and Western Railroad, 167.
Ducat, Lieut.-Col. A. C., 135.
Dyer, Gen. A. B., court of inquiry on, 238.

E.

Easton, Lieut.-Col. L. C., 135.
Elliot, Gen. W. L., 120, 121, 135.
Emerson, Assistant Surgeon, 18, 19.

Enemy fortifies in front of Nashville, 180.
Enemy reaches Nashville, 180.
Ewell, Gen. R. H., 14.

F.

Ferguson, Champ, 121.
Final illness of Gen. Thomas, 254.
Fish, Hon. Hamilton, 277.
Fitch, Lieut.-Commander, U.S.N., 186, 199.
Floyd, Gen. J. B., 65.
Flynt, Lieut.-Col. G. E., 110.
Flynt, Maj. G. E., 81.
Forrest, Gen. N. B., 176, 183, 200.
Fort Sumter, fire on, 38.
Fort Yuma, Cal., 28, 239.
Franklin, battle of, 179.
Fry, Gen. S. S., 53, 58, 61, 79.
Funeral services of Gen. Thomas, 261.

G.

Garfield, Gen. J. A., 104, 106.
Garrard, Gen. K., 146, 158, 163, 165, 167, 199, 212.
Gaw, Capt. W. B., 102, 104, 110.
Geary, Gen. J. W., 123, 126, 143, 146.
General orders announcing death of Gen. G. H. Thomas, 257.
Georgia campaign, report of, 158.
Getty, Gen. G. W., 14.
Gibbon, Gen. John, 276.
Gibson, Gen. W. H., 283.
Gillem, Gen. A. C., 62, 222.
Gold medal to Gen. Thomas, 229.
Grand rounds through Georgia, 173.
Granger, Gen. Gordon, 104, 107, 109, 118, 125, 127, 128.
Granger, Gen. R. S., 164, 221.
Grant, Gen. U. S., 24, 64, 66, 113, 115, 117, 118, 131, 133, 174, 181-185, 187-193, 197, 198, 200, 203, 205, 267, etc.
Greenwood, Capt., 38th Ohio Vols., 62.

INDEX. 319

Gross, Gen., 106, 125.
Gross, Surgeon F. H., 110.
Guenther, Lieut. F. L., 79-81.
Guerillas at McMinnville, Tenn., 120.

H.

Haggen, Dr., 254.
Hall, Hon. Hiliard, 280.
Halleck, Gen. H. W., 67, 186-190, 192, 193, 201, 203, 222.
Hancock, Gen. W. S., 24, 45.
Hardee, Gen. W. J., 151, 152.
Hardee, Maj. W. J., 29, 30, 36, 85.
Harker, Gen. C. G., 103, 109, 172.
Harlan, Col. J. M., 53, 58.
Harper's Ferry, 43.
Harrison, Col., 39th Ind. Vols., 88, 219.
Hatch, Gen. Edward, 177, 179, 199, 211, 216, 217.
Hazen, Gen. W. B., 87, 112.
Headquarters transferred to Louisville, 234.
Hedges, Lieut., U.S.A., 216.
Hewitt, Capt. J. M., 54.
Hood, Gen. J. B., 30, 85, 103, 151, 152, 154, 155, 175-180, 185, 200-202, 205, etc.
Hooker, Gen. Joseph, 111-113, 117, 123, 126, 127, 129, 130, 138-140, 143-150, 152.
Hoskins, Col. W. A., 53, 59.
Hough, Col. A. L., 284.
Houston, Gov. Sam, 36.
Howard, Gen. O. O., 117, 124, 125, 130, 137, 139-149, 155, 156, 168, 174.
Hunt, Capt. G. E., 62.
Hunton, Lieut.-Col. A. K., 62.

I.

Incidents of the battle of Mission Ridge, 131.
Indian campaign of Gen. Thomas, 33.

J.

Johnson, President Andrew, 235.
Jackson, Gen. J. S., 72.
Jackson, Gen. "Stonewall," 44.
Johnson, Gen. B. R., 14.
Johnson, Capt., 2d Ind. Cav., 104, 110.
Johnston, Gen. A. S., 29, 30, 32, 36, 64.
Johnston, Gen. Joseph E., 43, 151, 154.
Jones, Maj. F. J., 247.
Jones, Lieut. S. B., 62.
Jones, Col. Toland, 282.

K.

Kellogg, Capt. S. C., 102, 103, 105, 110, 135, 227.
Kelly, Lieut. M. J., 136, 227.
Kentucky saved to the Union, 245.
Killed and wounded at Mill Spring, 63.
Kilpatrick, Gen. J., 140, 141, 158, 163-165, 168.
Kimball, Gen. Nathan, 148, 209.
King, Gen. J. H., 99.
Kinney, Capt. D., 54, 59, 60.
Knipe, Gen., 211, 216.
Knoxville campaign, 51.

L.

Laibold, Col., 2d Missouri Vols., 162.
Last illness and death of Gen. Thomas, 255.
Lawrence, Maj. W. E., 54, 105, 110.
Lee, Gen. Fitzhugh, 30.
Lee, Rear-Admiral S. P., 221.
Letcher, Private Samuel, 62.
Lewis, Lieut.-Col. W. H., 16.
Liberty Gap, battle of, 84.
Lincoln, President A., 38, 50, 198.
Logan, Gen. J. A., 155, 192.
Long, Gen. Eli, 124, 127, 129.
Longstreet, Gen. James, 85.
Loomis, Col., 80, 81.
Louisville, occupation of, 69.

320 INDEX.

Loyalty of Gen. Thomas, 245.
Lugenbeel, Col. P., 14.

M.

Mack, Capt. O. A., 81, 82, 135.
Mackey, Gen. A. J., 82, 110, 151.
Manson, Gen. M. D., 53, 58, 60.
"March to the Sea," 173, 175.
Marshall, Gen. H., 49.
Matthews, Col. Stanley, 293.
Maxey, Senator S. B., 269.
McClellan, Gov. George B., 279.
McCook, Gen. A. G., 151, 290.
McCook, Gen. A. McD., 72-74, 76-79, 84, 86-88, 99, 104-108.
McCook, Col. Daniel, 97, 109, 172.
McCook, Gen. E. M., 139-141, 146, 147, 149, 160-162, 183.
McCook, Gen. R. L., 53, 59, 61, 66.
McCormick, Surgeon Charles, 254.
McCrary, Hon. G. W., 289.
McDowell, Gen. I., 42, 43.
McMichael, Maj. Wm., 135.
McPherson, Gen. J. B., 137, 138, 140-142, 145, 149, 150, 154.
Merrell, Capt. W. E., 135.
Merrill, Capt. Jesse, 136.
Michigan engineers, 58.
Military Division of the Pacific, 238.
Military Division of the Tennessee, 232.
Miller, Gen., 210.
Miller, Justice S. F., 271.
Mill Spring, report of battle, 57.
Mill Spring, killed and wounded, 63.
Minnesota, Second, regiment, 59.
Minty, Col., 86, 87, 107, 108.
Mission Ridge, report of battle, 120.
Mitchell, Gen. O. M., 51, 66, 68.
Moody, Capt. G. C., 110.
Mordecai, Capt. A., 227.
Morgan, Gen. J. D., 176, 177.
Morgan, Gen. M. R., 26, 284.
Morse, Lieut. A., 62.
Murray, Col., 121.
Murray, Surgeon Robert, U.S.A., 254.

N.

Nashville, arrival of troops at, 65.
Nashville, battle of, 194.
Nashville, order of battle, 209.
National cemeteries, 231.
Negley, Gen. J. S., 68, 76, 78, 79, 81, 87, 91-94, 100-102, 109.
Nelson, Gen. William, 47, 48, 66.
New Hope Church, battle of, 138.
Newton, Gen. John, 140, 148.

O.

Oakes, Gen. James, 30.
Oath of allegiance, 38.
"On to Richmond," 43.
Osterhaus, Gen. P. J., 124.
Otis, Judge E. A., 285.

P.

Pall-bearers, 263.
Palmer, Gen. Innis N., 30.
Palmer, Gen. J. M., 77, 78, 86, 98, 100, 102, 108, 112, 125, 127, 130, 134, 137, 139, 140, 142, 143, 145, 146-149, 151, 152, 158-160, 272.
Palmer, Col. W. J., 15th Pa. Vols., 224-226.
Parkhurst, Col. J. G., 79, 109, 227.
Patterson, Lieut. J. E., 62.
Patterson, Gen. Robert, 38-40, 42-44.
Paul, Lieut.-Col. J. R., 110.
Perin, Surgeon G., U.S.A., 135.
Perryville, battle of, 72.
Philadelphia City Troop, 41.
Pillow, Gen. G. J., 64.
Pittsburg Landing, 66.
Polk, Gen. Leonidas, 85, 88.
Pope, Gen. John, U.S.A., 268.
Porter, Lieut.-Col. A. P., 135.
Porter, Maj. Giles, 31.
Porter, Lieut. W. L., 136.
Post, Col. P. Sidney, 212, 214.

INDEX.

Pressure on Thomas, 205.
Prewitt's Knob, 68.
Prisoners captured at Nashville, 215.
Problem of reconstruction, 236.
Pulaski, Tenn., occupied, 178.
Pursuit of Hood, 201.
Pursuit of Johnston, 143.

R.

Railroad from Louisville to Knoxville, 50.
Railroad train arrives at Bridgeport, 85.
Ramsey, Col. R. H., 226.
Randall, Hon. S. J., 42.
Remains of Gen. Thomas taken to Troy, 260.
Result of battle of Nashville, 227.
Result of first day's battle at Nashville, 212.
Reynolds, Gen. J. J., 86, 87, 92, 95, 99-103, 105, 106, 109.
Reynolds, Lieut. J. K., 136.
Robinson, Col., 106.
Robinson, Lieut. G. A., 164.
"Rock of Chickamauga," 90.
Roper, Capt. G. S., 62.
Rosecrans, Gen. W. S., 72, 82-84, 87, 88, 90, 101, 104, 105, 113, 114.
Roster of Gen. Thomas's division, 53.
Rousseau, Gen. L. H., 47, 76, 77, 79, 80, 108, 164, 176, 177, 178.
Royall, Col. W. B., 30.
Rucker, Gen. E. W., 215.

S.

Scales, Hon. A. M., 281.
Scarcity of arms and ammunition, 47.
Schoepf, Gen. A., 53, 55, 56, 60, 68.
Schofield, Gen. J. W., 24, 138, 141, 142, 148-150, 178-180, 182, 189, 195, 209, 212-214, 217.
Scott, Gen. Winfield, 37, 42, 229.
Scribner, Col. B. F., 79, 99, 108.

Scully, Mr. J. W., 62.
Seward, Hon. W. H., 239.
Shankling, Lieut.-Col., 80.
Shanks, W. F. G., 113, 132.
Shepard, Col. O. L., 79.
Sheridan, Gen. P. H., 24, 77, 78, 85, 87, 89, 102, 103, 118, 119, 125, 128, 266.
Sherman, Gen. W. T., 14, 17, 24, 46, 50, 52, 117, 118, 122-125, 127, 128, 130, 137, 138, 156, 159, 173-175, 178, 183, 201, 202, 217.
Skinner, Maj. Ralston, 135.
Slocum, Gen. H. W., 166, 170, 171, 199.
Slowness of Thomas, 245.
Smith, Gen. A. J., 182, 183, 195, 199, 209, 211-214, 217.
Smith, Gen. E. K., 30, 85.
Smith, Capt. Frank G., 204.
Smith, Gov. W. E., 281.
Smith, Gen. W. F., 111, 120.
Snake Creek Gap, movement through, 136.
Society of Army of the Cumberland, resolutions of, 264.
Spaulding, Col., 215.
Spear, Gen., 80, 81.
Staff of Gen. Thomas, 115, 135, 136.
Standart, Capt. W. B., 54.
Stanley, Gen. D. S., 81, 86, 87, 103, 158, 159, 165, 166, 169, 170, 171, 178, 179.
Stanley, Col. F. R., 109.
Stanton, Hon. E. M., 181, 185, 198, 203, 205.
Starkweather, Gen., 76, 77, 79.
State-rights men foiled, 48.
Steedman, Gen. J. B., 53, 104, 107, 109, 114, 162, 164, 176, 177, 183, 210, 211, 213-215, 217.
Stitch, Private, 4th Ky. Vols., 62.
Stone, Capt. Henry, 226.
Stoneman, Gen. George, 30, 149, 161, 222.
Stone River, battle of, 73.
Stone River, casualties at, 82.
Stone River, report of battle of, 75.

21

Stoughton, Col. W. L., 109.
Swinton, William, pen-portrait of Gen. Thomas, 247.

T.

Taylor, Gen. Z., 23, 24, 229.
Tennessee nominates Thomas for President, 234.
Tennessee River, crossing of, 87.
Terrell, Gen. W. R., 72.
Terry, Gen. A. H., 24.
Texas, secession of, 36.
Thanks of Congress to Gen. Thomas, 229.
Thanks of Gen. Thomas to his army, 226.
Thanks of Tennessee Legislature, 229.
Third Military District, 237.
Thomas, Gen. George H., promoted, 37, 46, 133.
   address to his command, 207.
   declines all presents, 233.
   inspects his new command on the Pacific, 254.
   makes speech in Cincinnati, 240.
   report for month of May, 1864, 139.
   when and where born, 12.
   when and where married, 27.
   when appointed to a cadetship, 13.
Thompson, Col. C. R., 214.
Thornburgh, Maj. T. T., 16.
Thruston, Lieut.-Col. G. P., 104.
Townsend, Gen. E. D., 18, 189.
Trans-Mississippi Department, 176.
Troops at Crab Orchard, 55.
Troops from Virginia to Kentucky, 50.
Tullahoma captured, 85.
Turchin, Gen., 94.
Twiggs, Gen. D. E., 32, 33, 36.
Tyler, Hon. John, Jr., 283.

U.

Unveiling equestrian statue, 293.

V.

Van Cleve, Gen. H. P., 53, 86, 96.
Vandeveer, Gen. F., 53, 101, 108.
Van Dorn, Gen. Earl, 30, 33.
Von Schrader, Lieut.-Col. A., 81, 110.
Van Vliet, Gen. S., 14.

W.

Wade, Capt. R. D. A., 18, 20, 21.
Wagner, Col., 87, 148.
Walker, Col. M. B., 54, 76, 79.
Walthall, Gen., 219.
Ward, Gen., 47, 158.
Washburne, Gen. C. C., 176.
Whipple, Gen. W. D., 115, 135, 207, 226, 233.
Wilder, Col. J. T., 84, 86, 87, 97.
Wiles, Lieut.-Col. W. M., 135.
Willard, Capt. J. P., 101, 105, 110, 135, 227.
Williams, Gen., 142, 143, 147, 158, 159, 165.
Williams, Capt. T. C., U.S.A., 110.
Willick, Gen. A., 84, 106, 109.
Wilson, Gen. J. H., 182, 184, 195, 199, 204, 205, 208, 209, 211, 213, 215, 217, 272.
Withers, Senator R. E., 270.
Wood, Gen. T. J., 47, 66, 86, 101, 103–106, 109, 119, 125, 128, 140, 148, 149, 180, 195, 199, 204, 209, 212, 216, 217, 268.
Woolford, Col. Frank, 54, 57, 58.
Worth, Col. W. J., 20, 21.

Y.

Young, Capt. J. H., U.S.A., 136.

Z.

Zollicoffer, Gen. F. K., 49–51, 55, 61, 62.

Veterans Key

RICHARD BAREFORD

Veterans Key

Copyright © 2023 by Richard Bareford

All right reserved

ISBN: 9798882966644